The Ethics of
Money Production

JÖRG GUIDO HÜLSMANN

To the memory of
Hans Sennholz

The Ethics of Money Production

JÖRG GUIDO HÜLSMANN

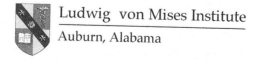 Ludwig von Mises Institute
Auburn, Alabama

ISBN: 978-1-61016-681-2

Contents

Preface ix

Introduction 1
    1. Money Production and Justice 1
    2. Remarks about Relevant Literature 7

Part 1: The Natural Production of Money 19

  1. Monies 21
    1. The Division of Labor without Money 21
    2. The Origin and Nature of Money 22
    3. Natural Monies 24
    4. Credit Money 28
    5. Paper Money and the Free Market 29
    6. Electronic Money 33

  2. Money Certificates 35
    1. Certificates Physically Integrated with Money ... 35
    2. Certificates Physically Disconnected from Money .. 38

  3. Money within the Market Process 43
    1. Money Production and Prices 43
    2. Scope and Limits of Money Production 45
    3. Distribution Effects 46
    4. The Ethics of Producing Money 49
    5. The Ethics of Using Money 51

4. Utilitarian Considerations on the Production of
   Money 55
   1. The Sufficiency of Natural Money Production 55
   2. Economic Growth and the Money Supply 60
   3. Hoarding 62
   4. Fighting Deflation 64
   5. Sticky Prices 68
   6. The Economics of Cheap Money 69
   7. Monetary Stability 72
   8. The Costs of Commodity Money 79

Part 2: Inflation 83

5. General Considerations on Inflation 85
   1. The Origin and Nature of Inflation 85
   2. The Forms of Inflation 88

6. Private Inflation: Counterfeiting Money
   Certificates 89
   1. Debasement 89
   2. Fractional-Reserve Certificates 91
   3. Three Origins of Fractional-Reserve Banking 93
   4. Indirect Benefits of Counterfeiting in a Free
      Society 97
   5. The Ethics of Counterfeiting 98

7. Enters the State: Fiat Inflation through Legal
   Privileges 103
   1. Treacherous Clerks 103
   2. Fiat Money and Fiat Money Certificates 106
   3. Fiat Inflation and Fiat Deflation 107

8. Legalized Falsifications 109
   1. Legalizing Debasement and Fractional Reserves . . 109
   2. The Ethics of Legalizing Falsifications 112

9. Legal Monopolies............................115
    1. Economic Monopolies versus Legal Monopolies . . 115
    2. Monopoly Bullion 116
    3. Monopoly Certificates........................118
    4. The Ethics of Monetary Monopoly 119

10. Legal-Tender Laws............................125
    1. Fiat Equivalence and Gresham's Law 125
    2. Bimetallism................................129
    3. Legal-Tender Privileges for Money Certificates . . . 131
    4. Legal-Tender Privileges for Credit Money 138
    5. Business Cycles 139
    6. Moral Hazard, Cartelization, and Central Banks . . 142
    7. Monopoly Legal Tender 145
    8. The Ethics of Legal Tender...................148

11. Legalized Suspensions of Payments................153
    1. The Social Function of Bankruptcy.............153
    2. The Economics of Legalized Suspensions 156
    3. The Ethics of Legalized Suspensions 157

12. Paper Money................................159
    1. The Origins and Nature of Paper Money 159
    2. Reverse Transubstantiations 162
    3. The Limits of Paper Money 164
    4. Moral Hazard and Public Debts 166
    5. Moral Hazard, Hyperinflation, and Regulation . . . 168
    6. The Ethics of Paper Money 172

13. The Cultural and Spiritual Legacy of Fiat Inflation . . . 175
    1. Inflation Habits 175
    2. Hyper-Centralized Government................176
    3. Fiat Inflation and War......................177
    4. Inflation and Tyranny 179
    5. Race to the Bottom in Monetary Organization 179
    6. Business under Fiat Inflation..................179
    7. The Debt Yoke 182

8. Some Spiritual Casualties of Fiat Inflation 185

9. Suffocating the Flame 188

Part 3: Monetary Order and Monetary Systems 193

14. Monetary Order 195

   1. The Natural Order of Money Production 195

   2. Cartels of Credit-Money Producers 197

15. Fiat Monetary Systems in the Realm of the
Nation-State 199

   1. Toward National Paper-Money Producers:
European Experiences. 199

   2. Toward National Paper-Money Producers:
American Experiences. 203

   3. The Problem of the Foreign Exchanges 206

16. International Banking Systems, 1871–1971 209

   1. The Classical Gold Standard 209

   2. The Gold-Exchange Standard 214

   3. The System of Bretton Woods 216

   4. Appendix: IMF and World Bank after
Bretton Woods 219

17. International Paper-Money Systems, 1971– ? 223

   1. The Emergence of Paper-Money Standards 223

   2. Paper-Money Merger: The Case of the Euro. 228

   3. The Dynamics of Multiple Paper-Money
Standards 230

   4. Dead End of the World Paper-Money Union 235

Conclusion 237

   1. Two Concepts of Capitalism 237

   2. Monetary Reform. 240

References 243

Index of Names 257

Index of Subjects 273

Preface

It has been a long-standing project of mine to give a concise exposition of monetary theory, with special emphasis on the ethical and institutional aspects of money production. Money and banking have been covered more than any other subject in economics. Still there is reason to hope that the following pages will not be superfluous, for they combine three elements that have not previously been integrated into a single work.

First, this book applies the tradition of philosophical realism to the analysis of money and banking. The great pioneer of this approach was the fourteenth century mathematician, physicist, economist, and bishop, Nicholas Oresme, who wrote the first treatise ever on inflation and, in fact, the very first treatise on an economic problem. Oresme exclusively dealt with the debasement of coins, a form of inflation that is unimportant in our age. But the principles he brought to bear on his subject are still up to date and have by and large remained unsurpassed. In modern times, Oresme's work has found its vindication in the writings of the Austrian School.

The Austrian theory of banking and fiat money is the second element of our analysis. The Austrian School is justly famous as a standard-bearer of the realist tradition in economics, and also as a champion of free-market policies. Seven generations of Austrian economists have explained why private property rights provide a fundamental framework for social cooperation in a truly humane economy. They have stressed the counterproductive effects that result when property rights are violated by private individuals and governments. And they have granted no exception in the field of money and banking, demonstrating that without private initiative and its correlate—personal responsibility—the production of money is perverted into an instrument of exploitation. Only the free and responsible initiatives of private individuals, associations, and firms can create monetary institutions of the sort that truly benefit society and its members.

The third element characterizing our approach is the analysis of the ethics of money and banking in line with the scholastic tradition of St. Thomas Aquinas and Nicholas Oresme. Scholasticism sought to integrate Aristotelian insights into the intellectual tradition of Christianity, under the conviction that science and ethics—and the projects of reason and faith generally—can be considered distinct branches of a unified system of knowledge. Murray Rothbard credits Thomism with a critical development in the field of ethics, for it

> demonstrated that the laws of nature, including the nature of mankind, provided the means for man's reason to discover a rational ethics. To be sure, God created the natural laws of the universe, but the apprehension of these natural laws was possible whether or not one believed in God as creator. In this way, a rational ethic for man was provided on a truly scientific rather than on a supernatural foundation.[1]

It was this scholastic line of thought that gave rise to economics as a science. As Joseph Schumpeter wrote:

> It is within [the scholastics'] systems of moral theology and law that economics gained definite if not separate existence, and it is they who come nearer than does any other group to having been the "founders" of scientific economics.[2]

Thus the scholastic approach seems to be an appropriate starting point for an examination of the ethics of money

---

[1]Murray N. Rothbard, *Economic Thought Before Adam Smith: An Austrian Perspective on the History of Economic Thought* (Aldershot, England: Edward Elgar, 1995), p. 58.

[2]Joseph A. Schumpeter, *History of Economic Analysis* (New York: Oxford University Press, 1954), p. 97.

production as well, both from the point of view of the history of ideas and for their contemporary application.

The aforementioned three elements might at first seem to be odd bedfellows. I hope to show, however, that there is a reason why these three strains of thought have grown up alongside each other. We will see how, when they are applied to this one area, they serve as complementary aspects of a general realist theory of money—an ontology of money, as it were—and that all these aspects lead to the conclusion that a free market in money production is ethically superior to its logical alternative: money production based on legal exemptions and privileges.

My special thanks go to Professor Jeffrey Herbener and Dr. Emmanuel Polioudakis for extensive commentary on the first draft of the manuscript and to Mr. Joseph Potts for revising and commenting on the final version. I am also indebted to Professor Larry Sechrest, Professor Roderick Long, Dr. Nikolay Gertchev, Dr. Jan Havel, Dr. Arnaud-Pellissier-Tanon, Dr. Lawrence Vance, and Mr. Robert Grözinger for their helpful comments, and to the Professors Thomas Woods, Joseph Salerno, William Barnett, Robert Higgs, and Christoph Strohm, as well as to Mssrs. Reinhard Stiebler, Brad Barlow, and Philipp Bagus for generous assistance in unearthing relevant literature. Many years ago my teacher Hans H. Lechner awakened my interest in the study of monetary policy, as I gratefully acknowledge. While writing the present book, I have been blessed with encouragement from Mr. Llewellyn Rockwell and my colleagues Hans-Hermann Hoppe, Mark Thornton, Jesús Huerta de Soto, Marco Bassani, Pascal Salin, Bertrand Lemennicier, and Philippe Nemo. Finally, I am grateful to Mr. Jeffrey Tucker for his unflagging support, as well as to my dear wife Nathalie for love and friendship while writing this book.

Jörg Guido Hülsmann
Angers, France
August 2007

Introduction

1. MONEY PRODUCTION AND JUSTICE

The production of goods and services is not a purely technological matter. It always relies on a legal and moral framework, and feeds back on this framework. A firm or an industry can pursue its activities in a way that confirms and nourishes the basic legal and moral presuppositions of human cooperation; yet it can also, intentionally or unintentionally, contradict and destroy these foundations.

Ethical problems of production have been assessed in a great number of industries, ranging from agriculture to textile manufacturing in developing countries to pharmaceuticals. Today only a few important industries have escaped such scrutiny. The most important of these is the production of money. Money is omnipresent in modern life, yet the production of money does not seem to warrant any moral assessment.

To be sure, central bank representatives are lecturing the public on the importance of business ethics; but their concerns do not seem to apply to themselves.[1] Similarly, the subject of business ethics is in a boom phase on campuses; but it is applied mainly to industrial corporations. And the churches and other religious institutions pronounce on many matters of politics; but monetary phenomena, such as paper money,

---

[1] See, for example, Jack Guynn, "Ethical Challenges in a Market Economy" (speech delivered at Bridgewater College, Bridgewater, Virginia, April 11, 2005). The author is the president and CEO of the Federal Reserve Bank of Atlanta.

central banks, dollarization, currency boards, and so on, are hardly mentioned at all. For example, Catholic social teaching only vaguely says that economic activity presupposes a "stable currency"[2] and that the "stability of the purchasing power of money [is] a major consideration in the orderly development of the entire economic system."[3]

There are very detailed statements of Christian doctrine when it comes to the morals of *acquiring and using money*; for example, the Christian literature on usury and on the ethics of seeking money for money's sake is legendary. But important though these problems may be, they are only remotely connected to the moral and cultural aspects of the *production of money*, and especially to the modern conditions under which this production takes place. Here we face a wide gap.

Things are not much better if we turn to the discipline that is supposed to be most concerned about money production, namely, economic science. There are innumerable economic writings on money and banking, but the number of works that are truly helpful in understanding the moral and spiritual issues of money production is rather small. The more recent literature in this field has tended to be especially myopic in regard to our concerns.

Monetary economics deals with discount and open-market policies, and with the typical goals of policy-makers, such as price stability, economic growth, full employment, and so on. But it does not usually offer any wider historical, theoretical, and institutional perspective. For example, few textbooks actually address the workings of a gold standard; yet a basic acquaintance with this institution is necessary to

---

[2]John Paul II, *Centesimus Annus* (1991), §§19, 48.

[3]John XXIII, *Mater et Magistra* (1961), §129. There is also no entry on our subject in the recent official compilation of documents pertaining to Catholic social doctrine; see Pontifical Council for Justice and Peace, *Compendium of the Social Doctrine of the Church* (Vatican: Libreria Editrice Vaticana, 2004).

understand the present state of monetary affairs in the Western world, as well as our political options.

The same textbooks also tend to suffer from an overly narrow conception of economic analysis, focusing on the relations between a few macroeconomic aggregates, such as the money supply, the price level, and national production. This focus might have a certain pedagogical justification, but it is nevertheless much too restrictive to do justice to our subject. The production of money has an enormous impact on the relationships between human persons and groups such as families and private associations. The rules of money production determine to a large extent the transformation of monetary systems through time.[4] All of this is important from a moral and spiritual point of view. Yet it simply vanishes from our intellectual radar screen if we look on money and banking only through macroeconomic spectacles.

Finally, few works actually make the step of integrating economic and moral categories. The great bulk of the literature either offers no moral assessment of monetary institutions at all, or it sets out on moral criticism of existing institutions without a thorough grasp of economics. Unfortunately, the latter shortcoming is particularly widespread, even among concerned and well-intentioned theologians and teachers of business ethics.

Let us emphasize that this gap concerns most notably the moral aspects of *modern* monetary institutions—in particular banks, central banks, and paper money. The Bible provides rather clear-cut moral guidance in regard to the production of money in ancient times, in particular with regard to gold and silver coin making.[5] Similarly, the medieval scholastics had

---

[4]Few works in current literature stress this point. See Angela Redish, *Bimetallism—An Economic and Historical Analysis* (Cambridge: Cambridge University press, 2000); T.J. Sargent and F.R. Velde, *The Big Problem of Small Change* (Princeton, N.J.: Princeton University Press, 2002).

[5]For an overview, see Rousas J. Rushdoony, "Hard Money and Society in the Bible," in Hans Sennholz, ed., *Gold Is Money* (Westport, Conn.: Greenwood, 1975).

developed a very thorough moral doctrine dealing with the old ways of making money. The first scientific treatise on money, Nicholas Oresme's *Treatise on the Alteration of Money*, made important breakthroughs and is filled with insights that are still relevant in our day.[6] Prior to his writings, the teaching office of the Catholic Church had addressed these problems, most notably Pope Innocent III's *Quanto* (1199), which denounced debasement of coins made out of precious metals.

But then the gap appears as soon as we turn to modern conditions. The old precepts about coin making do not exhaust the problems we confront in the age of paper money. And perhaps we encounter here the main reason why contemporary popes did not follow up on their medieval predecessors with any statement addressing the monetary institutions of our age.

In our book we purport to show how high the price of this gap is. Our exposition will be arranged around the *economics* of money production.[7] Adam Smith and many of his followers have

---

[6]See Nicholas Oresme, "A Treatise on the Origin, Nature, Law, and Alterations of Money," in Charles Johnson, ed., *The De Moneta of Nicholas Oresme and English Mint Documents* (London: Thomas Nelson and Sons, 1956).

[7]The notion that economic considerations must be taken account of in moral deliberation is not foreign to Christian thought. For a discussion of the scholastic doctrine of "Common Good" and the related problem of scaling values, see Jacob Viner, "Religious Thought and Economic Society," *History of Political Economy* 10, no. 1 (Spring 1978): 50–61. The ethical implications of social science—especially economics—have recently been discussed with much vigor in Leland B. Yeager, *Ethics as Social Science: The Moral Philosophy of Social Cooperation* (Cheltenham, U.K.: Edward Elgar, 2001). The existence of such implications is also recognized and emphasized in Catholic social doctrine. To put the matter in very simple terms: while the general mission of the Church (evangelization) stresses certain universal principles of faith and morals, the application of these principles to concrete problems (such as money production) must also rely on information provided by the social sciences. See Second Vatican Council, *Gaudium et Spes*, No. 36 (1965); Hervé Carrier, *Nouveau regard sur la doctrine sociale de l'église* (Vatican: Pontifical

called economics a moral science, and rightly so. Economics not only deals with moral beings—human persons—but it also addresses a great number of questions that have direct moral relevance. In the present case, this concerns most notably the question of whether any social benefits can be derived from the political manipulation of the money supply, or the question of how inflation affects the moral and spiritual disposition of the population. The economics of money production will lead us quite naturally to considerations of a juridical, moral, historical, and political nature. Our goal is not to be exhaustive, but to paint a broad picture in sufficient detail.

Accordingly, we will first deal with what we will call the "natural production of money" (Part One) and discuss the ways it can be improved in light of moral considerations. Then we will turn to inflation, the perversion of natural money production (Part Two). Here we will place great emphasis on the difference between two types of inflation. On the one hand, there is private inflation, which springs up spontaneously in any human society, but which is combated by the power of the state. On the other hand, there is fiat inflation, which as its name says actually enjoys the protection of the state and is therefore an institutionalized perversion of money production. In the final part (Part Three) we will then apply these distinctions in a brief analysis of the monetary systems of the West since the seventeenth century.

We will argue that natural money production can work; that it has worked wherever it has been tried; and that there are no tenable technical, economic, legal, moral, or spiritual reasons to suppress its operation. By contrast, there are a great number of considerations that prove conclusively the harmful and evil character of inflation. And in our time inflation has become persistent and aggravated because various legal provisions actually protect the monetary institutions that produce this inflation.

Council "Justice and Peace," 1990), pp. 42–44, 200–02 ; Pontifical Council for Justice and Peace, *Compendium of the Social Doctrine of the Church,* §9, pp. 4–5.

Money production is therefore a problem of justice in a double sense. On the one hand, the modern institutions of money production depend on the prevailing legal order and thus fall within one of the innermost provinces of what has been called social justice.[8] On the other hand, the prevailing legal order is itself the very problem that causes perennial inflation. Legal monopolies, legal-tender laws, and the legalized suspension of payments have unwittingly become instruments of social injustice. They breed inflation, irresponsibility, and an illicit distribution of income, usually from the poor to the rich. These legal institutions cannot be justified and should be abolished at once. Such abolition is likely to entail the elimination of the predominant monetary institutions of our age: central banks, paper money, and fractional-reserve banking.[9] Yet far from seeing herein merely an act of destruction,

---

[8]The concept of social justice has been developed by Luigi Taparelli d'Azeglio, *Saggio teoretico di diritto naturale appogiato sul fatto* (5 vols., Palermo: Antonio Muratori, 1840–43). Pius XI adopted it for his exposition of Catholic social doctrine in *Quadragesimo Anno*. He said in particular:

> The public institutions themselves, of peoples . . . ought to make all human society conform to the needs of the common good; that is, to the norm of social justice. If this is done, that most important division of social life, namely, economic activity, cannot fail likewise to return to right and sound order. (§110)

And the man who wrote the first draft of this encyclical emphasized that social justice was supposed to have an impact on economic institutions via the legal framework: "it shall bring about a legal social order that will result in the proper economic order." Oswald von Nell-Breuning, *Reorganization of Social Economy: The Social Encyclical Developed and Explained* (Milwaukee: Bruce, 1936), p. 250. For an excellent discussion of social justice see Matthew Habiger, *Papal Teaching on Private Property, 1891 to 1991* (Lanham, Md.: University Press of America, 1990), pp. 103–29.

[9]Fractional-reserve banks do not keep all the money that their customers deposit with them, but lend a part of the deposit to other people; in most textbooks this is called "bank money creation." The customer's bank account is therefore only partially (fractionally) backed by corresponding money under direct control of the bank. Below we will deal with this type of business in more detail.

such an event can be greeted as a restoration of monetary sanity and as a necessary condition for a more humane economy.

It is true that these are rather radical conclusions. However, one must not shy away from taking a strong stance in the face of great evil; and great evil is precisely what we confront in the present case. Our goal is not to press a partisan program, however. We seek merely to acquaint the reader with the essential facts needed for a moral evaluation of monetary institutions.[10]

2. REMARKS ABOUT RELEVANT LITERATURE

The argument for natural money production and against inflation goes back many centuries, to the fourteenth century French bishop, Nicholas Oresme.[11] Before him, St. Thomas

---

[10]A good number of authors who have analyzed the modern problems of money production from a Christian point of view have arrived at very similar conclusions, and did not hold back these views out of any misconceived notion of temperance. Fr. Dennis Fahey started his book quoting from a letter to the Apostolic Delegate in Great Britain. The letter was from the pen of a group of mainly Catholic businessmen and scholars. The authors state that they had "studied the fundamental causes of the present world unrest" and "have long been forced to the conclusion that an essential first step . . . is the immediate resumption by the community in each nation of its prerogative over the issue of money including its modern credit substitutes." *Money Manipulation and Social Order* (Dublin: Browne & Nolan, 1944). And Fr. Anthony Hulme concluded his exquisite study quite along the same lines:

> The work was written to show that there is a problem, to show that the problem is chiefly one of creation of interest bearing debt which is permitted to be used as basis for money, to show the way in which this is permeated by the rights to a return on money lent. (*Morals and Money* [London: St. Paul Publications, 1957], p. 160)

[11]On Oresme see in particular Émile Bridrey, *La théorie de la monnaie au XIVe siècle, Nicolas Oresme* (Paris: Giard & Brière, 1906), Pierre Souffrin and Alain P. Segonds, eds., *Nicolas Oresme, Tradition et innovation chez un intellectuel du XIVe siècle* (Paris: Les Belles Lettres, 1988); Lucien Gillard, "Nicole Oresme, économiste," *Revue historique* 279 (1988); Jeanne Quillet, ed., *Autour de Nicole Oresme, Actes du Colloque Oresme organisé à l'Université de Paris XII* (Paris : Bibliothèque de l'histoire de la philosophie,

Aquinas and others had considered various aspects of the problem. But none of them had tackled it from a consistent point of view and none of them had presented their ideas in a treatise. There were the beginnings of a doctrine, but this doctrine was scattered throughout the writings of Aquinas, Buridan, and others.[12] Oresme's great achievement was to integrate these previous works, as well as his own penetrating insights, into a treatise—the first treatise on money ever. The great historian of medieval economic thought Victor Brants pointed out that there is certainly merit in assembling such a work. And Brants observed very justly that Oresme was unsurpassed for centuries; he expressed "ideas that were very much on the point, more on the point than those that would dominate long after him."[13] In hindsight we can certainly say that Oresme's "Treatise" has stood the test of time. Translations into English, German, and French are still in print and

---

1990); Bertram Schefold, ed., *Vademecum zu einem Klassiker der mittelalterlichen Geldlehre* (Düsseldorf: Wirtschaft & Finanzen, 1995). Recent surveys of the literature are in J.H.J. Schneider, "Oresme, Nicolas," *Biographisch-Bibliographisches Kirchenlexikon* 6 (Nordhausen: Bautz, 1993); and in Hendrik Mäkeler, "Nicolas Oresme und Gabriel Biel: Zur Geldtheorie im späten Mittelalter," *Scripta Mercaturae* 37, no. 1 (2003). A recent work stressing the political implications of Oresme's "Treatise" is C.J. Nederman, "Community and the Rise of Commercial Society: Political Economy and Political Theory in Nicholas Oresme's *De Moneta*," *History of Political Thought* 21, no. 1 (2000).

12A very thorough study of Aquinas's monetary thought and its sources of inspiration is in Fabian Wittreck, *Geld als Instrument der Gerechtigkeit. Die Geldrechtslehre des Hl. Thomas von Aquin in ihrem interkulturellen Kontext* (Paderborn: Schöningh, 2002). More generally on the "School of Paris" (to which Aquinas belonged) see Odd Langholm, *Economics in the Medieval Schools: Wealth, Exchange, Value, Money and Usury According to the Paris Theological Tradition, 1200–1350* (Leiden: Brill, 1992).

13In the original: "des idées très justes, plus justes que celles qui dominèrent longtemps après lui." Victor Brants, *L'économie politique au Moyen-Age: esquisse des théories économiques professées par les écrivains des XIIIe et XIVe siècles* (reprint, New York: Franklin, [1895] 1970), p. 187, footnote 2; and p. 190.

monetary economists all over the world admire the work for its conciseness, clarity, and depth.

Later on the case for natural money production and against inflation was taken up and refined in various directions through the writings of the "proto-currency school" branch of the School of Salamanca (Saravia de la Calle, Martín Azpilcueta, Tomás de Mercado).[14] Yet none of these authors seems to have produced a treatise that could match Oresme's earlier work.

Another two centuries later, however, economists such as Richard Cantillon, David Hume, Étienne de Condillac, John Wheatley, David Ricardo, and William Gouge published noteworthy contributions on problems of money production.[15] These writers had more or less dropped the scholastic

---

[14]See Huerta de Soto, "New Light on the Prehistory of the Theory of Banking and the School of Salamanca," *Review of Austrian Economics* 9, no. 2 (1996). Modern translations of these writings are not readily available. However, thanks to the Acton Institute, two works of the School of Salamanca have recently been translated and published in English: Juan de Mariana, "A Treatise on the Alteration of Money," *Journal of Markets and Morality* 5, no. 2 ([1609] 2002); and Martín de Azpilcueta, "Commentary on the Resolution of Money," *Journal of Markets and Morality* 7, no. 1 ([1556] 2004). Since we cannot go into detail, let us merely remark that both works lack the lucidity and penetration that can be found in Oresme's treatise. Moreover, Azpilcueta's work does not really deal with money, but with exchange in general and in particular with the concept of just price. It considers monetary problems (such as the distinction between the monetary and nonmonetary use of coins) only to the extent that they affect this concept. To the present author it is a mystery why the original title "comentario resolutorio de cambios" has been rendered as "commentary on the resolution of money." A literal translation would be "commentary settling problems of the theory of exchange."

[15]See Richard Cantillon, *La nature du commerce en général* (Paris: Institut national d'études démographiques, 1997); David Hume, *Essays* (Indianapolis: Liberty Fund, 1987); Étienne Condillac, *Le commerce et le gouvernement*, 2nd ed. (Paris: Letellier, 1795); John Wheatley, *The Theory of Money and Principles of Commerce* (London: Bulmer, 1807); David

concern for the spiritual dimension of the question, but they pioneered a realistic economic analysis of fractional-reserve banking and paper money. Some of these writings are still in print today and have thus stood the test of time. We do not disparage their merit and their brilliance in noting that they, too, in the new field of banking and paper money, could not quite match the achievement of the old master, Oresme, in the field of commodity money.

In our age, the authors who have contributed most to the analysis of our problem were two agnostic Jews, Ludwig von Mises (1881–1973) and Murray N. Rothbard (1926–1995), who in turn were followers of the founder of the Austrian School of economics, Carl Menger (1840–1920).[16] Mises integrated the theory of money and banking within the overall theory of subjective value and pioneered a macroeconomic analysis in the realist tradition. In Rothbard's work, then, the Austrian theory of money found its present apex. Rothbard not only developed

---

Ricardo, *Works and Correspondence* (Cambridge: Cambridge University Press, 1951–73), vol. 4; William Gouge, *A Short History of Paper Money and Banking in the United States* (New York: Kelley, 1968).

[16]See Carl Menger, *Grundsätze der Volkswirtschaftslehre* (Vienna: Braumüller, 1871); idem, *Untersuchungen über die Methode der Socialwissenschaften und der politischen Oekonomie insbesondere* (Leipzig: Duncker & Humblot, 1883), pp. 161–78; idem, "Geld" (1892); Ludwig von Mises, *Theorie des Geldes und der Umlaufsmittel* (Leipzig: Duncker & Humblot, 1912); *Human Action* (Auburn, Ala.: Ludwig von Mises Institute, [1949] 1998); Nurray N. Rothbard, *Man, Economy, and State*, 3rd ed. (Auburn, Ala.: Ludwig von Mises Institute, 1993); idem, *What Has Government Done to Our Money?*, 4th ed. (Auburn, Ala.: Ludwig von Mises Institute, 1990); idem, *The Mystery of Banking* (New York: Richardson & Snyder, 1983); idem, *The Case Against the Fed* (Auburn, Ala.: Ludwig von Mises Institute, 1994). See also F.A. Hayek, *Free Choice in Currency* (London: Institute of Economic Affairs, 1976); Henry Hazlitt, *The Inflation Crisis and How to Resolve It* (Irvington-on-Hudson, N.Y.: Foundation for Economic Education, [1978] 1995); Hans Sennholz, *Age of Inflation* (Belmont, Mass.: Western Islands, 1979); idem, *Money and Freedom* (Spring Mills, Penn.: Libertarian Press, 1985). Among the earlier noteworthy contributions to the Austrian theory of money and banking see in particular Fritz Machlup, *Die Goldkernwährung* (Halberstadt: Meyer, 1925); F.A. Hayek, *Monetary Nationalism and International Stability* (New York: Kelley, [1937] 1964).

and refined the doctrine of his teacher Mises; he also brought ethical concerns back into the picture, stressing natural-law categories to criticize fractional-reserve banking and paper money. Our work is squarely built on the work of these two writers. Important living authors in this tradition are Pascal Salin, George Reisman, and Jesús Huerta de Soto.[17]

The affinity between Austrian School economics and the scholastic tradition is fairly well known among experts.[18] The

---

[17]See in particular Pascal Salin, *La vérité sur la monnaie* (Paris: Odile Jacob, 1990); George Reisman, *Capitalism* (Ottawa, Ill.: Jameson Books, 1996); Jesús Huerta de Soto, *Money, Bank Credit, and Economic Cycles* (Auburn, Ala.: Ludwig von Mises Institute, 2006). See also Mark Skousen, *Economics of a Pure Gold Standard*, 3rd ed. (Irvington-on-Hudson, N.Y.: Foundation for Economic Education, 1996); Walter Block, "Fractional Reserve Banking: An Interdisciplinary Perspective," Walter Block and Llewellyn H. Rockwell, Jr., eds., *Man, Economy, and Liberty* (Auburn, Ala.: Ludwig von Mises Institute, 1988); Hans-Hermann Hoppe, *The Economics and Ethics of Private Property* (Boston: Kluwer, 1993), chap. 3; idem, "How Is Fiat Money Possible?—or, The Devolution of Money and Credit," *Review of Austrian Economics* 7, no. 2 (1994); Hans-Hermann Hoppe, Jörg Guido Hülsmann, and Walter Block, "Against Fiduciary Media," *Quarterly Journal of Austrian Economics* 1, no. 1 (1998): 19–50; Jörg Guido Hülsmann, *Logik der Währungskonkurrenz* (Essen: Management Akademie Verlag, 1996); special issue on "L'Or, fondement monétaire du commerce international" in *Le point de rencontre—libéral et croyant*, vol. 49 (October 1996); special issue on "Deflation and Monetary Policy" in *Quarterly Journal of Austrian Economics* 6, no. 4 (2003).

[18]It is indeed more than a mere affinity. Rothbard and Huerta de Soto have explored the historical roots of Austrian economics in the economic writings of the late-scholastic School of Salamanca. See Murray Rothbard, "New Light on the Prehistory of the Austrian School," Edwin Dolan, ed., *The Foundations of Modern Austrian Economics* (Kansas City: Sheed & Ward, 1976), pp. 52–74; idem, *Economic Thought Before Adam Smith* (Cheltenham, U.K.: Edward Elgar, 1995), chap. 4; Alejandro Chafuen, *Faith and Liberty: The Economic Thought of the Late Scholastics*, 2nd ed. (New York: Lexington Books, 2003); Jesús Huerta de Soto, "New Light on the Prehistory of the Theory of Banking and the School of Salamanca"; idem, "Juan de Mariana: The Influence of the Spanish Scholastics," Randall Holcombe, ed., *15 Great Austrian Economists* (Auburn, Ala.: Ludwig von Mises Institute, 1999). See also Jean-Michel Poughon, "Les fondements juridiques de l'économie politique," *Journal des Économistes*

modern Austrian School distinguishes itself by a quest for realism that pervades both its arguments and the problems it deals with. Much more so than any other present-day paradigm in economic science, its cognitive approach and its practical conclusions are in harmony with the scholastic tradition. One historian of economic thought characterized the scholastic approach to the analysis of economic phenomena in the following words:

> they did not examine an economic problem as an autonomous phenomenon, consisting of measurable variables, but only as an adjunct of the social and spiritual order and in the context of the *cura animarum,* the care of souls.[19]

Austrians share the scholastic belief that there is no such thing as an economic science dealing with autonomous variables. Economic problems are aspects of larger social phenomena;

---

et des Études Humaines 1, no. 4 (1990). On the School of Salamanca, see in particular Marjorie Grice-Hutchinson, *The School of Salamanca* (Oxford: Clarendon Press, 1952); Wilhelm Weber, *Geld und Zins in der spanischen Spätscholastik* (Münster: Aschendorff, 1962); Ramon Tortajada, "La renaissance de la scolastique, la Réforme et les théories du droit naturel," A. Béraud and G. Faccarello, eds., *Nouvelle histoire de la pensée économique* (Paris: La Découverte, 1992), vol. 1, chap. 2.

[19]Julius Kirshner, "Raymond de Roover on Scholastic Economic Thought," introduction to R. de Roover, *Business, Banking, and Economic Thought in Late Medieval and Early Modern Europe* (Chicago: University of Chicago Press, 1974), p. 21. Kirshner's teacher, de Roover, stated:

> The great difference between scholastics and contemporary economics is one of scope and methodology: the Doctors approached economics from a legal point of view. They attached excessive importance to formalism, so that the study of economics nearly reduced itself to an investigation into the form and nature of contracts. (Ibid., p. 21)

At the end of the present work, the reader will be in a better position to judge the extent to which this approach is "excessive" or justifiable in the light of useful results.

and it is most expedient to deal with them as such, rather than to analyze them in some twisted separation.[20]

Not surprisingly, Austrian economics has inspired the few viable modern contributions to the moral analysis of money production. Apart from Rothbard's works, we need to mention in particular Bernard Dempsey's *Interest and Usury* (1943). From the pen of a trained Thomist philosopher and economist, this book is a path-breaking contribution to the moral analysis of fractional-reserve banking and thus covers some of the ground of our present study. Dempsey has shown that economic analysis can be successfully blended with the scholastic philosophical tradition into something like the natural theology of money and banking. The reason is that "there is no irreconcilable conflict of basic principle; both parties proceed from truths known from natural reason alone."[21]

Two decades later, Friedrich Beutter undertook a systematic moral assessment of inflation in our time and came to

---

[20]In a brilliant essay, the Lutheran theologian Wilhelm Kasch has argued that the present-day separation of monetary theory and theology has harmed both disciplines. It has driven theology toward a gnostic denial of the world; and it has turned monetary theory into a narrow auxiliary discipline of central-bank policy. Kasch points out that monetary theory, precisely because it is so narrowly conceived, is in the process of misunderstanding its subject matter and losing any scientific foundation, turning itself into a barren intellectual game. See Wilhelm Kasch, "Geld und Glaube. Problemaufriß einer defizitären Beziehung," idem, ed., *Geld und Glaube* (Paderborn: Schöningh, 1979). This problem persists to the present day. The discussion of the theological and moral aspects of money production typically revolves around the—vague—central-bank objective of monetary stability. See for example H. Hesse and O. Issing (eds.), *Geld und Moral* (Munich: Vahlen, 1994).

[21]Dempsey, *Interest and Usury* (Washington, D.C.: American Council of Public Affairs, 1943), p. 116; see also pp. 1–6. Based on this work, Fr. Dempsey received his Ph.D. in economics at Harvard under Schumpeter. On Dempsey's economics see Stephen D. Long, "Bernard Dempsey's Theological Economics: Usury, Profit, and Human Fulfillment," *Theological Studies* 12, no. 1 (1996); idem, *Divine Economy: Theology and the Market* (London: Routledge, 2000), pp. 195–214; John T. Noonan, *The Scholastic Analysis of Usury* (Cambridge, Mass.: Harvard University Press, 1957), pp. 403–06.

conclusions very much akin to those of Nicolas Oresme. He argued that inflation, in principle, is morally evil and that it could only be licit to overcome "epochal" conflicts and crises.[22]

In our day, Thomas Woods has brilliantly argued that Austrian economics on the one hand and Christian morals—Catholicism in particular—on the other hand are fully compatible. In *The Church and the Market* (2005), he gives a concise statement of the Austrian analysis of the labor market, of money and banking, of foreign aid, and of the welfare state; and he shows that this analysis provides crucial information for an adequate moral assessment of the market economy and of government interventionism.

Unfortunately, these works have been rather exceptional. During most of the past 150 years, Christian writers, and Catholic intellectuals in particular, have been quarreling with the economic institutions of the modern world; and this uneasy relationship had ample foundations in fact, as we will see in more detail. But whereas these thinkers refused to make peace with the secular world, they fatefully made their peace with pro-inflation doctrines that became fashionable again during the Great Depression. And this in turn vitiated their moral assessment of modern monetary institutions.

A good case in point is Anthony Hulme's book *Morals and Money*. Truly excellent in its exposition of what the Bible and the Christian moral tradition have to say about money, it also endorses age-old mercantilist fallacies about the workings of money within the economy. Hulme believes that the money supply has to grow along with output and that the slowing down of aggregate spending is disadvantageous, as is hoarding, deflation, and the diversion of spending streams into financial markets. This leads him straight to the conclusion that "our currency needs to be managed."[23] He deplores the inflation produced by fractional-reserve banks, but not

---

[22]See Friedrich Beutter, *Zur sittlichen Beurteilung von Inflationen* (Freiburg: Herder, 1965), pp. 173, 178–79.

[23]Hulme, *Morals and Money*, p. 71.

because it is inflationary (after all he believes that inflation is necessary), but because it benefits *private* agents. The solution to present-day monetary calamities is not to abolish the institutions of inflation root and branch, but to hand the inflation machine over to elected politicians.[24]

In short, misconceptions about the economic role of the money supply have vitiated the efforts of scholars to develop a cogent moral assessment of modern monetary institutions. We will therefore discuss the crucial question whether there are any social benefits to be derived from the manipulation of the natural production of money in a special chapter (chap. 4) of the present work.

Another group of noteworthy studies integrating moral concerns and Austrian economics comes from the pen of evangelical scholars who call themselves "Christian Reconstructionists." In particular, Gary North's *Honest Money* (1986) brilliantly combines biblical exposition and economics. Any serious attempt to come to grips with money and banking from a moral point of view must take account of the arguments presented in North's work.[25]

---

[24]The same characteristic set of ideas (acceptance of the basic case for inflation; therefore only rejection of "private" fractional-reserve banking, while endorsement of "public" fiat paper money) can be identified in all major Catholic authors until the early post-war period. See for example, Fathers Francis Drinkwater, *Money and Social Justice* (London: Burns, Oates & Washbourne, 1934); Charles Coughlin, *Money! Questions and Answers* (Royal Oak, Mich.: National Union for Social Justice, 1936); and Dennis Fahey, *Money Manipulation and Social Order* (1944); Oswald von Nell-Breuning and J. Heinz Müller, *Vom Geld und vom Kapital* (Freiburg: Herder, 1962). A critique of Coughlin and Fahey is in Thomas Woods, *The Church and the Market* (Lanham, Md.: Lexington Books, 2005), pp. 106–09. Hilaire Belloc and John Ryan maintained similar economic views as Coughlin and Fahey. For a present-day work of this orientation see Joseph Huber and James Robertson, *Creating New Money* (London: New Economics Foundation, 2000).

[25]This should not be taken as an all-out endorsement of North's more general enterprise of developing a "Christian economics." The present author does not believe that there is such a discipline, just as there is no Bolshevist mathematics or Muslim quantum physics.

Other authors have argued along similar lines, yet without attaining the level of sophistication displayed in North.[26] Money and banking are fascinating subjects. They have attracted a panoply of writers who have neither the knowledge nor the intellectual ability to master this field. The quantitative dominance of these poor writings might have contributed to throwing the entire enterprise of integrating ethics and monetary economics into disrepute.

But there is also another strong mechanism at work that helps account for the dearth of scholarship along these lines: professional and institutional bias.

The general thrust of the above-mentioned works is to cast serious doubts on the necessity and expediency of the government-sponsored production of money through central banks and monetary authorities. The authors argue that money and banking should best be subject to the general stipulations of the civil law. The government should not run or supervise banks and the production of paper money. Its essential mission is to protect property rights, especially the property of bank customers; any further involvement produces more harm than good. Now it is one of the home truths of the economics profession that virtually all of its members are government employees. Even more to the point, a great number of *monetary* economists are employees of central banks and other monetary authorities; and even those monetary economists who are "only" regular professors at state universities derive considerable prestige, and sometimes also large chunks of their income, from research conducted on behalf of monetary authorities.

---

[26]Among the better works of this group we might mention Howard Kershner's *God, Gold, and Government* (Englewood Cliffs, N.J.: Prentice-Hall, 1957), R.J. Rushdoony's *Institutes of Biblical Law* (Nutley, N.J.: Craig Press, 1973) and *The Roots of Inflation* (Vallecito, Calif.: Ross House Books, 1982), Ian Hodge's *Baptized Inflation* (Tyler, Texas: Dominion Press, 1986), and Tom Rose's *God, Gold, and Civil Government* (2002). See also Roland Baader, *Geld, Gold und Gottspieler* (Gräfelfing: Resch, 2004).

Economists relish in pointing out the importance of economic incentives in the determination of human behavior. While virtually no section of society has escaped their scathing criticism, until very recently few of them have been concerned about their own incentives. Yet the facts are plain: championing government involvement in money and banking pays the bills; promoting the opposite agenda shuts the doors to an academic career. No consistent economist could expect monetary economists to lead campaigns against central banks and paper money.[27]

He who acquaints himself with the modern scientific literature on money and banking must not close his eyes to these facts.

---

[27]See Lawrence H. White, "The Federal Reserve System's Influence on Research in Monetary Economics," *Econ Journal Watch* 2, no. 2 (2005): pp. 325–54. Significantly, the only recent successful campaign for monetary reform that was led by professional economists had to avoid the involvement of "experts" employed with monetary authorities. When Fritz Machlup, Milton Friedman, and others prepared the reform of the Bretton Woods system in the late 1960s, they studiously excluded any intellectuals employed by or affiliated with the IMF. Institutional backing came from outside the monetary establishment, namely, from the American Enterprise Institute. The movement eventually rallied in the town of Bürgenstock in Switzerland. See the eyewitness account of one of the members of the Bürgenstock Group in Wolfgang Kaspers, "The Liberal Idea and Populist Statism in Economic Policy: A Personal Perspective," Hardy Bouillon, ed., *Do Ideas Matter? Essays in Honour of Gerard Radnitzky* (Brussels: Centre for the New Europe, 2001), p. 118.

Part 1

The Natural Production of Money

1

Monies

1. THE DIVISION OF LABOR WITHOUT MONEY

To understand the origin and nature of money, one must first consider how human beings would cooperate in a world without money—in a *barter* world. Exchanging goods and services in such a barter world confronts the members of society with certain problems. They then turn to monetary exchanges as a means for alleviating these problems. In short, money is a (partial) solution for problems of barter exchanges. But let us look at this in just a little more detail.

The fundamental law of production is that joint production yields a greater return than isolated production. Two individuals working in isolation from one another produce less physical goods and services than if they coordinated their efforts. This is probably the most momentous fact of social life. Economists such as David Ricardo and Ludwig von Mises have stressed its implication: even if there are no other reasons for human beings to cooperate, the greater productivity of joint efforts tends to draw them together. The higher productivity of the division of labor, as compared to isolated production, is therefore the basis of a general "law of association."[1]

---

[1]David Ricardo first formulated this law as a law of comparative cost within the context of the theory of foreign trade. Later economists such as Pareto, Edgeworth, Seligman, and Mises argued that it was in fact a general law of exchange. Mises coined the expression "law of association."

Without money, people would exchange their products in barter; for example, Jones would barter his apple against two eggs from Brown. In such a world, the volume of exchanges—in other words, the extent of social cooperation—is limited through technological constraints and through the problem of the double coincidence of wants. Barter exchanges take place only if each trading partner has a direct personal need for the good he receives in the exchange. But even in those cases in which the double coincidence of wants is given, the goods are often too bulky and cannot be subdivided to accommodate them to the needs. Imagine a carpenter trying to buy ten pounds of flour with a chair. The chair is far more valuable than the flour, so how can an exchange be arranged? Cutting the chair into, say, twenty pieces would not provide him with objects that are worth just one twentieth of the value of a chair; rather such a "division" of the chair would destroy its entire value. The exchange would therefore not take place.

2. THE ORIGIN AND NATURE OF MONEY

These problems can be reduced through what has been called "indirect exchange." In our example, the carpenter could exchange his chair against 20 ounces of silver, and then buy the ten pounds of flour in exchange for a quarter ounce of silver. The result is that the carpenter's need for flour, which otherwise would have remained unsatisfied, is now satisfied through an additional exchange and the use of a "medium of exchange" (here: silver). Thus indirect exchange provides our carpenter with additional opportunities for cooperation with other human beings. It extends the division of labor. And it thereby contributes to the material, intellectual, and spiritual advancement of each person.

In the history of mankind, a great variety of commodities—cattle, shells, nails, tobacco, cotton, copper, silver, gold,

---

See David Ricardo, *Principles of Political Economy and Taxation* (London: Penguin, 1980), chap. 7, footnote; Ludwig von Mises, *Socialism* (Indianapolis, Ind.: Liberty Fund, 1981), pp. 256–61; idem, *Nationalökonomie* (Geneva: Union, 1940), pp. 126ff.; idem, *Human Action* (Auburn, Ala.: Ludwig von Mises Institute [1949] 1998), pp. 158–63.

and so on—have been used as media of exchange. In the most developed societies, the precious metals have eventually been preferred to all other goods because their physical character- istics (scarcity, durability, divisibility, distinct look and sound, homogeneity through space and time, malleability, and beauty) make them particularly suitable to serve in this func- tion.

When a medium of exchange is *generally accepted* in soci- ety, it is called "money." How does a commodity such as gold or silver turn into money? This happens through a gradual process, in the course of which more and more market partic- ipants, each for himself, decide to use gold and silver rather than other commodities in their indirect exchanges. Thus the historical selection of gold, silver, and copper was not made through some sort of a social contract or convention. Rather, it resulted from the spontaneous convergence of many individ- ual choices, a convergence that was prompted through the objective physical characteristics of the precious metals.

To be spontaneously adopted as a medium of exchange, a commodity must be desired for its nonmonetary services (for its own sake) and be marketable, that is, it must be widely bought and sold. The prices that are *initially* being paid for its nonmonetary services enable prospective buyers to estimate the *future* prices at which one can reasonably expect to resell it. The prices paid for its nonmonetary use are, so to speak, the empirical basis for its use in indirect exchange. It would be extremely risky to buy a commodity for indirect exchange without knowing its past prices; as a consequence, the spon- taneous emergence of a medium of exchange is virtually impossible whenever such knowledge is lacking. On the other hand, when it exists, then there can arise a monetary demand for the commodity in question. The monetary demand then adds to the original nonmonetary demand, so that the price of the money-commodity contains a monetary component and a nonmonetary component. Although in a developed economy the former is likely to outweigh the latter quite substantially, it is important to keep in mind that the monetary use of a com- modity ultimately depends on its nonmonetary use. The medieval scholastics called money a *res fungibilis et primo usu consumptibilis.*[2] It was in the very nature of money to be a marketable thing that had its primary use in consumption.

3. NATURAL MONIES

We may call any kind of money that comes into use by the voluntary cooperation of acting persons "natural money."[3] To cooperate voluntarily in our definition means to provide mutual support without any violation of other people's property, and to enjoy the inviolability of one's own property.[4]

---

[2]A thing that is fungible and primarily used in consumption. See Oswald von Nell-Breuning, "Geld," *Lexikon für Theologie und Kirche*, 2nd ed. (Freiburg: Herder, 1960), vol. 4, p. 633. This insight was anticipated in Aristotle's *Politics*, book 1, chap. 9, who placed great emphasis on the fact that people make money out of a thing that is one of the most useful things anyway, and which can be most conveniently handled. The same point was later a staple of economic thought. See in particular, John Law, *Money and Trade Considered etc.* (Edinburgh: Anderson, 1705), chap. 1; Adam Smith, *Wealth of Nations* (New York: Modern Library, 1994), bk. 1, chap. 4, pp. 24–25; Carl Menger, *Grundsätze der Volkswirtschaftslehre* (Vienna: Braumüller, 1871), chap. 8, p. 253; Ludwig von Mises, *Theory of Money and Credit* (Indianapolis: Liberty Fund, 1980), chap. 1, p. 44.

[3]The concept of natural money is not much used in the contemporary literature, but it has a venerable tradition in economics. See for example William Gouge, *A Short History of Paper Money and Banking* (reprint, New York: Augustus M. Kelley, [1833] 1968), pp. 7–17, where the author speaks of "real money"; Frédéric Bastiat, "Maudit Argent," *Journal des économistes* (April 1849); appeared in translation in *Quarterly Journal of Austrian Economics* 5, no. 3 (2002); idem, *Harmonies économiques*, 2nd ed. (Paris: Guillaumin, 1851), chap. 1 on natural and artificial organization; and Angel Rugina, *Geldtypen und Geldordnungen* (Stuttgart: Kohlhammer, 1949), pp. 46–47. See also Carlo Lottieri, *Denaro e comunità* (Naples: Alfredo Guida, 2000), pp. 72ff.

[4]See Mises, *Human Action*, chaps. 8 and 15; Murray N. Rothbard, *The Ethics of Liberty*, 2nd ed. (New York: New York University Press, 1998); Hans-Hermann Hoppe, *A Theory of Socialism and Capitalism* (Boston: Kluwer, 1989); idem, *The Economics and Ethics of Private Property* (Boston: Kluwer, 1993); idem, *Democracy—The God That Failed* (New Brunswick, N.J.: Transaction, 2001).

The role of private property as a fundamental institution of human society is of course a staple of historical experience and social science. It is also a staple of Christian social thought, rooted in the Sixth and Ninth Commandments. Within the Catholic Church, the popes emphasized that private property must be held inviolable, not out of any juridical dogmatism in favor of the well-to-do, but because they perceived such inviolability to be the first condition to improve the living standards of the masses.[5] They upheld this notion knowing full well that property owners are often bad stewards of their assets. They upheld it even in the cases in which the owners do not, as a matter of fact, use their private means to promote the good of all of society. And they upheld it in those cases in which the owners did not even have the slightest intention to pursue the common good. In short, the popes championed the distinction between justice and morals—between the *right* to own property and the *moral* obligation to make good use of this property.[6] A violation of one's moral obligation could not possibly justify the slightest infringement of property rights. Private property is sacred even if it is abused or not used:

> That justice called commutative commands sacred respect for the division of possessions and forbids invasion of others' rights through the exceeding of the limits of one's own property; but the duty of owners to use their property only in a right way does not come under this type of justice, but

---

[5]Pope Leo XIII wrote: "The first and most fundamental principle, therefore, if one would undertake to alleviate the condition of the masses, must be the inviolability of private property" (*Rerum Novarum*, §§11, 15). His successors have similarly emphasized the moral character of private property. For example, John XXIII stated that "private ownership must be considered as a guarantee of the essential freedom of the individual, and at the same time an indispensable element in a true social order" (*Mater et Magistra*, §111).

[6]See on this distinction Thomas Aquinas, *Summa theologica*, IIa–IIae, q. lxvi, art. 2, answer; Leo XIII, *Rerum Novarum*, §22.

under other virtues, obligations of which 'cannot be enforced by legal action.' Therefore, they are in error who assert that ownership and its right use are limited by the same boundaries; and it is much farther still from the truth to hold that a right to property is destroyed or lost by reason of abuse or non-use.[7]

In the case of a society in which private property is inviolable, we may speak of a "completely free society" and its economic aspect may then be called a "free market" or a "free economy." Such an economy, if perfected by charity, truly promotes "economic and civil progress."[8] The monetary corollary of such a society is, as we have said, natural money—or rather all the different natural monies that would exist in such a society, for there are good reasons to assume that a free society would harbor a variety of different monies, which would all be natural monies in our sense. Notice that natural money is an eminently social institution. This is so not only in the sense that it is used in interpersonal exchanges (all monies are so

---

[7]Pius XI, *Quadragesimo Anno*, §47. He is quoting Leo XIII's encyclical *Rerum Novarum*. Generally speaking, the Catholic attitude toward property has two characteristic features. First, each property owner is morally commanded to use his property as though it were the property of all. Middle-class Christians should use their property with "liberality" and rich Christians should use it with "magnificence." See *Summa theologica*, II–II, q. 66, a. 2, ad 3, and II–II, q. 134, a. 2 and a. 3. Second, private property rights are derived from a "fundamental property right"— the fact that God destined the earth to serve all of mankind. See *Rerum Novarum*, §§7 and 8; *Gaudium et Spes*, §69. Austrian economists have placed great emphasis on the fact that private property in the means of production has much more beneficial social effects than coerced communal ownership. See in particular Mises, *Socialism*, pp. 27–32. In other words, the destination of the means of production to serve the broad masses is an built-in feature of a free economy. On property rights in Christian dogma, see John Paul II, *Centesimus Annus*, §§30–43; see also Matthew Habiger, *Papal Teaching on Private Property, 1891 to 1991* (New York: University Press of America, 1990); Pontifical Council for Justice and Peace, *Compendium of the Social Doctrine of the Church* §171–84, pp. 96–104.

[8]John Paul II, *Centesimus Annus*, §42.

used), but also in the sense that they owe their existence exclusively to the fact that they satisfy human needs better than any other medium of exchange. As soon as this is no longer the case, the market participants will choose to discard them and adopt other monies. This freedom of choice assures, so to speak, a grass-roots democratic selection of the best available monies—the natural monies.

Where property rights are violated, especially where they are violated in a systematic manner, we may no longer speak of a completely free society. It is possible that natural monies would still be used in such societies, namely, to the extent that the violations of property rights do not concern the choice of money. But wherever people are not free to choose the best available monies, a different type of money comes into existence—"forced money." Its characteristic feature is that it owes its existence to violations of property rights. It is used, at least to some extent, because superior alternative monies cannot be used without exposing the user to violence. It follows that such monies are tainted from a moral point of view. They may still be beneficial and used in indirect exchanges, but they are in any case less beneficial than natural monies, because they owe their existence to violations of private property, rather than to their relative superiority in satisfying human needs alone.

Gold, silver, and copper have been natural monies for several thousand years in many human societies. The reason is, as we have said, that their physical characteristics make them more suitable to serve as money than any other commodities. Still we call them natural monies, not because of their physical characteristics, but because free human beings have spontaneously selected them for that use. In short, one cannot tell on *a priori* grounds what the natural money of a society is. The only way to find this out is to let people freely associate and choose the best means of exchange out of the available alternatives. Looking at the historical record we notice that, at most times and most places, people have chosen silver. Gold and copper too have been used as monies, though to a lesser extent.

4. CREDIT MONEY

Natural money must possess two qualities. It must first of all be valuable *prior* to its monetary use, and it must furthermore be physically suitable to be used as a medium of exchange (at any rate more suitable than the alternatives). The historical monies we have mentioned so far derive their prior value from their use in consumption. Even in the case of the precious metals this is so. It is true that they are not destroyed in consumption, as for example tobacco and cotton, but they are nevertheless consumed as jewelry, ornament, and in a variety of industrial applications.

Now there are other monies that do not derive their prior value from consumption. The most important cases are paper money and electronic money, to which we will turn below. But there is also credit money, the subject of the current section. As the name says, credit money comes into being when financial instruments are being used in indirect exchanges. Suppose Ben lends 10 oz. of silver to Mike for one year, and that in exchange Mike gives him an IOU (I owe you). Suppose further that this IOU is a paper note with the inscription "I owe to the bearer of this note the sum of 10 oz., payable on January 1, 2010 (signature)." Then Ben could try to use this note as a medium of exchange. This might work if the prospective buyers of the note will also trust Mike's declaration to pay back the credit as promised. If Mike's reputation is good with certain people, then it is likely that these people will accept his note as payment for their goods and services. Mike's IOU then turns into credit money.

Credit money can never have a circulation that matches the circulation of the natural monies. The reason is that it carries the risk of default. Cash exchanges provide immediate control over the physical money. But the issuer of an IOU might go bankrupt, in which case the IOU would be just a slip of paper.

Not surprisingly, therefore, credit money has reached wider circulation only when the credit was denominated in terms of some commodity money, when the reputation of the issuer was beyond doubt, and when it was the only way to quickly provide the government with the funds needed to conduct large-scale war. This was for example the case with the American Continentals that financed the War of Independence and with the French *assignats* that financed the wars of the French revolutionaries against the rest of Europe. In the early days, credit money had also been issued in other forms than paper. In particular, IOUs made out of leather have been repeatedly used as money starting in the ninth century.[9]

Credit money is only a derived kind of money. It receives its value from an expected future redemption into some commodity. In this respect it crucially differs from paper money, which is valued for its own sake. And this brings us to the next topic.

5. PAPER MONEY AND THE FREE MARKET

So far we have singled out the precious metals to illustrate our discussion because, historically, the precious metals have been the money of the free market, and also because to the present day no other commodities seem to be more suitable to be used as media of exchange. But the contention that gold, silver, and copper are the best available monies seems to be contradicted by the fact that, today, there is virtually no country in the world that uses precious metals as monies. Rather, all countries use paper monies.[10] This universal practice seems to have a ready explanation in the observation that paper money is even more advantageous than the precious metals, for at least three reasons: (1) its costs of production are

---

[9]See Rupert J. Ederer, *The Evolution of Money* (Washington, D.C.: Public Affairs Press, 1964), pp. 92–93; Elgin Groseclose, *Money and Man: A Survey of Monetary Experience* (New York: Frederick Ungar, 1961), p. 119.

[10]Paper money must not be confused with credit money made out of paper, or with money certificates made out of paper. The latter can be redeemed into commodity money; the former cannot. Note that economists have used the expression "paper money" both in the narrow sense in which we use it here and in a larger sense, which covers paper money in the narrow sense as well as credit money and paper certificates for money.

far lower; (2) its quantity can be easily modified to suit the needs of trade; and (3) its quantity can be easily modified to stabilize the value of the money unit.

Before we turn to analyzing these alleged advantages in more detail, we have to deal with the even more fundamental question of whether paper money is a market phenomenon in the first place. Does it owe its existence to the free choice of the money users, or to legal privileges? If the former is the case, there seems to be no fault with paper money—quite to the contrary. But if it exists only due to compulsion and coercion; that is, due to violations of property rights—its alleged advantages must be examined very carefully.

Now if we turn to the empirical record, we confront the stark fact that, in no period of human history, has paper money spontaneously emerged on the free market.[11] No Western writer before the eighteenth century seems to have even considered that the existence of paper money was possible. The idea arose only when paper certificates for gold and silver gained a larger circulation, especially in the context of large-scale government finance.[12] In the eighteenth, nineteenth, and twentieth centuries, various experiments with paper money

---

[11]A good overview is in John E. Chown, *A History of Money* (London: Routledge, 1994), part 3. See also George Selgin, "On Ensuring the Acceptability of a New Fiat Money," *Journal of Money, Credit, and Banking* 26 (1994); Kevin Dowd, "The Emergence of Fiat Money: A Reconsideration," *Cato Journal* 20, no. 3 (2001). Note again that paper money must not be confused with credit money.

[12]Note that the Bank of England was established in 1694, a few years after the creation of the Bank of Sweden. Probably it was the French philosopher Montesquieu who first held that a pure "sign money," or, as he called it, "ideal money" was possible. See Charles de Montesquieu, *De l'esprit des lois* (Paris: Gallimard/Pléiade, 1951), book 22, chap. 3, p. 653. However, he thought that anything but "real money" (commodity money) would invite abuses, an opinion shared by many later illustrious economists such as David Ricardo and Ludwig von Mises. An exception was James Steuart, who actually endorsed a pure "money of account." See James Steuart, *An Inquiry Into the Principles of Political Economy* (London: Millar & Cadell, 1767), book 3, chap. 1.

have taken place in the West.[13] Governments have issued paper money along with the legal obligation for each citizen to accept it as legal tender. They overrode the stipulations made in private contracts and forced creditors, say, to accept payments in paper "greenbacks" rather than in gold or silver. In most cases, however, governments have transformed previously existing paper certificates for gold and silver into paper money by outlawing the use of gold and silver, and of all other suitable commodities and certificates. The experience of other cultures and times tells the same story. Paper money had been introduced in China in the twelfth century, equally through compulsion and coercion by the ruler.[14] In all known historical cases, paper money has come into existence through government-sponsored breach of contract and other violations of private-property rights. It has never been a creature of the free market.

The historical record does not of course provide a decisive verdict on the question whether paper money can spontaneously emerge on a free market. Can we settle the issue on theoretical grounds? Here the following consideration comes into play. By its very nature, paper money provides only monetary services, whereas commodity money provides two kinds of services: monetary and commodity services. It follows that the prices paid for paper money can shrink to zero, whereas the price of commodity money, will always be positive as long as it attracts a nonmonetary demand. If the prices paid for a paper money fall to zero, then this money can never be re-monetized again, because short of an already-existing

---

[13]It is still useful to read contemporary analyses of these events. See for example William Gouge, *A Short History of Paper Money and Banking in the United States*, part 2; Adolph Wagner, *Die russische Papierwährung* (Riga: Kymmel, 1868), chap. 8, pp. 116–80; Karl Heinrich Rau, *Grundsätze der Volkswirtschaftslehre*, 7th ed. (Leipzig & Heidelberg: Winter, 1863), §310–17, pp. 391–415; William Graham Sumner, *History of Banking in the United States* (New York: Augustus M. Kelley, [1896] 1971).

[14]See Jonathan Williams et al., *Money: A History* (London: Palgrave Macmillan, 1998), chap. 6.

price system the market participants could not evaluate the money unit. Thus the use of paper money carries the risk of total and permanent value annihilation. This risk does not exist in the case of commodity money, which always carries a positive price and which can therefore always be re-monetized.

It does not take much fantasy to predict the practical implications of this fact. In a truly free market, paper money could not withstand the competition of commodity monies. The more farsighted and prudent market participants would get rid of their paper money first, and the others would follow in due course. At the end of this process, which could be consummated in but a few seconds, but which could conceivably also last a few years, the paper currency would be completely eradicated.[15]

The preceding analysis leads to the conclusion that no money can remain in circulation only because it has been in circulation up to now. The ultimate source of its value—the rock bottom of its value—must be something else than the mere fact that, so far, people have been willing to accept it.[16] All kinds of psychological motivations might provide such a source for a while, but they will all collapse under the pressure of a substitution process of the kind we have described above. What then? Can the armed power of the government keep money in circulation? The government's fiat can indeed confer value on paper money—the value of not getting into trouble with the police.[17] But this observation only confirms

---

[15]See Hülsmann, *Logik der Währungskonkurrenz* (Essen: Management Akademie Verlag, 1996), pp. 260–74, 307.

[16]See Benjamin Anderson, *The Value of Money* (reprint, Grove City, Penn.: Libertarian Press, [1917]), chap. 7 "Dodo-Bones," p. 125.

[17]Georg Holzbauer argued that the value of paper money was ultimately rooted in the fact that the government forces its citizens to use those paper slips to pay taxes. It thus had a "tax foundation." See Georg Holzbauer, *Barzahlung und Zahlungsmittelversorgung in militärisch besetzten Gebieten* (Jena: Fischer, 1939), pp. 85–87. For a similar argument see Yuri Kuznetsov, "Fiat Money as an Administrative Good," *Review of Austrian Economics* 10, no. 2 (1997): 111–14.

our point that paper money is not a market phenomenon. It cannot flourish in the fresh air of a free society. It is used only when police power suppresses its competitors, so that the members of society are given the stark choice of either using the government's paper money or forgoing the benefits of a monetary economy altogether.[18]

6. ELECTRONIC MONEY

The preceding observations can be directly applied to the case of electronic money. An economic good that is defined entirely in terms of bits and bytes is unlikely ever to be produced spontaneously on a free market, for the very same reasons that we just discussed in the case of paper money. And despite the dedicated efforts of various individuals and associations, no such money has in fact ever been produced since the creation of the Internet made electronic payments possible. At present, only *government* money has been produced in electronic form; and as in the case of paper money, governments could do this only because they have the possibility to suppress competition.

On the free market, the new information technologies have been unable to create any new monies. They have been able to develop various new instruments to *access and transfer* money. These new electronic techniques of *dealing with* money are very efficient and beneficial, but they must not be confused with the creation of electronic money.

---

[18]Below we will examine whether fiat paper money is viable in the long run, and how it stands up to moral standards.

2

Money Certificates

1. Certificates Physically Integrated with Money

The precious metals would have become monies even if coinage had never been invented, because even in the form of bullion their physical advantages outweigh those of all alternatives. There is however no doubt that coinage added to the benefits derived from indirect exchange, and that it therefore contributed to the spreading of monetary exchanges. Coinage allows the exchange of precious metals without engaging in the labor-intensive processes of weighing the metal and melting it down. One can determine a metal weight by simply counting the coins.[1]

Coinage endows a mass of precious metal with an imprint that certifies its weight. The typical imprint says something to the effect that the coin weighs a total of so and so many grams or ounces (gross weight), with this or that proportion or absolute content of precious metal (fine weight). This is why coin names were typically the names of weights, for example, the pound, the mark, the franc, or the ecu.

Notice that the service depends entirely on the trustworthiness of the certifier, that is, of the minter. If the market participants cannot trust the certificate, they will rather do without the coin and go through the extra trouble of weighing

---

[1]See Aristotle, *Politics*, bk. 1, chap. 9.

the metal and possibly melting it down to determine its content of fine metal. A trustworthy coin economizes on this trouble and thus adds to the value of the bullion contained in the coin; for example, a trustworthy 1-ounce silver coin is more valuable than 1 ounce of silver bullion.[2] People therefore pay higher prices for coins than for bullion, and the minter lives off this price margin.[3]

Because the value of the certificate depends on the trustworthiness of the minter, coins are typically used within limited geographical areas. Only the people who know the minter are likely to accept his coins. All others will insist on being paid in bullion or in coins they trust. This does not mean that in practice every village needs a different set of coins. The geographical radius within which a coin is used *can* grow very large and it can even become world encompassing if the minter has an excellent reputation. This was for example the case with the Mexican dollar coins that in the early nineteenth

---

[2]An early writer who stressed this fact was Nicholas Copernicus. See Copernicus, "Traité de la monnaie," in L. Wolowski, ed., *Traité de la première invention des monnoies, de Nicole Oresme . . . et Traité de la monnoie, de Copernic* (Paris: Guillaumin, 1864), pp. 52–53. "L'empreinte de garantie ajoute quelque valeur à la matière elle-même" (p. 53).

[3]Most historical coins have been fabricated in government mints. This has misled many people into believing that the superior value of coins as compared to bullion demonstrates that the legal sanctioning of a coin is the source of its superior value as compared to bullion. For example, the ancient Greeks called money "noumisma" (from "nomos"—the law); and at the beginning of the twentieth century, the German professor Knapp popularized what he called the "state theory of money." The idea that government fiat was a source of value has inspired many extravagant theories and political schemes. As we shall see, the truth is that government-enforced legislation can provide a few privileged coin makers with a monopoly rent. But this has nothing to do with coinage *per se*. Even without any legal sanction, trustworthy coins are more valuable than bullion. This value difference springs, as we have seen, from the service of certification. Historically, private coinage came first and only later did governments take over. See Arthur Burns, *Money and Monetary Policy in Early Times* (New York: Augustus M. Kelley, [1927] 1965), pp. 75–77, 442–44.

century circulated freely in most parts of the U.S. and which have bequeathed their name to the present-day currency of this country.

Historically, minters have offered additional services that complement the certification of weights. Thus one of the perennial problems of coining precious metals is that used coins might contain a smaller quantity of precious metal than freshly minted coins. If this happens, people are inclined to hold back the good coins for themselves and to trade only the bad coins. To overcome this problem, minters could offer their coins in combination with an insurance service: they could offer to exchange any slightly used coin against a new one. This policy would guarantee the stability and homogeneity of the coinage through time. Thus the insured coins would trade at even higher prices, from which price differential (the premium) the replacement expenses can be paid.

A great number of monetary thinkers from the Middle Ages to our times have held that coinage should be entrusted to the princes or governments, who, because they were the natural leaders of society, were also the people to be naturally trusted. The medieval scholastics knew full well that the princes frequently abused this trust, placing for example an imprint of "one ounce" on a coin that contained merely half an ounce, pocketing the other half of an ounce for themselves. Therefore Nicholas Oresme postulated that the princes did not have the right to alter the coins at all, unless they had the consent of the entire community, that is, the entire community of money users.

Economic science has put us in a position to understand that competitive coinage is an even better way of preserving the trustworthiness of coins. There is no economic reason not to allow every private citizen to enter the minting business and to offer his own coins. It is true that a private minter too might abuse the trust his customers put in him and his coins. But punishment is immediate: he will lose all these customers. People will start using other coins issued by people they have reason to trust more. In a way, this competitive process also fulfills Oresme's postulate that the entire community of money users decide about coinage. He held that "money is the property of the commonwealth."[4] On a free market, the money owners can assert this property right smoothly and swiftly. Each person who no longer trusts the minter A simply stops using A's coins and begins to use the coins of minter B. Thus he leaves the A community and joins the B community.

Competition in coinage is no panacea. Abuses are always possible and in many cases they cannot easily be repaired. The virtue of competition is that it offers the prospect of minimizing the scope of possible abuses. And its great charm is that it involves the entire community of money users, not just some appointed or self-appointed office holders. Down here on earth this seems to be all we can hope for.

2. CERTIFICATES PHYSICALLY DISCONNECTED FROM MONEY

If certificates may add to the value of bullion then certificates may have a value on their own. Therefore they can also be traded without being physically integrated with the precious metal of which they certify the quantity. Then they are money substitutes.

Issuing such money substitutes was the generally accepted practice in the cities of Amsterdam and Hamburg for almost two centuries. The Bank of Amsterdam (established in 1609) issued paper notes that certified that the holder of the note was the legal owner of so-and-so much fine silver deposited in the vaults of the bank. These banknotes could be redeemed any time at the counters of the Bank, on the simple demand of the present owner.[5] As a consequence, they were traded in lieu of the silver itself. Rather than exchanging physical silver, people made their purchases with the banknotes

---

[4]Nicholas Oresme, "A Treatise on the Origin, Nature, Law, and Alterations of Money," in Charles Johnson, ed., *The De Moneta of Nicholas Oresme and English Mint Documents* (London: Thomas Nelson and Sons, 1956), p. 16.

[5]It is not necessary for us to dwell here on the nuances of early "bank money." The most accessible presentation is in Adam Smith, *Wealth of Nations*, bk. 4, chap. 3, part 1, appendix.

that certified ownership of a sum of silver deposited at the Bank.

Apart from paper notes, the main types of such substitutes are token coins, certificates of deposit, checking accounts, credit cards, and electronic bank accounts on the Internet. Despite the physical variety of these types, each of them features three fundamental characteristics: intermediation, titles, and the holding of "reserves."[6]

Certification in the present case is not as integral as in the case of imprints that are struck in to the money material itself—the regular coins that we discussed above. Rather, the money substitute relates to a quantity of money that is removed from the eyes of the partners to the exchange. The money itself is held at some other place, namely, at the bank or treasury department or whichever other organization has issued the certificate. Thus there is in the present case not only monetary intermediation in the weak sense that a third party certifies quantities of money exchanged by the other two parties; but also in the strong sense that this third party actually physically controls the money at the time of the exchange.

Furthermore, money substitutes do not merely certify the physical existence of a certain amount of precious metal; they are also a legal title to that amount. The rightful owner of a one-ounce-of-silver banknote, for example, is the rightful owner of one ounce of silver deposited in the vaults of the institution that issued the banknote.

Finally, the money supplies held by the issuer of the substitutes are called the "reserves." This terminology is established in economic science, but it should be used with some caution. Many students of money and banking believe that certificates such as book entries in bank accounts are the real monies, because they are actually used in daily exchanges,

---

[6]For most of the problems we will discuss in the present work, these common features are more important than the differences. For brevity's sake, we will therefore mostly address the case of banknotes. In certain important respects banknotes differ from other money substitutes. We will discuss these differences at the appropriate place in Part Two.

whereas the money held by the institutions that make the account entries are just the reserves. But the truth is quite different. In all such cases, the so-called reserves are in fact the real money, whereas the account entries are only money substitutes.[7]

What are the advantages and disadvantages of certificates disconnected from the money itself? The main advantage is that the costs of storage, transportation, and certification (minting) can be reduced. The main disadvantage is that the potential for abuse is greater than in the case of coinage. Fraudulent bankers can embezzle on the property of their customers far more easily than fraudulent minters. A look at the history of institutions reveals that this temptation was virtually impossible to resist, especially when certification was not competitive. In the case of the Bank of Hamburg it took almost 150 years before abuse set in (at any rate, before it became manifest). Other bankers fell from grace much more quickly. For example, the goldsmiths who in the mid-1600s had taken

---

[7]One also needs to keep in mind that objects like banknotes can have very different economic natures. Today virtually all banknotes are government-enforced paper monies. But in former times, they were usually certificates for gold or silver. U.S. Federal Reserve notes had been gold certificates until August 1971 (under the 1944 Bretton Woods system, foreign central banks could redeem them until 1971, when the system collapsed). Since then, they have been paper money. Thus although on the level of their physical appearance they remained unchanged, dollar notes did change their economic nature. Similarly, a token coin bears more physical resemblances to a gold coin than to a paper certificate. But from an economic point of view, paper certificates and token coins are in one class of phenomena: they are both substitutes that are physically disconnected from money. The coin form *per se* is here irrelevant. In particular, notice that tokens also need to be distinguished from coins that contain a more or less large amount of precious metal in alloy. In the latter case, the certificate is still physically connected with the money material. In short, the physical aspects of things are often irrelevant from an economic point of view. The point has been stressed for example in Oswald von Nell-Breuning, "Geldwesen und Währung im Streite der Zeit," *Stimmen der Zeit* 63, no. 10 (July 1933). We will discuss this important phenomenon in more detail in Part Two.

over the certification business in the city of London, after the English king had robbed the gold deposited in the Tower, very soon started using the deposits in their lending operations. Thus they turned themselves into "fractional-reserve bankers," meaning that only a part (a fraction) of their issue was covered by underlying money reserves.

In short, the potential abuse of substitutes is a very considerable disadvantage. One may therefore justly doubt that on a free market they could have gained any larger circulation. Even David Ricardo, the great champion of paper currency, admitted that it was unlikely that such substitutes could withstand the competition of coins. The only sure way to bring paper notes into circulation was to impose them on the citizenry: "If those who use one and two, and even five pound notes, should have the option of using guineas, there can be little doubt which they would prefer."[8]

But our point is not to speculate about the significance that paper certificates would have on the free market. We merely wish to point out that paper certificates and token coins might conceivably play a role here, and that they have been used very widely in the past, though very often under some sort of imposition. In a free society, the market participants would constantly weigh the advantages and disadvantages of the various certification products. It is true that they would not be able to prevent all abuses. But again, the point is that a competitive system minimizes the possible damage.

---

[8]David Ricardo, "Proposals for an Economical and Secure Currency," *Works and Correspondence*, Piero Sraffa, ed. (Cambridge: Cambridge University Press, 1951–73), vol. 4, p. 65. In Ricardo's eyes, free choice in money could not be permitted because consumer preference for gold and silver coins would mean that, "to endulge a mere caprice, a most expensive medium would be substituted for one of little value." Ibid. We will deal with the costs of commodity money in a subsequent section.

3

Money within the Market Process

1. Money Production and Prices

The basic economic fact of human life is the universal condition of scarcity. Our means are not sufficient to realize all of our ends. In particular, our time is limited and thus we have to make up our mind how to use it, whether in paid work, in family or communal activities, or in personal leisure. But all other means at our disposal are limited too: our cash holdings, our financial assets, the size and quality of our cars and houses, and so on. Thus whatever we do, we have to choose how to use these resources, which also means that we decide at the same time how not to use them.

Now the use of all means of action is conditioned by the law of diminishing marginal value. According to this law, the relative importance of any unit of an economic good for its owner—or, as economists say, the marginal value of any unit—diminishes as we come to control a greater overall supply of this good, and vice versa. The reason is that each additional unit enables us to pursue new objectives that we would not otherwise have chosen to pursue. Therefore, these objectives are necessarily less important for the acting person than the objectives that he would have pursued with the smaller supply. It follows, for example, that the marginal value of an additional mouthful of water is very different for a person travelling in a desert than for the same person swimming in a lake. And the marginal value of a 200 square-foot room added to our house is very different, depending on whether the present size of our house is 500 or 5,000 square feet. Similarly, the marginal value of an additional dollar depends on how many dollars its owner already holds in his cash balance.

It follows that the *production* of any additional unit of money makes money less valuable for the owner of this additional unit than it would otherwise have been. In particular, it becomes less valuable for him as compared to all other goods and services. As a consequence, he will now tend, *as a buyer* of goods and services, to pay more money in exchange for these other goods and services; and *as a seller* of goods and services, he will now tend to ask for higher money payment.

In short, money production entails a tendency for money prices to increase. This tendency will at first show itself in the prices paid by the money producer himself. But then it will spread throughout the rest of the economy because those individuals who sold their goods and services to the money producer now also have larger cash balances than they otherwise would have had. For them too, therefore, the relative value of money will decline and they too will therefore tend to pay higher prices for the goods and services that *they* desire. It follows that still other people will have higher cash balances than otherwise and thus a new round of price increases sets in, and so on. This process continues until all money prices have been adjusted to the larger money supply. It is true that, for reasons that are too special to warrant our attention at this place, some prices might decrease in this process. But the overall tendency is for prices to increase. Thus the overall tendency of money production is to increase prices beyond the level they would otherwise have reached. This implies in turn that the purchasing power of any unit of money diminishes.

Let us emphasize again that the process through which money production tends to increase the price level is spread out in time. It therefore affects the different prices at different points of time—there is no simultaneous increase of all prices. Furthermore, there is no reason why prices should change uniformly or in some fixed proportion to the change of the money supply. Hence, money production entails a tendency for prices to increase, but this increase occurs step by step in a process spread out through time and affects each price to a different extent.[1]

2. Scope and Limits of Money Production

How much money will be produced on the market? How many coins? How many paper certificates? The limits of mining and minting, and of all other monetary services are ultimately given through the preferences of the market participants. As in all other branches of industry, miners and minters will make additional investments and expand their production if, and only if, they believe that no better alternative is at hand. In practice this usually means that they will expand coin production if the *expected monetary return* on investments in mines and mint shops is at least as high as the monetary returns in shoe factories, bakeries, and so on.

The returns of the various branches of human industry ultimately depend on how the individual citizens choose to use the scarce resources that they own. In their capacity as consumers, the citizens choose to spend their money on certain products rather than on other products, thus determining the revenue side of all branches of industry. In their capacity as owners of productive resources (labor, capital, land), the citizens choose to devote these resources to certain ventures rather than in other ventures, thus determining the cost side of all branches of industry. Ultimately, therefore, it is the individual citizens who through their personal choices determine the relative profitability of all productive ventures. Each citizen engages in cooperation with some of his fellows, and by the same token he also withholds cooperation from others. This selection process or market process encompasses all productive

---

[1]In contemporary monetary analysis, these effects are commonly called "Cantillon effects" after Richard Cantillon, the first economist to stress that increases of the money supply do not affect all prices and monetary incomes at the same time and to the same extent. See Richard Cantillon, *La nature du commerce en général* (Paris: Institute national d'études démographiques, 1997), part 2, chap. 7.

ventures and therefore creates a mutual interdependence between all persons and all firms.

On a free market, the production of money is fully embedded in this general division of labor. Additional coins are made as long as this production offers the best available returns on the resources invested in it. It is curtailed to the extent that other branches of industry offer better prospects.

Moreover, just as the choices of individual citizens determine the relative extent of the production of money, as compared to other productions, they also determine the number of different coins that will be produced. Above we stated that money was *a* generally accepted medium of exchange. It is not merely conceivable that several monies will be in parallel use; this has been in fact the universal practice until the twentieth century. In the Middle Ages, gold, silver, and copper coins, as well as alloys thereof, circulated in overlapping exchange networks. At most times and places in the history of Western Europe, silver coins were most widespread and dominant in daily payments, whereas gold coins were used for larger payments and copper coins in very small transactions. In ancient times too, this was the normal state of affairs.

The parallel production and use of different coins made out of precious metals is therefore the natural state of affairs in a free economy. Oresme constantly warned of altering coins, but he stressed that the introduction of a new type of coins was not such an alteration so long as it did not go in hand with outlawing the old coin.[2]

3. Distribution Effects

When it comes to describing the distribution effects resulting from money production, economists ever since the times of Nicholas Oresme and Juan de Mariana typically cite just

---

[2]See Nicholas Oresme, "A Treatise on the Origin, Nature, Law, and Alterations of Money," in Charles Johnson, ed., *The De Moneta of Nicholas Oresme and English Mint Documents* (London: Thomas Nelson and Sons, 1956), chaps. 2, 3, and 13; and chap. 9, pp. 13–14.

one such effect. They point out that the increased money supply brings about a tendency for the increase of all money prices—a fall of the purchasing power of money. Then they argue that the reduced purchasing power benefits debtors, because the amount of debt they have to pay back is now worth less than before, and that this benefit therefore necessarily comes at the expense of the creditors.

This way of presenting things is not fully correct. It is true that an increased money supply tends to bring about higher money prices, and thus diminishes the purchasing power of each unit of money. But it is not true that this process necessarily operates in favor of the debtor and to the detriment of the creditor. A creditor may not be harmed at all by a 25 percent decrease in the purchasing power of money if he has anticipated this event at the point of time when he lent the money. Suppose he wished to obtain a return of 5 percent on the capital he lent, and that he anticipated the 25 percent depreciation of the purchasing power; then he would be willing to lend his money only for 30 percent, so as to compensate him for the loss of purchasing power. In economics, this compensation is called "price premium"—meaning a premium being paid on top of the "pure" interest rate for the anticipated increase of money prices. This is exactly what can be observed at those times and places where money depreciation is very high.[3]

A creditor might actually benefit from lending money even though the purchasing power declines. In our above example, this would be so if the depreciation turned out to be 15 percent, rather than the 25 percent he had expected. In this case, the 30 percent interest he is being paid by his debtor contains three components: (1) a 5 percent pure interest rate, (2) a 15 percent price premium that compensates him for the depreciation, and (3) a 10 percent "profit."

---

[3] Late scholastic Martín de Azpilcueta argued that price premiums were not *per se* usurious, but legitimate compensations for loss of value. See Martín de Azpilcueta, "Commentary on the Resolution of Money," Journal of Markets and Morality 7, no. 1 (2004) §48–50, pp. 80–83.

The same observations can be made, *mutatis mutandis*, for the debtors. They do not necessarily benefit from a depreciating purchasing power of money, and they can even earn a "profit" when money's purchasing power increases if the increase turns out to be less than that on which the contractual interest rate was based. It all depends on the correctness of their expectations.

There is however another distribution effect of the production of money. This effect is far more important than the one we have just described because it does not depend on the market participant's expectations. It is an effect that the market participants cannot avoid by greater smartness or circumspection.

To understand this distribution effect we must consider that exchange and distribution are not disconnected activities. In the market process, they are but one and the same event. Brown sells his apple for Green's pear. After the exchange, the distribution of apples and pears is different from what it otherwise would have been. Every exchange thus entails a modification of the "distribution" of resources that would otherwise have come into being. It follows that any production of additional goods and services is bound to have such an impact on distribution. The new supply of product redirects the distribution of wealth in favor of the producer.

Consider the case of money production. Here too the additional quantities that leave the production process, when sold, first benefit the first owner: the producer. He can buy more goods and services than he otherwise could have bought, and his spending on these things in turn increases the incomes of his suppliers beyond the level they would otherwise have reached. But the additional money production reduces the purchasing power of money. It follows that it *also* creates losers, namely, those market participants whose monetary income does not rise at first, but who have to pay right away the higher prices that result when the new money supply spreads step by step into the economy.

Money production therefore *redistributes real income from later to earlier owners of the new money*. As we have pointed out, this redistribution cannot be neutralized through expectations. Even the market participants who are aware of it cannot prevent it from happening. They can merely try to improve their own *relative* position in it, supplying early owners of the new money, preferably the money producer himself.

This distribution effect is a key to understanding monetary economies. It is the primary cause of almost all conflicts revolving around the production of money. As we shall see in more detail, it is therefore also of central importance for the adequate moral assessment of monetary institutions.

To avoid possible misunderstandings, however, let us emphasize that the distribution effects springing from production are not *per se* undesirable. They are an essential element of the free market process, which puts a premium on continual production in the service of consumers and does not reward inactivity.

4. THE ETHICS OF PRODUCING MONEY

Aristotle emphasized the beneficial character of monetary exchanges, which facilitate and extend the division of labor. He merely denounced the practice of turning money into a fetish and desiring it for its own sake.[4] The scholastic writers of the Middle Ages adopted by and large the same point of view, but they also went beyond Aristotle, who focused on the ethics of using money, by discussing the ethics of money production.[5]

The scholastics did not question the legitimacy of producing money *per se*. As in the case of using money, however, they stated that money production had to respect certain ethical rules. Nicholas Oresme and others stressed that all coins

---

[4]See Aristotle, *Politics*, bk. 1, chap. 9. This was also the position of the Church Fathers and later Christians. For an overview see Christoph Strohm, "Götze oder Gabe Gottes? Bemerkungen zum Thema 'Geld' in der Kirchengeschichte," *Glaube und Lernen* 14 (1999): 129–40.

[5]This was a natural development of the distinction between the right to private property and the moral obligation to use one's property in a Christian way. See above, section on natural monies.

should be clearly distinguishable from one another. In particular, it would not be licit that a minter produces coins that by their name, imprint, or other features resemble other coins that contain more precious metals.[6] In other words, the benefits of competition in coinage result from a strict application of the Ninth Commandment: "You shall not bear false witness against your neighbor."

This is the reason why coins up to the early modern period traditionally had weight names such as mark and franc. But this proved to be an improvident choice because coined metal, as we have seen, has by the very nature of things a different value than bullion metal.[7] The word "ecu" for example was on the one hand used in the same sense in which we use today the word "ounce"—it was the name of a weight. But it was also the name of a gold coin that (originally) was supposed to be the equivalent of one ounce of silver. Just imagine what it would mean if, today, we had a silver currency consisting of 1-ounce silver coins that we called "ounces." The expression "ounce" would then be unsuitable to be used in setting up contracts because it is ambiguous. It makes a difference whether we are talking about certified weights, as in coins, or uncertified weights as in gold nuggets. One would therefore have to specify in each contract whether payment is to be made in weight-ounces or coin-ounces. But then the practice of using weight names for coins loses its point. The mere weight name as such is *not* specific enough.

---

[6]Oresme, "Treatise," chap. 13, insisted, for example, that coins containing alloys should have a different color.

[7]Juan de Mariana and other medieval theologians have postulated that the value of coined metal *should* be made equal to the value of bullion. Many secular writers such as John Locke and Charles de Montesquieu have espoused the same point of view. And even first-rate economists such as Jean-Baptiste Say and Murray Rothbard came close to endorsing this position when they postulated that coins be named after their fine content of precious metal. But all these views are misguided because, as we have said, the value difference between coins and bullion of equal weight is not a perversion of human judgment that could be overcome with a moral postulate, but a fact that lies in the very nature of things.

This does not mean, of course, that the weight contents of fine metal should not be imprinted on the coin. Quite to the contrary, this is exactly what successful minters have done in the past, what they do now, and what they will do in the future. The point is that it makes no sense to *call* a coin after its content of fine metal; such a name does not reduce ambiguities, but increases them.

Coinage in a competitive system would have to rely on a scrupulous differentiation of the coin producers. It would not be sufficient that each minter print on his coin something like "this coin contains five grams of fine silver" because, as we have seen, some minters would offer additional services such as the exchange of used for new coins. At the very least, therefore, the name of the minter and any supplementary information needed to identify him would be required. Present-day gold coins such as the Krugerrands, the Eagles, and the Maple Leafs already fulfill this requisite: they feature both a unique name and they state the weight of fine gold contained in the coin.

5. THE ETHICS OF USING MONEY

The Catholic tradition warned in the strictest terms against abuses of money, but it did not deny that, if practiced within the right moral boundaries, the use of money and the paying and taking of interest were natural elements of human society.[8] Jesus himself, when explaining the rewards given to the faithful in the coming Kingdom of Heaven, used an illustration involving the positive use of money and banking. He stated that the Kingdom of Heaven would parallel the reward given for good stewardship of money, and that hell would wait for those who made no use of money at all. Two stewards who used the money entrusted to them in trade and made a 100 percent profit, found the praise of the master and were invited to share in his joy. But one steward who buried the money given to him in the ground was severely chided as "wicked" and "lazy." The master pointed out that he could have turned

---

[8]This position was foreshadowed in Aristotle, *Politics*, bk. 1, chap. 9.

the money into some profit by simply putting it in a bank: "Should you not then have put my money in the bank so that I could have got it back with interest on my return?" He therefore commanded his other servants to take the money away from this servant and to throw him out of the house: "And throw this useless servant into the darkness outside, where there will be wailing and grinding of teeth" (Matthew 25: 26–30).

Thus the use of money and banking may very well be considered legitimate from a Christian point of view. In any case, in the present work we are primarily interested in the economics and ethics of producing money rather than of *using* money in credit transactions.[9] We can therefore avoid discussing one of the most vexatious problems of Catholic social doctrine, namely, the problem of usury. In very rough terms, usury is excessively high interest on money lent. This raises of course the question how one can distinguish legitimate from illegitimate "excessive" interest. Theologians have pretty much exhausted the range of possible answers. Some medieval theologians went so far as to claim that any interest was usury. Others such as Conrad Summenhardt held that virtually no interest payment that the market participants voluntarily agreed upon could be considered usury.

The teaching office of the Catholic Church has repudiated the former opinion without taking a position on the latter. It rejects "usury" but allows the taking of "interest" on several grounds that are independent of (extrinsic to) the usury problem.[10] It does not endorse on *a priori* grounds just any credit

---

[9]Nicholas Oresme distinguished three ways of gaining through money in unnatural ways: (1) the art of the money-changer: banking and exchange, (2) usury, and (3) the alteration of the coinage. "The first way is contemptible, the second bad and the third worse." See Oresme, "Treatise," chap. 17, p. 27.

[10]For an overview see Eugen von Böhm-Bawerk, *Capital and Interest* (South Holland, Ill.: Libertarian Press, 1959), vol. 1, chaps. 2 and 3; John T. Noonan, *The Scholastic Analysis of Usury* (Cambridge, Mass.: Harvard University Press, 1957); Raymond de Roover, *Business, Banking, and Economic Thought in Late Medieval and Early Modern Europe* (Chicago:

bargain made on the free market. It affirms that taking and paying interest is not *per se* morally wrong, but at the same time retains the authority to condemn some interest payments as usurious. This concerns especially the case of consumer credit, because taking interest might here be in violation of charity. Similarly, while interest on business loans is *per se* legitimate, some business loans might be illegitimate because of particular circumstances. Below we will follow Bernard Dempsey in arguing that interest payments deriving from fractional-reserve banking are tantamount to "institutional usury."[11]

University of Chicago Press, 1974); and H. du Passage, "Usure," *Dictionnaire de Théologie Catholique* 15 (Paris: Letouzey et Ane, 1909–1950). See also A. Vermeersh, "Interest," *Catholic Encyclopedia* 8 (1910); idem, "Usury," *Catholic Encyclopedia* 15 (1912); and Bernard Dempsey, *Interest and Usury* (Washington, D.C.: American Council of Public Affairs, 1943). A good discussion of "interesse" as compared to "usury" is in Victor Brants, *L'économie politique au Moyen-Age* (reprint, New York: Franklin, 1970), pp. 145–56. Further discussion of the history of this concept is in Ludwig von Mises, *Socialism* (Indianapolis: Liberty Fund, 1981), part 4, chap. 3 and 4; Murray N. Rothbard, *Economic Thought Before Adam Smith* (Cheltenham, U.K.: Edward Elgar, 1995), pp. 42–47, 79–81; Jesús Huerta de Soto, *Money, Bank Credit, and Economic Cycles* (Auburn, Ala.: Ludwig von Mises Institute, 2006), pp. 64–69.

[11]See Dempsey, *Interest and Usury*, p. 228.

4

Utilitarian Considerations on the Production of Money

1. THE SUFFICIENCY OF NATURAL MONEY PRODUCTION

So far we have described how a commodity money system would work in a free market and how this system appears from an ethical point of view. We have also argued that our present paper currencies and electronic currencies could not survive in a truly free market against the competition of commodity monies. They continue to be used because they enjoy the privilege of special legal protection against their natural competitors, gold and silver. At no time in history has paper money been produced in a competitive market setting. Whenever and wherever it came into being, it existed only because the courts and the police suppressed the natural alternatives.

In other words, to have a paper money means to allow the government to significantly curtail the personal liberties of its citizens. It means to curtail the freedom of association and the freedom of contract in a way that affects the citizens on a daily basis and on a massive scale. It means send in the police and to use the courts to combat human cooperation involving "natural monies" such as gold and silver, monies in use since biblical times.

These circumstances weigh heavily against paper money. Using the armed forces of the state to put an entire nation before the stark choice of either using the government's money, or renouncing the benefits of monetary exchanges altogether—this is certainly not a light matter, but one that requires a compelling and unassailable rationale. To make a moral case for paper money or electronic money, one has to demonstrate that they convey significant advantages for the community of their users (the "nation"), advantages that might compensate for their severe moral shortcomings. The question, then, is whether such advantages exist. Can paper money and electronic money be justified on utilitarian grounds? To this question we now turn.

It is a significant fact that, before the time when paper money first came into being, no philosopher of money ever criticized the then-existing commodity monies on utilitarian grounds. It is true that Plato proposed to outlaw private ownership of natural monies—gold and silver—on political grounds, namely, to ensure that each individual was economically dependent on government.[1] But even Plato did not claim that gold and silver were somehow inadequate as monies, or that monies imposed by the government could render greater monetary services. And neither do we find any such thought in Aristotle or in the writings of the Church fathers and the scholastics. Quite to the contrary! Bishop Nicholas Oresme argued that the money supply was irrelevant for monetary exchanges *per se*. Changes of the nominal money supply—the "alteration of names"—did not make money more suitable to be used in indirect exchanges, nor less; such changes merely affected the terms of deferred payments (credit contracts), which was also why Oresme opposed them.[2]

---

[1]See Plato, *The Laws*, book 5, 741b–44a. He argued that the money most suitable for his totalitarian ideal city would be fiat money that had no value outside of the city walls.

[2]See Oresme, Nicholas Oresme, "A Treatise on the Origin, Nature, Law, and Alterations of Money," in Charles Johnson, ed., *The De Moneta of Nicholas Oresme and English Mint Documents* (London: Thomas Nelson and Sons, 1956), chap. 11, p. 18.

Thus before the sixteenth century there was apparently no problem of hoarding, or of sticky prices, and apparently no need to stabilize the price level, the purchasing power, or aggregate demand. But the champions of paper money are far from seeing any significance in this fact. Gold and silver, they argue, were sufficient for the primitive economies prevailing until the High Middle Ages. But the capitalist economies that emerged in the Renaissance required a different type of money. And the new theories explaining this need arose along with the new paper currencies. So what do we make of these new theories? We have to examine them one by one, even though in the present work we can only address the major ones, trusting that the reader will rely for everything else on other works.

But before we explain the fallacies involved in the most widespread justifications of paper money, let us point out that post-1500 monetary writings not only swamped the world with such justifications, but also provided the rejoinders. We have already mentioned that Oresme argued that the money supply was irrelevant, in the sense that the services derived from monetary exchange did not depend on the quantity of money used. The intellectuals of the Renaissance and of the mercantilist period could never quite get around this fundamental insight. Even those who otherwise justified various inflationist schemes had to acknowledge it.[3] Then the classical economists stated very clearly that, in principle, any quantity of money would do; even though they qualified this proposition in the light of various false doctrines they had inherited from their mercantilist predecessors.[4] The first economist

---

[3]John Locke famously argued that, in a closed economy, "any quantity of that Money . . . would serve to drive any proportion of Trade . . ." "Some Considerations of the Consequences of the Lowering of Interest and Raising the Value of Money" (1691), in P.H. Kelly, ed.,*Locke on Money* (Oxford: Clarendon Press, 1991), vol. 1, p. 264. The caveat was that the money supply had to be constant, lest money would not be an unalterable measure of the value of things. We will discuss this problem below.

[4]David Ricardo, emulating Locke's argument, said about the consequences of an increase in the number of transactions: "There will be

who had a clear scientific grasp of the issue was John Wheatley, the brilliant critic of the monetary thought of Hume, Steuart, and Smith.[5] But Wheatley never presented a systematic doctrine in print. In the twentieth century, Ludwig von Mises and Murray Rothbard filled this gap. The practical offshoot of their monetary analysis is that no social benefits can be derived from government control over the money supply. In Rothbard's words:

> We conclude, therefore, that determining the supply of money, like all other goods, is best left to the free market. Aside from the general moral and economic advantages of freedom over coercion, no dictated quantity of money will do the work better, and the free market will set the production of gold in accordance with its relative ability to satisfy the needs of consumers, as compared with all other productive goods.[6]

Again, as we have pointed out, this is anything but a novelty in the history of thought. Oresme clearly saw that increases of the nominal money supply would enrich the princes at the expense of the community. But except for very rare and exceptional emergency situations, this was not the

---

more commodities bought and sold, but at lower prices; so that the same money will still be adequate to the increased number of transactions, by passing in each transaction at a higher value." The problem was, in Ricardo's opinion, that the increased purchasing power of money would invite additional money production, and thus the standard of value would be modified. Moreover, this change would affect deferred payments. David Ricardo, "Proposals for an Economical and Secure Currency," *Works and Correspondence*, Piero Sraffa, ed. (Cambridge: Cambridge University Press, 1951–1973), p. 56.

[5]See John Wheatley, *The Theory of Money and Principles of Commerce* (London: Bulmer, 1807). On Wheatley see Thomas Humphrey, "John Wheatley's Theory of International Monetary Adjustment," *Federal Reserve Bank of Richmond Economic Quarterly* 80, no. 3 (1994); Wheatley's treatise is still referenced today in Paul Lagasse et al. eds., *Columbia Encyclopedia Britannica*, 6th ed. (Gale Group, 2003), entry on "Money."

[6]Murray N. Rothbard, *What Has Government Done to Our Money?*, 4th ed. (Auburn, Ala.: Ludwig von Mises Institute, 1990), pp. 34f.

price to be paid for some benefit that could not otherwise be obtained. Nominal increases of the money supply were unnecessary from the point of view of the entire common- wealth. The nominal alteration of the coinage, said Oresme,

> ... does not avoid scandal, but begets it ... and it has many awkward consequences, some of which have already been mentioned, while others will appear later, nor is there any necessity or convenience in doing it, nor can it advantage the commonwealth.[7]

The truth is often deceptively simple. It is the errors that are manifold and complicated. So it is at any rate in the case of money. The simple truth is that there is no need for political intervention to impose monies different from the ones that the market participants would have chosen anyway. But many doctrines have been concocted to justify precisely such inter- vention.[8] It is not necessary for us to refute all of them in the present work. In what follows we will discuss only the seven most widespread errors.

---

[7]Oresme, "Treatise," chap. 18, p. 29. He went on:

> A clear sign of this is that such alterations are a modern invention, as it was mentioned in the last chapter. For such a thing was never done in [Christian] cities or kingdoms for- merly or now well governed. ... If the Italians or Romans did in the end make such alterations, as appears from bad ancient money sometimes to be found in the country, this was proba- bly the reason why their noble empire came to nothing. It appears therefore that these changes are so bad that they are essentially impermissible.

Compare this astounding historical judgment to Ludwig von Mises's "Observations on the Causes of the Decline of Ancient Civilization," in *Human Action* (Auburn, Ala.: Ludwig von Mises Institute, 1998), pp. 761–63.

[8]For an overview of the most widely accepted present-day criticisms of natural money see James Kimball, "The Gold Standard in Contempo- rary Economic Principles Textbooks: A Survey," *Quarterly Journal of Aus- trian Economics* 8, no. 3 (2005).

2 ECONOMIC GROWTH AND THE MONEY SUPPLY

The most widespread monetary fallacy is probably the naïve belief that economic growth is possible only to the extent that it is accompanied by a corresponding growth of the money supply.[9] Suppose the economy growths at an annual rate of 5 percent. Then according to that fallacy it is necessary to increase the money supply also by 5 percent because otherwise the additional goods and services could not be sold. The champions of this fallacy then point out that such growth rates of the money supply are rather exceptional for precious metals. Gold and silver are therefore unsuitable to serve as the money of a dynamic modern economy. We better replace them with paper money, which can be flexibly increased at extremely low costs to accommodate any growth rates of the economy.

---

[9]Often this belief is based on the "assignment theory of money" according to which each unit of money is some sort of a receipt. The receipt testifies that its owner has delivered a quantity of goods or services into the economy as into a large social warehouse; and by the same token the receipt assigns the owner the right to withdraw an equivalent quantity of goods or services from the economy as from a social warehouse. This assignment theory goes back to John Law in the early eighteenth century, was developed in the second half of the nineteenth century, and eventually inspired several champions of inflation such as Wieser and Schumpeter. Among Catholic authors subscribing to this doctrine see in particular Heinrich Pesch, *Lehrbuch der Nationalökonomie* (Freiburg i.Br.: Herder, 1923), vol. 5, p. 175, where the author discusses the factors determining the money supply "needed" in the economy, highlighting the "total value of all goods and services circulating in the economy." Pesch overlooks that the market value of goods and services is not independent of the money supply. For example, a larger money supply entails higher prices and thus a higher "total value of all goods and services." See also Étienne Perrot, *Le chrétien et l'argent—Entre Dieu et Mammon* (Paris: Assas éditions/Cahiers pour croire aujourd'hui, Supplement no. 13, 1994), p. 16 where the author defines the nature of money as being an IOU redeemable on demand. For a critique of the assignment theory of money, see Jean-Baptiste Say, *Traité d'économie politique*, 6th ed. (Paris: Guillaumin, 1841), chap. 27, pp. 278–87; Ludwig von Mises, *Theory of Money and Credit* (Indianapolis: Liberty Fund, 1980), appendix, pp. 512–24.

This argument is wrong because any quantity of goods and services can be exchanged with virtually any money supply. Suppose the money supply in our example does not change. If 5 percent more goods and services are offered on the market, then all that happens is that the money prices of these goods and services will decrease. The same mechanism would allow economic growth even when the quantity of money *shrinks*. Any rate of growth can therefore be accommodated by virtually any supply of natural monies such as gold and silver.

The qualification "virtually" takes account of the fact that there are certain technological limitations on the use of the precious metals. Suppose there are high growth rates over an extended period of time. In this case, it might be necessary to reduce coin sizes to such an extent that producing and using these coins becomes unpractical. This problem is very real in the case of gold. It has never existed in the case of silver— which is also why many informed writers consider silver to be the money par excellence. In any case, such technological problems pose no problem. As Bishop Oresme explained more than 700 years ago, the thing to do in such cases is simply to abandon the use of the unpractical coins, say gold coins, and switch to another precious metal, say silver.[10] And, we may add, on the free market there are strong incentives to bring about such switching promptly and efficiently. No political intervention is necessary to support this process.

A more sophisticated variant of the growth-requires-more-money doctrine grants that any quantities of goods and services could be traded at virtually any money supply. But these advocates argue that, if entrepreneurs are forced to sell their products at lower prices, these prices might be too low in comparison to cost expenditure. Selling product inventories at bargain prices entails bankruptcy for the entrepreneurs.

But this variant is equally untenable, because it is premised on a mechanistic image of entrepreneurship. Fact is

---

[10]See Oresme, "Treatise," chap. 13, pp. 20f.

that entrepreneurs can anticipate any future reductions of the selling prices of their products. In the light of such anticipations they can cut offering prices on their own cost expenditure and thus thrive in times of declining prices. This is not a mere theoretical possibility but the normal state of affairs in periods of a stable or falling price level. For example, in the last three decades of the nineteenth century, both Germany and the U.S. experienced high growth rates at stable and declining consumer-price levels.[11] The same thing is observed more recently in the market for computers and information technology, the most vibrant market since the 1980s, which has combined rapid growth with constantly falling product prices.

3. Hoarding

The foregoing considerations also apply to the phenomenon of hoarding. It is impossible to use money without holding a certain amount of it; thus every participant in a monetary economy hoards money. The reason why the pejorative term "hoarding" is sometimes used in lieu of the more neutral "holding" is that, in the mind of the commentator, the amounts of money held by this or that person are excessive. The crucial question is of course: by which standard?

It is possible to give a meaningful definition of hoarding in moral terms. Some people have a neurotic propensity to keep their wealth in cash. They are misers who hoard their money even when spending it would be in their personal interest. They neglect clothing, housing, education, charity, and so on; and thus they deprive themselves of their full human potential, and in turn deprive others of the benefits that come from social bonds with a developed human being. Notice that this definition of hoarding as pathological behavior does not refer

---

[11]See Milton Friedman and Anna Schwartz, *A Monetary History of the United States* (Chicago: University of Chicago Press, 1963); Ulrich Nocken, "Die Große Deflation: Goldstandard, Geldmenge und Preise in den USA und Deutschland 1870–1896," Eckart Schremmer, ed., *Geld und Währung vom 16. Jahrhundert bis zur Gegenwart* (Stuttgart: Franz Steiner, 1993), pp. 157–89.

to absolute amounts of money held. Rather it concerns the amounts of money held relative to alternative ways of investing one's wealth. There are indeed many situations in which it is advisable—both for an individual person and for groups—to hold large sums of cash. For centuries, holding large numbers of gold and silver coins was an important way for people to save their own private pension funds, and in many times and places it was the only way to provide for old age and emergency situations. Similarly, in times of stock market and real-estate booms, it is generally prudent to keep a large amount of one's wealth in cash. It is true that there are other situations in which even very small sums of money held might be excessive. The point is that the question whether one's cash balances are just "money held" or whether they are pathological "money hoards" must be determined for each individual case.

The right way to deal with excessive money hoarding is to talk to the persons in question and persuade them to change their behavior. What if these persons remain stubborn? Is it then advisable to apply political means such as expropriation or an artificial increase of the money supply? The answer to these questions is in the negative. Hoarding *per se* might be pathological, but it does not deprive other people of what is rightfully theirs. And in particular it does not prevent the efficient operation of the economy.

As we have stated above, the absolute money supply of an economy is virtually irrelevant. The economy can work, and work well, with virtually any quantity of money. Hoarding merely entails a reduction of money prices; hoarding on a mass scale merely entails a large reduction of money prices. Consider the (completely unrealistic) scenario of a nation hoarding so much silver that the remaining silver would have to be coined in microscopically small quantities to be used in the exchanges.[12] In a free society, the market participants

---

[12]This is probably close to the scenario that most critics of hoarding have in mind. Thus we read in an influential contemporary book on

would then simply switch to other monies. Rather than paying with silver coins they would start using gold coins and copper coins.

Now suppose that, despite the foregoing considerations, a government bent on fighting money hoards would set out to artificially increase the money supply anyway. Would this policy reach its goal? Not necessarily. There is at least an equal likelihood that the policy would actually promote hoarding. The increased money supply would raise the money prices being paid on the market above the level they would otherwise have reached. And this makes it necessary for people to hold larger cash balances. Now it is true that the increase in individual cash balances is not necessarily in strict proportion to the increase of the price level. Thus it is possible that people will, relatively speaking, *reduce* their demand for money as a consequence of the policy. But it is just as likely that the policy will have no such effect, or that it actually produces the opposite effect.

Thus we conclude that hoarding cannot serve as a pretext for the artificial extension of the money supply. In some extreme cases it might merit the attention of spiritual leaders and psychologists. But it is never a monetary problem.

4. FIGHTING DEFLATION

Still another variant of the same basic fallacy that we just discussed is the alleged need to fight deflation.

Catholic social doctrine: "In early literature, a common symbol for economic evil was the miser, who through avarice hoarded his money. The miser was evil because, in a static world, with valuables in short supply, what one person hoarded was subtracted from the common store." Michael Novak, *The Spirit of Democratic Capitalism* (New York: Simon & Schuster, 1982), p. 98; see also pp. 266–67. The author then goes on to point out that the social problem of hoarding has been resolved in modern times through what he believes is the dynamism of capitalism, which incites people to spend rather than hoard their money. We will have the occasion to deal with this "dynamism" in some more detail below. At this point, let us notice that hoarding is never, *per se*, a social problem in the first place.

The word "deflation" can be defined in various ways. According to the most widely accepted definition today, deflation is a sustained decrease of the price level. Older authors have often used the expression "deflation" to denote a decreasing money supply, and some contemporary authors use it to characterize a decrease of the inflation *rate*. All of these definitions are acceptable, depending on the purpose of the analysis. None of them, however, lends itself to justifying an artificial increase of the money supply.

The harmful character of deflation is today one of the sacred dogmas of monetary policy.[13] The champions of the fight against deflation usually present six arguments to make their case.[14] One, in their eyes it is a matter of historical experience that deflation has negative repercussions on aggregate production and, therefore, on the standard of living. To explain this presumed historical record, they hold, two, that deflation incites the market participants to postpone buying because they speculate on ever lower prices. Furthermore, they consider, three, that a declining price level makes it more difficult to service debts contracted at a higher price level in the past. These difficulties threaten to entail, four, a crisis within the banking industry and thus a dramatic curtailment of credit. Five, they claim that deflation in conjunction with "sticky prices" results in unemployment. And finally, six, they consider that deflation might reduce nominal interest rates to such an extent that a monetary policy of "cheap money," to stimulate employment and production, would no longer be possible, because the interest rate cannot be decreased below zero.

---

[13]The public speeches of the chiefs of monetary policy furnish ample evidence in support of this contention. Professor Bernanke, the present chairman of the Federal Reserve, is especially outspoken on this issue.

[14]For an overview, see Federal Reserve Bank of Cleveland, *Deflation— 2002 Annual Report* (May 9, 2003); R.C.K. Burdekin and P.L. Siklos, eds., *Deflation: Current and Historical Perspectives* (Cambridge: Cambridge University Press, 2004). On the latter volume, see Nikolay Gertchev's excellent review essay in *Quarterly Journal of Austrian Economics* 9, no. 1 (2006): 89–96.

However, theoretical and empirical evidence substantiating these claims is either weak or lacking altogether.[15]

First, in historical fact, deflation has had no clear negative impact on aggregate production. Long-term decreases of the price level did not systematically correlate with lower growth rates than those that prevailed in comparable periods and/or countries with increasing price levels. Even if we focus on deflationary shocks emanating from the financial system, empirical evidence does not seem to warrant the general claim that deflation impairs long-run growth.[16]

Second, it is true that unexpectedly strong deflation can incite people to postpone purchase decisions. However, this does not by any sort of necessity slow down aggregate production. Notice that, in the presence of deflationary tendencies, purchase decisions in general, and consumption in particular, does *not* come to a halt. For one thing, human beings act under the "constraint of the stomach." Even the most neurotic misers, who cherish saving a penny above anything else, must make a minimum of purchases just to survive the next day. And all others—that is, the great majority of the population—will by and large buy just as many consumers' goods as they would have bought in a nondeflationary environment. Even though they expect prices to decline ever further, they will buy goods and services at some point because they prefer enjoying these goods and services sooner rather than later (economists call this "time preference"). In actual fact, then,

---

[15]For recent Austrian analyses of deflation, see the special issue on "Deflation and Monetary Policy" in *Quarterly Journal of Austrian Economics* 6. no. 4 (2003). See also Murray N. Rothbard, *America's Great Depression*, 5th ed. (Auburn, Ala.: Ludwig von Mises Institute, 2000), part 1; idem, *Man, Economy, and State*, 3rd ed. (Auburn, Ala.: Ludwig von Mises Institute, 1993), pp. 863–65.

[16]See George Selgin, *Less Than Zero* (London: Institute for Economic Affairs, 1997); Michael D. Bordo and Angela Redish, "Is Deflation Depressing? Evidence from the Classical Gold Standard," NBER Working Paper #9520 (Cambridge, Mass.: NBER, 2003); A. Atkeson and P.J. Kehoe, "Deflation and Depression: Is There an Empirical Link?" *American Economic Review, Papers and Proceedings* 94 (May 2004): 99–103.

consumption will slow down only marginally in a deflationary environment. And this marginal reduction of consumer spending, far from impairing aggregate production, will rather tend to *increase* it. The simple fact is that all resources that are not used for consumption are saved; that is, they are available for investment and thus help to extend production in those areas that previously were not profitable enough to warrant investment.

Third, it is correct that deflation—especially unanticipated deflation—makes it more difficult to service debts contracted at a higher price level in the past. In the case of a massive deflation shock, widespread bankruptcy might result. Such consequences are certainly deplorable from the standpoint of the individual entrepreneurs and capitalists who own the firms, factories, and other productive assets when the deflationary shock hits. However, from the aggregate (social) point of view, it does not matter who controls the existing resources. What matters from this overall point of view is that resources remain intact and be used. Now the important point is that deflation does not destroy these resources physically. It merely diminishes their monetary value, which is why their present owners go bankrupt. Thus deflation by and large boils down to a redistribution of productive assets from old owners to new owners. The net impact on production is likely to be zero.[17]

Fourth, it is true that deflation more or less directly threatens the banking industry, because deflation makes it more difficult for bank customers to repay their debts and because widespread business failures are likely to have a direct negative impact on the liquidity of banks. However, for the same reasons that we just discussed, while this might be devastating for some banks, it is not so for society as a whole. The crucial point is that bank credit does *not create* resources; it channels existing resources into *other* businesses than those which

---

[17]One might argue that, even though deflation had no negative impact on production, the aforementioned redistribution is unacceptable from a moral point of view. We will discuss some aspects of this question in the second part of the present book, in the section dealing with the economics of legalized suspensions of payments.

would have used them if these credits had not existed. It follows that a curtailment of bank credit does not destroy any resources; it simply entails a different employment of human beings and of the available land, factories, streets, and so on.

In the light of the preceding considerations it appears that the problems entailed by deflation are much less formidable than they are in the opinion of present-day monetary authorities. Deflation certainly has much disruptive potential. However, as will become even more obvious in the following chapters, it mainly threatens institutions that are responsible for inflationary increases of the money supply. It reduces the wealth of fractional-reserve banks, and their customers—debt-ridden governments, entrepreneurs, and consumers. But as we have argued, such destruction liberates the underlying physical resources for new employment. The destruction entailed by deflation is therefore often "creative destruction" in the Schumpeterian sense.[18]

Finally, we still need to deal with the aforementioned fifth argument—deflation in conjunction with sticky prices results in unemployment—and with the sixth argument—deflation makes a policy of cheap money impossible. Because these arguments are of a more general nature, we will deal with them separately in the next two sections.

5. STICKY PRICES

In the past eighty years, the sticky-prices argument has played an important role in monetary debates. According to this argument, the manipulation of the money supply might be a suitable instrument to re-establish a lost equilibrium on certain markets, most notably on the labor market. Suppose that powerful labor unions push up nominal wage rates in all industries to such an extent that entrepreneurs can no longer profitably employ a great part of the workforce at these wages. The result is mass unemployment. But if it were possible to substantially increase the money supply, then the selling prices

---

[18]See Joseph A. Schumpeter, *Capitalism, Socialism, and Democracy* (London: Allen & Unwin, 1944), chap. 7.

of the entrepreneurs might rise enough to allow for the re-integration of the unemployed workers into the division of labor. Now, the argument goes, under a gold or silver standard, this kind of policy is impossible for purely technical reasons because the money supply is inflexible. Only a paper money provides the technical wherewithal to implement pro-employment policies. Thus we have here a *prima facie* justification for suppressing the natural commodity monies and supporting a paper money standard.

This argument grew into prominence during the 1920s in Austria, Germany, the United Kingdom, and other countries. After World War II, it became something like a dogma of economic policy. But this does not alter the fact that it is sheer fallacy, and it is not even difficult to see the root of the fallacy. The argument is in fact premised on the notion that monetary-policy makers can constantly outsmart the labor unions. The managers of the printing press can again and again surprise the labor-union leaders through another round of expansion-ist monetary policy. Clearly, this is a silly assumption and in retrospect it is very astonishing that responsible men could ever have taken it seriously. The labor unions were not fooled. Faced with the reality of expansionist monetary policy, they eventually increased their wage demands to compensate for the declining purchasing power of money. The result was stagflation—high unemployment plus inflation—a phenomenon that in the past thirty years has come to plague countries with strong labor unions such as France and Germany.

6. THE ECONOMICS OF CHEAP MONEY

Another widespread fallacy is the idea that paper money could help to decrease the interest rate, thus promoting economic growth. If new paper tickets are printed and then first offered on the credit market, so the argument goes, the supply of credit is increased and as a consequence the price of credit—interest—declines. Cheap money is now available for businessmen all over the country. They will invest more than they otherwise would have invested, and therefore economic growth will be enhanced.

There are actually a good number of different fallacies involved in this argument, and it is impossible for us to deal with all of them here.[19] Suffice it to say that capitalists invest their funds only if they can expect to earn a return on investment—interest—and that they do not seek merely nominal rates of return, but real returns. If they expect the "purchasing power" of the money unit (PPM) to decline in the future, they will make investments only in exchange for a higher nominal rate of return. Thus suppose Mrs. Myers plans to lend the sum of 100 oz. of silver for one year to a businessman in her neighborhood, but only in exchange for a future payment of 103 oz. Suppose further that she expects silver to lose some 5 percent of its purchasing power within the following year. Then Mrs. Myers will ask for another 5 oz. (making the total future payment 108 oz.), so as to compensate her for the loss of purchasing power.

Now the question is whether (1) printing new money tickets will in fact decrease the real interest rate and (2) whether, if it does decrease the real interest rate, this will be an economic boon.

To answer the first question, we have to bring anticipations back into the picture. If the capitalists realize that new paper notes are being printed, they can expect a decline of the PPM and thus they will ask for a higher price premium. If the price premium is an exact compensation for the decline of the PPM, the real interest will be unaffected. In this case, the artificial increase of the money supply would entail merely a different distribution of capital among businessmen, and thus a different array of consumer goods being produced. Some businessmen and their customers will win, whereas other businessmen and their customers will lose. But there will be no overall improvement.

---

[19]For full detail see Mises, *Human Action*, esp. chap. 20; Murray N. Rothbard, *Man, Economy, and State* (Auburn, Ala.: Ludwig von Mises Institute, 1993), chap. 11; Jesús Huerta de Soto, *Money, Bank Credit, and Economic Cycles* (Auburn, Ala.: Ludwig von Mises Institute, 2006), chaps. 4–6.

Now suppose that the capitalists *over*estimate the future decline of the PPM. In this case, the real interest rate would actually *increase* and many businessmen would be deprived of credit they could otherwise have obtained. Again, the consequence would be a different distribution of capital among businessmen, and thus a different array of consumer goods being produced. But there would be no overall improvement or deterioration.

Yet it is also possible that the capitalists *under*estimate the future decline of the PPM. This might be the case, in particular, when they are unaware of the fact that more paper notes are being printed. It is this scenario that the advocates of cheap money commonly have in mind. But the hope that tricking capitalists into accepting lower real interest rates entails more economic growth is entirely unfounded. It is true that in the case under consideration the real interest rate would decline under the impact of new paper money being offered on the credit market. It is also true that this event is likely to incite businessmen to borrow more money and to start more investment projects than they otherwise would have started. Yet it would be a grave error to infer that this is tantamount to enhanced economic growth. The case is exactly the reverse.

At any point of time, the available supplies of factors of production put a limit on the number of investment projects that can be successfully completed. What the artificial decrease of the real interest rate does is to increase the number of projects that are *launched*. But the total volume of investments that can be *completed* has not thereby increased, because this volume depends exclusively on the productive resources that are objectively available during the time needed for completion. The artificial decrease of the interest rate therefore lures the business community into all kinds of investments that cannot be completed. In terms of a biblical example, they could be said to start building all kinds of towers, only to discover after a while that they just had the resources to build the foundations, but not to finish the towers themselves (Luke 14:28–30). The labor and capital invested in the foundations are then lost, not only for the investor, but for the entire commonwealth. They could have been fruitfully invested in a smaller number of projects, but the artificial decrease of the interest rate prevented this. In short, economic growth is diminished below the level it could otherwise have reached.

To sum up, it is by no means sure that politically induced increases of the money supply will lead to a decrease of the interest rate below the level it would have reached in a free economy. The success of cheap-money policy is especially unlikely when the policy is not adopted on an *ad-hoc* basis, but turned into a guiding principle of economic policy. But the fundamental objection to this policy is that it is counterproductive even if it succeeds in decreasing the interest rate. The consequence would be more waste and thus less growth.

7. MONETARY STABILITY

The second-most widespread monetary fallacy relates to the problem of monetary stability. The conviction that money should be an anchor of stability in the economic world is very old. But to understand this postulate in a proper way, it is necessary to distinguish two very different meanings of "monetary stability."

The first meaning stresses the stability of the physical integrity of commodity money (in particular, the physical composition of coins made out of precious metals) through time. In this sense, monetary stability does have a precise meaning. From a purely formal point of view, it can therefore be a possible postulate of ethical monetary policy. It is a postulate relating to the production of money. No producer shall make coins bearing the same imprint but containing different quantities of precious metal. Monetary stability in this sense is not only unobjectionable, but truly a presupposition of a well-functioning economy. And it is this sense of monetary stability that was stressed in the Bible and in authoritative texts of the Middle Ages.[20]

---

[20]The Old Testament is crystal clear on the importance of the physical integrity of coinage: "Varying weights, varying measures, are both an abomination to the LORD" (Proverbs 20:10). Innocent III emphasized the same point in the only authoritative papal pronouncement on

Notice that monetary stability in the sense of a stable physical integrity of commodity money results in a relatively stable "purchasing power" of the money unit (PPM). When mining is less profitable than other branches of industry—which tends to be the case when the price level is high—then less money will be produced and money prices will tend to decline. And when mining is more profitable—usually when the price level is low—then more money will be produced and money prices will therefore tend to rise. All of this is of no importance whatever for the benefits that can be derived from monetary exchanges. It is true that a great decrease of the PPM is conceivable when extremely rich and cost-efficient new mines are discovered. But notice two things. First, in a free economy, the market participants can very easily protect themselves against any unwanted eradication of the PPM by simply adopting other monies. Second, as a matter of fact, no such violent depreciations of the PPM have ever occurred in the case of precious metals. The famous "gold and silver inflation" of the sixteenth and seventeenth century increased Europe's money stock according to certain estimates by not

---

medieval currency questions: in the bull *Quanto* (1199). Nicholas Oresme wrote an entire treatise that exposed the physical alteration of the coinage as a fraudulent and harmful practice. And the other great medieval authority on monetary questions, Ptolemy of Lucca, stressed the same point, arguing that the alteration of coinage "would work to the people's detriment, since money should be the measure of things . . . but the more the money or coinage is changed the more the value or the weight changes." Ptolemy of Lucca, *On the Government of Rulers* (Philadelphia: University of Pennsylvania Press, 1997), p. 134.

Notice that the authority of Ptolemy's text for subsequent generations derived to a large extent from the fact that it was believed to be the work of Saint Thomas Aquinas. But according to the prevailing opinion in contemporary scholarship, Saint Thomas wrote only the first twenty chapters of this book; the rest (including the passage we cited above) was from the pen of Ptolemy. The chapters written by Saint Thomas have been republished in several modern editions under the title of the original manuscript: *On Kingship, To the King of Cyprus*. See in particular the 1949 edition from the Pontifical Institute of Mediaeval Studies in Toronto, which contains a very useful introduction.

more than 50 percent[21]; according to others by up to 500 percent.[22] However, this happened over a period of some 150 years. Thus the average growth rate of the money supply lay somewhere between 0.3 and 3.3 percent *per annum*. By contrast, in our days of paper money, even the countries enjoying a "conservative" monetary policy experience far greater increases of the money supply. For example, in the U.S. and in the European Union, the stock of "base money" (paper notes plus accounts held at the central banks) has been increased by annual rates of between 5 and 10 percent during the past five years.

Now let us turn to the second meaning of monetary stability. It connotes the stability of the purchasing power of the money unit (the PPM). The first thinker to formulate the postulate of a stable PPM was Saint Thomas Aquinas in the thirteenth century. He argued:

> The particular virtue of currency must be that when a man presents it he immediately receives what he needs. However, it is true that currency also suffers the same as other things, viz., that it does not always obtain for a man what he wants because it cannot always be equal or of the same value. Nevertheless it ought to be so established that it

---

[21]Around the year 1500, the total stock of money in Europe was about 3,500 tons of gold and 37,500 tons of silver. Over the next 150 years, Spain imported some 181 tons of gold and some 16,886 tons of silver from its mines in South America (other producers were negligible as compared to these figures). A major part of these Spanish imports were re-exported to the Far East and to the Middle East. See Geoffrey Parker, "Die Entstehung des modernen Geld- und Finanzwesens in Europa 1500–1730," C.M. Cipolla and K. Borchardt, *Europäische Wirtschaftsgeschichte*, vol. 2, *Sechzehntes und siebzehntes Jahrhundert* (Stuttgart: Gustav Fischer, 1983), pp. 335–36. The author quotes from F.P. Braudel und F. Spooner, "Prices in Europe from 1450 to 1750," E.E. Rich and C.H. Wilson, eds., *The Cambridge Economic History of Europe* (Cambridge: Cambridge University Press, 1967), vol. 4.

[22]See Friedrich-Wilhelm Henning, *Handbuch der Wirtschafts- und Sozialgeschichte Deutschlands* (Paderborn: Schöningh, 1991), vol. 1, pp. 546–48.

retains the same value more permanently than other things.[23]

Notice that Saint Thomas realized perfectly well that a stable PPM was not a natural outcome of the market process. It was in his eyes an ethical *postulate*. However, no major writer before him believed that a stable PPM was a meaningful policy objective. Aristotle had observed that the prices of all things are in a continuous flux, and that money was no exception.[24] And that was it. Even after Aquinas, most scholastics sided on this issue with the Greek philosopher rather than with Saint Thomas. To the extent that late scholastics such as Martín de Azpilcueta, Tomás de Mercado, Pedro de Valencia, and others stressed a postulate of monetary stability at all, they meant the stable physical composition of coins.[25] Only starting from the seventeenth century, did secular writers from John Locke to David Ricardo to Irving Fisher come to endorse the postulate of a stable PPM. Today, this postulate lies at the heart of most contemporary writings on the problem of monetary stability. It is also a widely accepted definition among contemporary Catholic writers on monetary affairs.[26] However, despite its popularity it is fraught with ambiguities and is liable to lead to wrong policy conclusions.

---

[23]Saint Thomas Aquinas, *Commentary on the Nicomachean Ethics*, vol. 1 (Chicago: Regnery, 1964), bk. 5, lect. 9, col. 987, pp. 427–28.

[24]Aristotle, *Nicomachean Ethics*, bk. 5, chap. 8

[25]See Marjorie Grice-Hutchinson, *Economic Thought in Spain*, L. Moss and C. Ryan, eds. (Aldershot, U.K.: Edward Elgar, 1993), pp. 84–85 and appendix. A contemporary historian of economic thought observed that, as far as money was concerned, realist and nominalist philosophers paradoxically switched roles. Oresme was the realist philosopher and Aquinas a nominalist. See André Lapidus, "Une introduction à la pensée économique médiévale," A. Béraud and G. Faccarello, eds., *Nouvelle histoire de la pensée économique* (Paris: La Découverte, 1992), vol. 1, chap. 1, pp. 50–51; see also idem, "Metal, Money, and the Prince: John Buridan and Nicholas Oresme after Thomas Aquinas," *History of Political Economy* 29 (1997).

[26]See, for example, Oswald von Nell-Breuning and J. Heinz Müller, *Vom Geld und vom Kapital* (Freiburg: Herder, 1962), p. 76; Karl Blessing,

It is a matter of course that a stable PPM is "a major consideration in the orderly development of the entire economic system."[27] The question is merely how to balance this consideration with other considerations of a moral and economic nature. On the free market, as we have seen, there is a tendency for the selection of the best monies, including in terms of PPM stability. As long as the citizens are free to choose their money, they can avoid exposure to any violent fluctuations of the PPM by simply switching to other monies. The question, then, is whether the stabilization of the purchasing power of money is such an overriding goal that it would justify the establishment of government control over the money supply, in order to "fine-tune" the purchasing power to an extent that would not spontaneously result from the market process. The ideal of such fine tuning inspired a great intellectual movement in the early twentieth century. Under the leadership of the American economist Irving Fisher and others, this movement paved the way for the complete triumph of paper money.[28]

In practice, the Fisherian stabilization movement was an abject failure. Throughout the entire twentieth century, in all countries, the purchasing power of money managed by public authorities declined and oscillated as never before in the entire history of monetary institutions. However, despite this rather devastating empirical record, one could hold that, in theory at least, the case for monetary stabilization is still valid and that it simply needs to be applied much better than in the past. In order to assess this contention it is necessary to examine whether, in principle at least, one *can* fine-tune the PPM,

---

"Geldwertstabilität als gesellschaftspolitisches Problem," K. Hoffman, W. Weber, and B. Zimmer eds., *Kirche und Wirtschaftsgesellschaft* (Cologne: Hanstein, 1974). In *Centesimus Annus*, Pope John Paul II stressed the importance of stable money, but did not define what he meant by this notion. He merely stated: "The economy . . . presupposes a stable currency" (§48).

[27]John XXIII, *Mater et Magistra*, §129.

[28]See Irving Fisher, *Stabilized Money: A History of the Movement* (London: George Allen and Unwin, 1935).

and whether such fine-tuning could possibly be warranted in the first place. To these questions we now turn.

First of all notice that the notion of "purchasing power of money" (PPM) cannot be given an impartial definition. The PPM is in fact the total *array* of things for which a unit of money can be exchanged. If the price of telephones increases while the price of cars drops, it is impossible to say by any impartial standard whether the PPM has increased or decreased. One can of course make up some algorithm that "weighs" the prices of cars and telephones and so on, and brings them under a common mathematical expression or index. But such indices are not some sort of constant measuring stick of economic value. For one thing, the constituents of the price index are in need of incessant adaptation (they need to be *changed*) to take account of the changes in the array of goods and services offered on the market in exchange for money. Moreover, and most importantly, no such index conveys generally valid information. Different persons buy different goods; therefore, some of them might experience a rise of prices (of the prices *they* have to pay) while others experience a drop of (their) prices in the very same period. The quantitative statement of the index reflects just an average of very different concrete situations. But it is concrete circumstances, not some average, that count for human decision-making.

We cannot do more here than scratch the surface of these technical problems.[29] Our point is that, from a purely formal point of view, monetary stability in the sense of a stable PPM cannot be easily translated into a clear-cut political postulate. The very concept of PPM is fraught with ambiguities that can only be overcome by more or less arbitrary decisions of those charged to apply it. The political implications are momentous. The PPM criterion gives great and arbitrary powers to those charged with making up the algorithm.

---

[29]For a detailed exposition see Rothbard, *Man, Economy, and State,* chap. 11. See also Gottfried von Haberler, *Der Sinn der Indexzahlen* (Tübingen: Mohr, 1927).

Now let us assume for the sake of argument that these very considerable problems did not exist. Let us assume that monetary stability in the sense of a stable PPM could in fact be unequivocally defined. Then the question is: Would it be expedient to postulate a stable PPM? As we have said, this question is answered affirmatively by a great number of contemporary writers on monetary economics. The basic rationale is that one of the chief functions of money is to serve as a standard of value. Businessmen and others use money prices in their economic calculations, and to make these calculations as accurate as possible it is necessary to have a stable standard of value.

When is money a stable standard of value? Here we encounter a certain variety of opinions. For example, according to Locke and others, this was the case if the national money supply did not change. According to David Ricardo and others, it was the case if the money unit preserved its purchasing power. According to Hayek and others, it was the case if the total amount of money spending did not change.[30] But it does not matter much which of the above definitions we adopt. The basic rationale for a stable standard of value is a spurious one in all cases.[31]

The nature of business calculation is not to *measure* the absolute "value" of a firm's assets, but to *compare* alternative courses of action. Suppose Jones has a capital of 1,000 ounces

---

[30]Today, the position espoused by Ricardo is the dominant one, except for an important nuance: Ricardo held that gold was the most suitable money even though, in theory, paper money could have even greater PPM stability than gold. He held this position because paper money would open the floodgates for abuses through government. On balance, therefore, Ricardo opted for gold. The yellow metal was an imperfect standard of value, but it was better than any alternative was or promised to be. After Ricardo, however, concerns about tyranny seem to have dwindled in monetary discussion. Most present-day economists have come under the influence of Irving Fisher, who in a life-long campaign dismissed fears about managed paper monies.

[31]See Mises, *Theory of Money and Credit*; idem, *Geldwertstabilisierung und Konjunkturpolitik* (Jena: Fischer, 1928); idem, *Human Action*, part 3.

of gold and that he can use them to either set up a shoe factory or establish a bakery. He expects the shoe factory to yield 1,100 ounces or 10 percent gross return, and the bakery to yield 1,200 ounces or 20 percent gross return. This comparison is the essence of business calculation. Stability of the PPM does not at all come into play. Jones can calculate with equal success under a stable, a growing, or a declining PPM.[32] His calculus can be exact when the national money supply increases, decreases, or remains frozen. And it can be exact irrespective of whether the total amount of money spending changes or remains the same as before.

In the light of these considerations, it appears that older writers such as Oresme were right all along to neglect the stable PPM criterion, and to keep their attention focused on monetary stability in the sense of the physical integrity of coinage.

8. The Costs of Commodity Money

One great disadvantage of natural monies such as gold and silver seems to be their relatively high cost of production. According to a widespread opinion that became popular through the writings of classical economists Adam Smith and David Ricardo, paper money could do the monetary job just as well, and at much lower production costs.

It is true that producing a 1-ounce silver coin, which we might call "one dollar," entails much higher costs than producing a banknote that bears the same name. But it does not follow that this is necessarily a disadvantage. The natural costs that go in hand with producing gold and silver are in fact a supreme reason why these metals are better monies than paper. The fact that they are costly means that they cannot be multiplied at will; and this in turn means that commodity monies such as gold and silver feature a *built-in natural insurance* against an excessively depreciating purchasing power of

---

[32]The same thing holds true for deferred payments.

money.[33] In this crucial respect they are far superior to paper-money notes, which can be multiplied *ad libitum* and which, as universal experience shows, have been multiplied and are currently being multiplied in far greater proportions than gold and silver ever have.

Hence, the comparison between commodity monies and paper money should not be cast in too narrow terms. Relevant benefits do not just consist in some arbitrarily narrow "exchange service," as we have just argued, but include things like guarantees against inflation. And the relevant costs are not just the cost of fabricating the different monetary objects, but total costs entailed by each system. Even the most ardent advocates of paper money have conceded that our current monetary regime is hardly a bargain. For example, consider that central banks and other monetary authorities have built up huge bureaucracies, and that the Fed-watching industry (people employed to interpret and forecast the policy of the monetary authorities) is similarly important.[34] These two items alone add up to a significant payroll next to which the expenses for mining and minting look much less "costly" than the Ricardians portray. And notice the irony that mining and minting are still with us in the age of paper money!

---

[33]See A. Wagner, *Die russische Papierwährung—eine volkswirtschaftliche und finanzpolitische Studie nebst Vorschlägen zur Herstellung der Valuta* (Riga: Kymmel, 1868), pp. 45–46. The author states that for this reason paper money is no suitable currency and categorically recommends a return to commodity money wherever paper has been introduced, such as in Imperial Russia of his time.

[34]See Milton Friedman, "The Resource Cost of Irredeemable Paper Money," *Journal of Political Economy* 94, no. 3, part 1 (1986): 642–47. Compare Friedman's paper with the statements contained in William Gouge, *A Short History of Paper Money and Banking*, pp. 66–67. See also Roger W. Garrison, "The Costs of a Gold Standard," Llewellyn H. Rockwell, Jr., ed., *The Gold Standard* (Auburn, Ala.: Ludwig von Mises Institute, 1992), pp. 61–79. In 2004, the Federal Reserve System employed a staff of some 23,000. Similarly, the German Bundesbank employed some 11,400 civil servants (*Stammpersonal*) in 2007 and the Banque de France had some 11,800 civil servants (*titulaires*) in 2006.

There is of course nothing wrong with experimenting with cheaper alternatives to gold and silver coins. Nothing would preclude such experiments in a free society. All we can say is that in the past all such experiments have lamentably failed. And the advocates of paper money therefore hardly ever seriously considered establishing their pet scheme on a competitive basis. Ricardo and his followers advocate the *coercive* replacement of a more costly good by a cheaper one. Clearly, in all other spheres of life, we would reject any such proposal as extravagant and outrageous. We do not coerce all members of society into driving only the cheapest cars because they satisfy some arbitrarily conceived "transportation needs" at lowest cost. We do not impose rags and hovels on people who prefer clothes and houses. Neither is there a reason to impose paper money on those who prefer the monies of the ages.

Thus another standard justification for paper money does not hold water. And the same demonstration can be delivered for all other economic theories that purport to explain why it should be beneficial to suppress the natural commodity monies and to replace them with a political makeshift such as paper money. We could go into much length delivering these demonstrations. The point of the foregoing pages was to exemplify the general thesis that there is no utilitarian rationale for the institution of paper money, the money of our times. This thesis will serve as the starting point for the following discussion of the various abuses that can be made, and which unfortunately have been made, in the realm of the production of money.

Part 2
Inflation

5

General Considerations
on Inflation

1. THE ORIGIN AND NATURE OF INFLATION

S o far we have presented the operation of a natural monetary system of competing commodity monies. We have
also argued that there is no utilitarian rationale for inter-
vening into the market process and altering the money supplies through political means.

Now we must turn to deal with the vitally important phenomenon of inflation. We can define it as an extension of the
nominal quantity of any medium of exchange beyond the
quantity that would have been produced on the free market.
This definition corresponds by and large to the way inflation
had been understood until World War II.[1] Yet it differs from
the way the word "inflation" is used in contemporary economics textbooks and in the financial press. Most present-day
writers mean by inflation a lasting increase of the price level

---

[1]This general understanding can be inferred from popular reference
works such as the *Funk and Wagnalls Standard College Dictionary* (1941),
which defined inflation as an "expansion or extension beyond natural
or proper limits or so as to exceed normal or just value, specifically
overissue of currency." The same dictionary defined an inflationist as an
"advocate or believer in the issuing of an abnormally large amount of
currency especially of bank or treasury notes not convertible into coin."

or, what is the same thing, a lasting reduction of the purchasing power of money. Let us hasten to point out that, as far as mere vocabulary is concerned, both meanings of the word are perfectly fine, if only they are used consistently. Definitions do not carry any intrinsic merit; but they can be more or less useful for the understanding of reality. Our definition of inflation singles out the phenomenon of an "increase of nominal quantity of any medium of exchange beyond the quantity that would have been produced on the free market" for the simple reason that this phenomenon is causally related to a large number of other phenomena that are relevant from an economic and moral point of view. As we shall see, inflation in our sense is the cause of unnatural income differentials, business cycles, debt explosion, moderate and exponential increases of the price level, and many other phenomena. This is why we hold our definition to be the most useful one for the purposes of the following analysis. The reader will soon be in a position to verify this contention.

Inflation is an extension of the nominal quantity of any medium of exchange beyond the quantity that would have been produced on the free market. Since the expression "free market" is shorthand for the somewhat long-winded "social cooperation conditioned by the respect of private property rights," the meaning of inflation is that it extends the nominal money supply through a *violation* of property rights. In this sense, inflation can also be called a forcible way of increasing the money supply, as distinct from the "natural" production of money through mining and minting. This was also the original meaning of the word, which stems from the Latin verb *inflare* (to blow up).

Why do people inflate the money supply in the first place? As we have seen, each new money unit benefits the first recipients; for example, under a silver standard, the miners and minters of silver. We here encounter a providential incentive for the natural production of money. But we must not ignore that the benefits that accrue to the first recipient also present a constant temptation to forcibly increase the money supply. The history of monetary institutions is very much the history of how people—governments and private citizens alike, but mostly governments—have given in to this temptation. People inflate the money supply because they stand to profit from it.

Economists are usually reluctant to dwell on the moral dimensions of social facts, and rightly so, because moral questions are outside their customary purview. But one does not need to be a moral philosopher to know that certain incomes are illegitimate; that they derive from a violation of the fundamental rule of civil society—respect for private property. And it would be irresponsible, even for an economist, not to point out that such illegitimate incomes can be obtained, and have been obtained very often, through an inflation of the money supply. Clearly, such incomes offend any notions of natural justice and are impossible to square with the precepts of Christianity. Thomas Woods is very much on point when he remarks: "If there is a principle of Catholic morality according to which such insidious wealth redistribution is acceptable, it is not known to the present writer."[2]

Let us emphasize that inflation is not problematic because in some larger sense it benefits some people at the expense of others. All human actions entail distributions of benefits. For example, if John and Paul court Anne, and Anne eventually decides to marry John, her decision comes "at the expense" of Paul. Similarly, a mining business gains "at the expense" of other businesses that would have come into existence if the miner had not paid higher wage rates for the workers, who have therefore agreed to work for him rather than for these other businesses. But the benefits accruing to John and to the miner in the foregoing examples do not come through an invasion of the physical borders of other people's property. Anne was not Paul's property; John could therefore justly marry her. The workers were not the property of any employer; our miner could therefore justly hire them.

---

[2]Thomas Woods, *The Church and the Market* (Lanham, Md.: Lexington Books, 2005), p. 95. For the same reason, Beutter calls inflation a "great evil." See Friedrich Beutter, "Geld im Verständnis der christlichen Soziallehre," W.F. Kasch, ed., *Geld und Glaube* (Paderborn: Schöningh, 1979), p. 132.

Things are very different in the case of a robber who through his action obtains some part of other people's property that they would not have consented to give him; thus he invades their property. And in the same sense, intentional misrepresentation can entail an invasion of property. When the counterfeiter manages to sell a false certificate, he too obtains some good or service that he would not have obtained without the fraud.[3]

2. The Forms of Inflation

Inflation is one of the subjects on which economists have spilled much of their ink. But virtually all of these economic analyses suffer from a much too narrow, materialistic definition of inflation. Neither the price level, nor any money aggregate gives us the key for a proper understanding of inflation. Rather, the most useful approach is to focus on the legal rules of money production. Are the market participants free to use and produce money as they see fit? Or are they prevented from doing this? These are the relevant questions. They lead straight to the moral-institutional definition of inflation that we have espoused above. Inflation is that part of the money supply that comes into being because of the invasion of private property rights.

In the first part of our present work, we have studied the production and use of money under the hypothesis that property rights are respected. Now we turn to analyzing step by step the various ways by which property rights can be violated, and have been violated, in order to artificially increase the money supply to the benefit of the perpetrators or their allies. We will first analyze inflation in a free society and then turn to inflation induced by government fiat. The former is relatively unimportant from a quantitative point of view, but we need to deal with it first for systematic reasons and also because it allows us to talk about a "good side" of inflation.

---

[3]For a discussion of fraud as a subclass of the crime of trespass, see Stephan Kinsella, "A Libertarian Theory of Contract," *Journal of Libertarian Studies* 17, no. 2 (2003).

6

Private Inflation: Counterfeiting Money Certificates

1. DEBASEMENT

Before the age of banking, debasement had been the standard form of inflation. Debasement is a special way of altering coins made out of precious metal. To debase a coin can mean either one of two things: (a) to reduce its content of fine metal without changing the imprint; and (b) to imprint a higher nominal figure on a given coin.

Debasement can be either intentional or unintentional. Suppose a coin maker erroneously puts the stamp "1 ounce of fine gold" on a quantity of less than one ounce. He then produces a false coin; the certificate does not correspond to the content. False certification might occur here and there, but in practice it is extremely rare. In virtually all the cases of debasement, the coin-maker acts in full conscience of his deed. He certifies that the coin contains a certain quantity of fine metal, but he knows full well that it contains in fact less than this quantity. Such intentional falsification of certificates is commonly called counterfeiting.

We have stressed that people cause inflation because it benefits them, though at the undue expense of their fellow citizens. This is of course also the reason why people become counterfeiters. The counterfeiter plans to sell the debased coin

without informing the buyer about the debasement, so as to
obtain in exchange for it the same amount of goods and services that one could buy with a sound coin. The fraudulent
intention behind most practical cases of debasement is obvious from the techniques that are usually applied. The debaser
does not take away some metal from the sound coin and turn
it into a smaller debased coin. Rather he substitutes some base
alloy for the precious metal he has taken away, to preserve the
false impression that the debased coin is a sound one.

In the Western world, debasement was the standard form
of inflation until the seventeenth century. It was widespread
and perennial in all phases of the history of ancient Rome and
under virtually all dynasties of medieval Christendom. And
the only reason for its absence in more recent times is that
modern counterfeiters could rely on the much more efficient
inflation techniques of fractional-reserve banking and paper
money.[1]

In many cases, the counterfeiters have been private individuals—ordinary criminals. But in the larger cases, the counterfeiters have been the very persons who were supposed to act
as guardians of the soundness of the currency—the government. For reasons that we will discuss in more detail when talking about fiat money, governments have played a far greater
role in debasing money than private citizens. Notice however
that inflation in the form of debasement was moderate in comparison to the extent of inflation in the age of banking, and

---

[1]For an in-depth analysis of twelve major inflations from antiquity to
the mid-twentieth century, see Richard Gaettens, *Inflationen*, 2nd ed.
(Munich: Pflaum, 1955). The major debasements discussed in this book
occurred in the Roman Empire (third century A.D.), Holy Roman
Empire (fifteenth century), Spain (seventeenth century), and again the
Holy Roman Empire (17th century). The other eight cases all concern
inflation through fractional-reserve banks and paper money producers.
More recently, Bernholz has reviewed the entire historical record of
hyperinflation (very strong inflation entailing a collapse of the monetary system; we will discuss this below) and found that all known cases
without exception have resulted from excessive paper money production. See Peter Bernholz, *Monetary Regimes and Inflation* (Cheltenham,
U.K.: Edward Elgar, 2003).

especially in comparison to inflation in our present age of paper money. From 1066 to 1601, the English silver pound was debased by one third.[2] In other words, in this period stretching over more than 500 years, the English kings inflated the money supply by the factor 0.3. By contrast, in the subsequent 200-year period, which saw the emergence of modern banking, that factor was in the order of 16. And in the mere 30-year period from January 1973 to January 2003, the U.S. dollar (M1) increased almost by a factor of 5.[3]

2. FRACTIONAL-RESERVE CERTIFICATES

Let us now turn to the important case of the inflation of certificates that are not physically integrated with the monetary metal. As in the case of debasement, we can here distinguish between intentional and unintentional inflation, emphasizing again that the latter case is of no great practical importance.[4] Virtually all the false certificates that are disconnected from the certified money are counterfeit certificates. The issuer of these certificates knows that he does not hold enough reserves of money to redeem all of his certificates at once. The amount of money he keeps on hand to satisfy any

---

[2]See John Wheatley, *The Theory of Money and Principles of Commerce* (London: Bulmer), p. 256. The last year in which a debasement took place was 1601 (p. 266). Wheatley notes that, starting in the mid-1500s, silver was imported from the Americas, where the mines of Potosi had been discovered in 1527. In the latter half of the 1600s, banking came into play.

[3]M1 increased from $252 billion (January 1, 1973) to $1,226 billion (January 1, 2003). During the same period, the federal debt increased from $449 billion (December 29, 1972) to $6,228 billion (September 30, 2002). Sources: Federal Reserve Bank of Saint Louis; Bureau of the Public Debt.

[4]The only realistic scenario for unintentional inflation is that of a note-issuing bank that is robbed without noticing the robbery. While the ignorance lasts, the quantity of its notes is larger than its reserves and thus there is inflation. As soon as the robbery is discovered and becomes publicly known, the owners of the bank will have to redeem the notes out of their own money, lest they go bankrupt. Either way, the inflation disappears.

demands for redemption represents just a fraction of the amount that he certified he had on hand. We can therefore call his certificates "fractional-reserve certificates." Although fractional-reserve token coins and other physical embodiments have played a certain role in monetary history, they cannot match the importance of fractional-reserve banknotes and fractional-reserve demand deposits. We will therefore largely focus on the latter.[5]

From a counterfeiter's point of view, falsifying money certificates that are physically connected with the certified quantity of money has two great shortcomings: it is relatively expensive, and it is relatively easy for the other market participants to discover the fraud and avoid using the coins. These problems dwindle once our counterfeiter turns to falsifying certificates that are not physically connected to the money. Falsifying banknotes, for example, might require a considerable initial investment in time and money to create a suitable prototype. But once the prototype is there, it can be reproduced in virtually unlimited numbers and at great profit, because the marginal cost of producing additional banknotes is close to zero. Moreover, in the case of paper certificates, extensions of the money supply are more difficult to perceive than in the case of certificates directly attached to the metal. Debased coins, even when the counterfeiting is done with great care, not only have a slightly imperfect imprint, but also differ from good coins in respect to color and, in the case of gold coins, to their sound when flipped with the thumbnail. Most importantly, the certificates can easily be tested any time by cutting or punching them, or by melting down the coin. Thus even for laymen it is relatively easy to distinguish sound coins from falsifications. Not so in the case of paper certificates.

---

[5]For an analysis of historical issues of false certificates by fractional-reserve banks from antiquity to the eighteenth century, see Jesús Huerta de Soto, *Money, Bank Credit, and Economic Cycles* (Auburn, Ala.: Ludwig von Mises Institute, 2006), chap. 2. There is some evidence that the "money changers" mentioned in the New Testament (see Matthew 25:27 and Luke 19:23) were in fact fractional-reserve bankers. See Anthony Hulme, *Morals and Money* (London: St. Paul Publications, 1957), p. 29.

3. THREE ORIGINS OF FRACTIONAL-RESERVE BANKING

As in the case of debasement, banknotes have been falsified both by ordinary criminals and by the "guardians" themselves. Banknotes came into existence on a larger scale when money warehouses were established in Venice and other northern Italian cities in the late sixteenth, and then in a number of commercial cities north of the Alps in the early seventeenth century, for example, in Amsterdam, Middelburg, Nuremberg, Hamburg, Delft, and Rotterdam. During the sixteenth century, inter-regional trade had grown to such an extent that the merchants were in touch with one another not only during the times of the great fairs, but throughout the entire year. Now it became necessary to settle accounts on a daily basis, and the most practical way to do this was through money warehouses. Each merchant held an account, and payments from and to other merchants were made by simple book entries at the local money warehouse.[6]

These institutions were called "banks," but in their beginnings they were not banks in the modern sense, but money warehouses. Some of them kept this character for a long time. For example, the Bank of Amsterdam (established in 1609) remained a warehouse until 1781, when it started issuing banknotes in excess of its money holdings, yet without changing the outer appearance of the banknotes. Thus in 1781 the Bank of Amsterdam started counterfeiting its own banknotes. It was no longer a money warehouse. It became a fractional-reserve bank.

Other banks did not wait nearly as long as the Bank of Amsterdam to enter the lucrative business of counterfeiting. The London goldsmith bankers, who multiplied in the 1630s,

---

[6]See Geoffrey Parker, "Die Entstehung des modernen Geld- und Finanzwesens in Europa 1500–1730," C.M. Cipolla and K. Borchardt, eds. *Europäische Wirtschaftsgeschichte*, vol. 2, *Sechzehntes und siebzehntes Jahrhundert* (Stuttgart: Gustav Fischer, 1983), pp. 349–50. The classic narrative of these events is in Richard Ehrenberg, *Das Zeitalter der Fugger: Geldkapital und Creditverkehr im 16. Jahrhundert* (Jena: Fischer, 1896).

very quickly made that move. So did the Bank of Stockholm (established 1656), which a few years after its inception managed to create a large circulation for its notes. But the same bank was also one of the first to experience the perennial nemesis of fractional-reserve banking—the bank run. The fundamental practical problem of fractional reserves is that it is impossible for the issuing bank to accommodate all demands for redemptions at the same time (as warehouse banks can). If the bank customers have the slightest suspicion that they might not get their money back, they "run" to the bank to be among the happy few who are still granted redemption of their banknotes. This happened to the Bank of Stockholm in 1664. But it did not stop the proliferation of fractional-reserve banking in the subsequent decades and centuries.

Thus fractional-reserve banking can arise as a perversion of money warehousing. But it can also originate as a perversion of credit banking. We have already talked about credit money and argued that it is unlikely to have any larger circulation because of the default risk and especially because most market participants prefer cash to credit instruments in spot exchanges. Now in order to make good for the latter deficiency, the banker might offer to redeem his IOUs on demand, that is, before maturity is reached. From the point of view of the customer, then, these IOUs can be turned into cash almost as securely as money certificates. We have to say "almost" because it would of course be impossible for our banker to comply with redemption requests that exceed his cash holdings—a problem that cannot arise in money warehousing, where every certificate is backed by a corresponding amount of money in the warehouse.

So how does this practice appear from a juridical and moral point of view? It depends on whether the banker is affirmatively candid about the nature of his business. If he takes care to inform his customers that the redeemable IOUs are not money certificates and that he—the banker—remains the rightful owner of the money for the entire duration of the credit, then the practice seems to be unobjectionable. By contrast, if he insinuates that his IOUs are money certificates, we would certainly have to say that this is a case of fraud.

Historically, it seems as though dissimulation has been more important than outright misrepresentation. On the oldest known paper note from the Bank of Scotland, dated 16 April 1776, we read: "The Governor & Company of the Bank of Scotland constituted by Act of Parliament Do hereby oblige themselves to pay to [name] or the Bearer Twelve pounds Scots on demand." The crucial wording here is "oblige themselves to pay"—on later banknotes we often find the expression "promise to pay." Thus the least thing we can say is that these notes are mute about the precise nature of the product. The "promise to pay" is not a feature that would distinguish a credit bank from a money warehouse.[7] To keep the market participants fully informed, it would be necessary to state as clearly as possible whether the promised payment will be made out of a small (fractional-reserve) cash fund, or out of a warehouse. Similarly, it would be necessary to state who will be considered to be the owner of the money in case the banker proves to be unable to comply with all redemption requests.[8] If our credit banker knowingly and deliberately dissimulates the precise nature of his IOUs, he abuses the good faith of his trading partners and thereby infringes upon their property

---

[7]Monetary historian Norbert Olszak observes that the first banknotes issued by the Bank of England were certificates of deposit. Then the wording on the notes was changed and they became "promissory notes." This process was completed by the middle of the eighteenth century. Olszak underlines its purpose: to get rid of "la stricte couverture métallique." Norbert Olszak, *Histoire des banques centrales* (Paris: Presses Universitaires de France, 1998), p. 24.

[8]If the customers were considered to be the owners of the money, the banker would be bankrupt in such a case. By contrast, if the banker were considered to be the owner of the money, he would stay in business and one would say that the customers have simply made a bad investment. Present-day legislation in the U.S. and the U.K. endorses the latter point of view. Few Americans know that the money they keep in their checking accounts is legally the property of the bankers, who have merely an obligation to "pay back" that money on demand.

rights. He thereby turns himself into a fractional-reserve banker.[9]

So far we have presented fractional-reserve banking as springing exclusively from the misguided choices of warehouse managers and credit bankers who fell prey to temptation. But it is also conceivable that these choices were in turn caused by a third event, in particular, by the threat of government-sponsored robbing of money warehouses. As Jesús Huerta de Soto has argued for the case of the sixteenth century banks of Seville, the ruthlessness of bankers was by no means the only cause for the introduction of the fractional-reserve principle:

> . . . it is no less true that the inauspicious imperial policy, by transgressing the most elementary principles of property rights and directly confiscating the stocks of money kept in the vaults, merely provided an even bigger incentive for the bankers to invest the greater part of the deposits received in loans, which became a habitual practice: if, in the final analysis, there was no guarantee that the public authorities would respect the part of the cash reserve which was kept in the bank (and experience showed that, when times were difficult, the Emperor did not hesitate to confiscate this reserve and substitute it by compulsory loans to the Crown), it was preferable to devote the greater part of the deposits to loans to private industry and commerce, thus avoiding expropriation and obtaining greater profitability.[10]

Thus the introduction of fractional-reserve banking might be seen as a free-market reaction against, and attenuation of,

---

[9]We mention this possible origin of fractional-reserve banking only for the sake of completeness. The question of how this type of business can emerge, and how it has emerged historically, is of secondary importance for the argument in the present work. A detailed analysis of fractional-reserve banking as a possible perversion of credit banking is in Jörg Guido Hülsmann, "Has Fractional-Reserve Banking Really Passed the Market Test?" *Independent Review* 7, no. 3 (2003).

[10]Jesús Huerta de Soto, "New Light on the Prehistory of the Theory of Banking and the School of Salamanca," *Review of Austrian Economics* 9, no. 2 (1996): 60.

government interventionism. It is true that, even under the threat of imminent expropriation, fractional-reserve banking might not be justifiable *per se*; but at least the presence of such a threat would diminish the guilt of the protagonists, and it would certainly explain their actions in other terms than original sin.

Much more historical research is needed to establish the relative importance of the three possible causes of fractional-reserve banking that we have discussed in the preceding pages. There are good reasons to believe that the third cause—government-sponsored robbing of money warehouses—has played a rather pervasive role. But we must leave the answer to that question to future research.

4. INDIRECT BENEFITS OF COUNTERFEITING IN A FREE SOCIETY

Counterfeiting is in the true sense of the word a popular inflation technique. All sorts of people who have dextrous hands or who can afford to hire people with such hands—bankers, governments, merchants, goldsmiths, artisans, etc.—can try it out. And the history of money illustrates that all sorts of such people have tried it out, with the harmful consequences analyzed above: unjust distributions of income and misallocations of capital. Thus counterfeiting exists in all types of economies, be it the market of a free society or the centrally planned economy of a totalitarian state. Unlike fiat money, of which we will speak below, it cannot be abolished through political measures. It can be repressed by the prospect of severe punishment. But it cannot be entirely eliminated by such external means, because it springs from the internal human condition of original sin.

Yet in a free society counterfeiting is not without certain positive consequences, even though the counterfeiters themselves do not plan to bring them about. In particular, the very danger of falling prey to a counterfeiter plays the useful social function of making the citizens vigilant about their money. The function of counterfeiters resembles the function of the many viruses that subsist in a healthy human body. Fighting the virus keeps the body alive and strong. Similarly, the ever-present danger of counterfeiting stimulates vigilance in monetary affairs and thus helps to preserve sound money. People watch their gold and silver coins closely because they know that counterfeiting affects them directly. They strive to learn more about distinguishing good coins from bad coins, and good banknotes from bad ones. They apply such knowledge and teach it to their families and others. And once they discover any sort of fraud, they stop using the fraudulent coins and banknotes, and switch to other certificates.

Counterfeiting is usually detected very quickly. When people are free to choose their money, it cannot create much damage. But this important natural limitation on inflation exists only in free societies, as we shall see in more detail.

5. The Ethics of Counterfeiting

Debasement and fractional-reserve banking are unjustifiable. No theory of ethics defends lies or, for that matter, counterfeiting. It is true that a few moral philosophers have tried to justify lies that are meant to prevent greater harm. But which harm could be avoided through counterfeiting? Or does counterfeiting convey any special advantages to the community of money users? Nobody has ever ventured to answer these questions affirmatively; and thus we do not need to deal with them here. As far as counterfeiting *per se* is concerned, there cannot be the slightest doubt about the Christian stance. The Eighth Commandment tells us about intentional falsification of certificates: "You shall not bear false witness against your neighbor." And many other passages from the Old Testament spell out what this means in the context of certificates that attest quantities of precious metals.[11]

---

11 Do not act dishonestly in using measures of length or weight or capacity. . . . You shall have a true scale and true weights, an honest ephah and an honest hin. I, the LORD, am your God, who brought you out of the land of Egypt. (Leviticus 19: 35–36)

You shall not keep two differing weights in your bag, one large and the other small; nor shall you keep two different

These general ethical principles were applied with great rigor to the case of money in Nicholas Oresme's "Treatise." The author noted that falsifying the imprint of a coin was a penal offense, and even a legitimate cause of war. He held that a "change of names" (debasement) was scandalous and should never be done. An alteration of the weight without changing the name was similarly "a foul lie and a fraudulent cheat."[12]

Bishop Oresme made no exception to his condemnation of false money certificates. Even the government could not, for any reason, falsify money certificates and thus inflate the money supply. He argued that any alteration of money through the government was unjust in itself, and that the government necessarily gained at the expense of the community.[13] The government thus turns into a tyrant:

> . . . from the moment when the prince usurps this essentially unjust privilege, it is impossible that he can justly take profit from it. Besides, the amount of the prince's profit is

---

> measures in your house, one large and the other small. But use a true and just weight, and a true and just measure, that you may have a long life on the land which the LORD, your God, is giving you. Everyone who is dishonest in any of these matters is an abomination to the LORD, your God. (Deuteronomy XXV: 13–16)
>
> Varying weights, varying measures, are both an abomination to the LORD. [. . .] Varying weights are an abomination to the LORD, and false scales are not good. (Proverbs 20: 10, 23)

[12]Nicholas Oresme, "Treatise on the Origin, Nature, Law, and Alterations of Money," in Charles Johnson, ed., *The De Moneta of Nicholas Oresme and English Mint Documents* (London: Thomas Nelson and Sons, 1956), chap. 12, p. 19. See also chaps. 5 and 11.

[13]As we have seen, Ptolemy of Lucca made the much weaker point that the community would lose through alterations of the coinage because such alterations change a standard measure (*On the Government of Rulers* [Philadelphia: University of Pennsylvania Press, 1997], p. 134). This harm corresponds to the damage created by meddling with measures of length, temperature, etc. Oresme saw that more was at stake here. The alteration of the coinage involved a physical transfer of money from the community to the government.

necessarily that of the community's loss. But whatever loss the prince inflicts on the community is injustice and the act of a tyrant and not of a king, as Aristotle says. And if he should tell the tyrant's usual lie, that he applies that profit to the public advantage, he must not be believed, because he might as well take my coat and say he needed it for the public service. And Saint Paul says that we are not to do evil that good may come. Nothing therefore should be extorted on the pretence that it will be used for good purposes afterwards.[14]

Oresme stresses here a fundamental fact. As we have pointed out above, the additional money benefits the first owners at the expense of all other money owners. It is true that this is so irrespective of whether the additional money results from natural production or from inflation. But inflation is not just an extension of the money supply. The crucial point is that it extends the money supply through a violation of property rights. Inflation provides not just gains; it provides illegitimate gains. Its alleged benefits are not really different from the benefits of robbery and fraud.[15]

---

[14]Oresme, "Treatise," chap. 15, p. 24. The text refers to Aristotle's *Politics*, V, x, 10 (1310b40) and *Nichomachean Ethics*, ix (1160b2), as well as to Saint Paul's Letter to the Romans 3:8. Oresme repeatedly made this point, stressing that the function of inflation is to enrich the government at the expense of other people (see for example chap. 12). Oresme argued that debasement could only be licit when two conditions were simultaneously given: (1) there would have to be a great emergency, and (2) the entire community, not just the government, would have to give its consent (chap. 22). Government should get its regular revenue elsewhere (chap. 24). Very similarly, Ludwig von Mises argued that inflation by its very nature contradicted the principle of popular sovereignty. The only way for the people to keep their government in check was to control the government's resources. If the government needed more money, therefore, it should approach the citizens to pay higher taxes. Inflating the money supply provided it with more resources than the citizens were ready to contribute. See Ludwig von Mises, *Theory of Money and Credit* (Indianapolis: Liberty Fund, 1980), pp. 466–69.

[15]Therefore there seem to be good grounds for arguing that inflation, independent of any attenuating circumstances, is an inherently bad action (*intrinsece malum*) in the sense of Catholic moral doctrine. See on this point John Paul II, *Veritatis splendor*, §80.

Oresme also argued that counterfeiting was a far more serious moral offense than the sins that are most frequently associated with the use of money, namely, money changing and usury. Money changing and usury might be tolerable under certain special circumstances. But counterfeiting was inherently unjust and therefore never permissible. It actually stimulated money changing and further counterfeiting by people who seized on the general confusion created by the initial counterfeiter.[16]

---

[16]See Oresme, "Treatise," chaps. 18–21, passim. Saint Thomas took it for granted that money forgers deserve death; see *Summa Theologica*, II–II, Q. 11, Art. 3.

7

Enters the State: Fiat Inflation through Legal Privileges

1. TREACHEROUS CLERKS

It is well known that the history of institutions cannot be adequately understood without considering the economic constraints and incentives of the protagonists. This holds true especially in the case of monetary institutions. The emergence of our present-day institutions in this field—central banks, paper money, and so on—must be seen in the context of government finance. Governments at nearly all times and places have been the main beneficiaries of inflation. Rather than protecting society from it, therefore, all of them have sooner or later given in to the temptation of using inflation for their own purposes. First they stopped combating it. Then they facilitated it, encouraged it, and finally promoted it with all their powers. They have obstructed and suppressed the production of money on the free market, set up institutions that were designed for perennial inflation, and constantly remodeled these institutions to increase their inflationary potential.[1] In all such cases, in which governments create

---

[1]See George Selgin and Lawrence White, "A Fiscal Theory of Government's Role in Money," *Economic Inquiry* 37 (1999). Selgin and White make exception only for fractional-reserve banking, which in their eyes

inflation or increase it beyond the level it would otherwise have reached, there is fiat inflation.

Governments inflate the money supply because they gain revenue from inflation. As we have pointed out, additional money benefits the first owners at the expense of all other money owners. Therefore, if government or its agents are the ones who bring about the extension of the money supply, they stand ready to gain from it, and they gain at the expense of the other citizens. In the fourteenth century, Nicholas Oresme argued that this fact was at the root of the frequent monetary interventions of the princes:

> I am of the opinion that the main and final cause why the prince pretends to the power of altering the coinage is the profit or gain which he can get from it; it would otherwise be vain to make so many and so great changes. . . . Besides, the amount of the prince's profit is necessarily that of the community's loss.[2]

The times have changed and the techniques of inflation have changed with them. But governments still intervene in

---

is a market institution. See idem, "How Would the Invisible Hand Handle Money?" *Journal of Economic Literature* 32, no. 4 (1994). This latter opinion not only stands on weak theoretical ground, but also flies into the face of the entire historical record of fractional-reserve banks, which have been promoted either directly through government interventions, or indirectly through banks and other monetary institutions that had special legal protection and support from tax money. See the detailed discussion in Jesús Huerta de Soto, *Money, Bank Credit, and Economic Cycles* (Auburn, Ala.: Ludwig von Mises Institute, 2006), chap. 8, sect. 4, pp. 675–714.

[2]Oresme, "Treatise," Nicholas Oresme, "Treatise on the Origin, Nature, Law, and Alterations of Money," in Charles Johnson, ed., *The De Moneta of Nicholas Oresme and English Mint Documents* (London: Thomas Nelson and Sons, 1956), chap. 15, p. 24. See also Juan de Mariana, (1609)"A Treatise on the Alteration of Money," *Markets and Morality*, vol. 5, no. 2 (2002), chap. 13. Is it necessary to point out that profiting from the community's loss involves necessarily a flagrant violation of distributive justice, which justice is based on the sanctity of private property? See on this Leo XIII, *Rerum Novarum*, §33, 46.

the production of money and money certificates in order to obtain additional income. The difference between our time and the age of Oresme is that present-day governments have received absolution from the scientific authorities of our day. Many princes blushed when they were caught debasing the currency of the country. But modern presidents, prime ministers, and chancellors can keep a straight face and justify inflation with the alleged need to stabilize the price level and to finance growth. All the recognized experts say so.[3] And it betrays a lack of courtesy to point out that "recognition" of an expert means that he is on the government's payroll.

Inflation can certainly also exist in a hypothetical society in which the government does not in the slightest way interfere with the production of money. The crucial point is that in such a case there are no legitimized institutions of inflation. Being a criminal activity, inflation has to flee the light of day and lingers only at the edges of such a society. As long as the citizens are free to produce and use the best money available, therefore, sound money prevails, whereas debased money and fractional reserves lead a fringe existence. Inflation can then cause occasional harm for individuals, but it cannot spread far and last long. Only the government has the power to make inflation a widespread, large-scale, and permanent phenomenon, because only the government has the power to systematically prevent the citizens from spontaneously adopting the best possible monies and money certificates. Unfortunately, as we shall see, this is exactly what governments have

---

[3]Contemporary textbooks and research articles of a non-Austrian inspiration argue that monetary policy (according to our definition: inflation) is beneficial or at least can be beneficial if properly handled. The arguments brought forth in these works are in most cases variants of the theories that we discussed in chapter 4. See for example Frederic S. Mishkin, *The Economics of Money, Banking, and Financial Markets*, 7th ed. (New York: Addison Wesley, 2003); Manfred Borchert, *Geld und Kredit* (Munich: Oldenbourg, 2001); Christian Ottavj, *Monnaie et financement de l'économie*, 2nd ed. (Paris: Hachette, 1999). For Austrian critiques of the idea that inflation can be beneficial, see the works by Mises, Rothbard, Sennholz, Reisman, Salin, and Huerta de Soto that we quoted in the introduction.

done in the past. The resulting damage has been immense, not only in terms of material wealth, but also in terms of the moral and spiritual development of the western world. We will therefore analyze the inflation that springs from government fiat in some detail.

Notice at present that the gain that the government and its allies derive from fiat inflation can most adequately be called "institutional usury," as Dempsey has pointed out.

2. FIAT MONEY AND FIAT MONEY CERTIFICATES

According to a widely held opinion, government has the power to impose money on its citizens. This is of course the premise of the so-called state theory of money, which we have criticized above, and according to which money is by its very nature fiat money—a creation of the state. As we have argued, the state theory of money is untenable on grounds of both theoretical reasons and historical experience.

But the scope of fiat money has also been explained in a more realistic version. These advocates do not claim that all kinds of money need the backing of the state. They merely contend that, in some cases, the power of the official apparatus of compulsion and coercion can establish money. In other words, there is here no dispute of the fact that free enterprise can produce natural monies. The point is that governments too can produce money, not by becoming entrepreneurs, but by forcing the citizens to use some money of the government's choice.

This version is correct, provided one does not subscribe to an exaggerated notion of what "forcing" and "imposing" means. The government cannot for example bring its citizens to abandon their traditional monies and to replace them henceforth with armchairs or with stones that weigh three tons each. Neither can it bring its citizens to use a paper money that loses 90 percent of its value per hour. Such a policy, even if it were pursued with utmost determination, would not establish money of the government's liking; it would merely destroy the entire network of indirect exchanges. Rather than using the inadequate money, the citizens would refuse to exchange at all. The result would be misery and death for millions, as well as chaos and overthrow of the government.

Similarly, the government cannot just print paper tickets and command their citizens to use them. As we have seen, a new kind of money can only be introduced into the market if it has some known value that exists prior to its monetary use. The government therefore has to somehow connect its paper money to the existing price system. So far, two ways of doing this have been tried out. One, the government can issue paper tickets that bear the same names as the units of the already existing monies, and oblige all citizens through legal tender laws to accept the paper as if it were natural money. This was how the American Union government introduced "greenbacks" in 1862.[4] Two, the government can grant legal privileges to some of the already existing monies or money certificates, and thereby turn them into fiat monies and fiat money certificates.

3. FIAT INFLATION AND FIAT DEFLATION

Privileged monies and certificates have a wider circulation than they would have attained on the free market. They are therefore inherently inflationary. Notice however that fiat inflation is not just any inflation initiated by a government. When governments secretly counterfeit money certificates, as they have often done in the Middle Ages, they do not create fiat inflation. Rather in these cases they are "private" counterfeiters just as any other counterfeiter outside of government. The characteristic feature of fiat inflation is that it is done openly and legally. As we shall see, however, official approval does not diminish the pernicious effects of inflation; and it is far from removing its ethical offensiveness.

---

[4]At the beginning, there was no talk about ever redeeming the greenbacks into gold or silver, and thus they were paper money during the early period. Later they become credit money, when the government announced its intention to redeem them at some point in the near future. When redemption started in 1879, the greenbacks became fractional-reserve money certificates.

The reverse side of the increased circulation of the privileged coins and banknotes is a decreased circulation of alternative media of exchange. The very meaning of monetary privilege is that it creates a competitive disadvantage for the monies and money certificates that would have been used if the privilege had not been established. Thus the fiat inflation of privileged coins and banknotes always and everywhere goes hand in hand with a fiat deflation of the other monies and money certificates.

The legal privileges that governments use to create fiat money and fiat money certificates fall into four large groups: legalized falsifications, legal monopolies, legal tender laws, and legalized suspensions of payments. Usually these privileges are not granted in separation from one another, but in some combination; for example, the late nineteenth century notes of the Bank of England were legal tender and had a monopoly. Still it is true that theoretically those four privileges could be granted independent of one another. For the sake of analytical clarity, we will therefore do both: study the independent impact of each of them, and discuss how they combine with one another. This will be our subject in the next four chapters. We will then conclude our analysis of inflation with a chapter on paper money, which has come into existence as a consequence of those four privileges, and another chapter on the cultural and spiritual consequences of fiat inflation.

8

Legalized Falsifications

1. Legalizing Debasement and Fractional Reserves

Above we have discussed how inflation can be created independent of government, namely, through the "private" falsification of money certificates. Such inflation, albeit widespread, is negligible from a quantitative point of view when compared to fiat inflation. The reason, as we have argued above, is that there are powerful forces at work to contain private falsification within fairly narrow limits. First, falsifying money certificates is a tort, and counterfeiting (intentional falsification) is a criminal activity punishable by law. Second, once a falsification has been discovered, the market participants are likely to abandon the use of the false certificates and begin to use other ones. Third, in the worst of all cases, the market participants can demand payments in bullion and verify the fine content of metal by themselves.

The legalization of false certificates removes the first of these three limitations. "Legalization" can mean that the government declares a debased coin—or a fractional-reserve banknote—to be a means of payment that every creditor is legally obliged to accept at par; we will deal with this case in some detail.

But the legalization of false certificates can also come in a more elementary form, namely, when the government becomes agnostic about the language of the country and thus refuses to enforce the laws. For example, it might adopt the point of view that the expression "one ounce of gold" is really just a string of letters that can be given just about any contractually binding meaning. It would follow that a mint can legally issue coins that feature the imprint "one ounce of gold," but which in fact contain just half an ounce, or no gold at all. The government could also adopt such an agnostic point of view *vis-à-vis* banknotes; or at least it could use ambiguous imprints such as the famous "promise to pay."[1] All such policies legalize false money certificates, if not in intention, then at least in fact. The present chapter deals with such cases.

First of all, let us observe that the government's agnosticism in these matters has in all known cases been rather self-serving. The legalization of false certificates usually occurred after the government itself had already debased the currency or because it planned to debase it, or because it sought to obtain credit from fractional-reserve banks. The result is always the same: counterfeiting henceforth goes unpunished, and thus the material incentives of counterfeiting develop a greater inflationary potential.

However, as we have noticed above, on an otherwise free market such policies very quickly lead to some sort of a correction through the remaining liberty of action. The citizens, cautious of the widespread falsifications and weary of the constant inflation under their laws, would start using money certificates that are produced abroad. Rather than using, say, the "coronas" produced by their own prince, they might start using the "ducats" of the neighboring country, where the falsification of certificates is still a legal offense. In short, laws that legalize false money create more inflation than would otherwise have existed; but *per se* they do not open the floodgates. However harmful and morally offensive such legislation might be, it cannot create large-scale fiat inflation.

---

[1]There is of course no such thing as a "false certificate" or an "ambiguous certificate" once the premise is accepted that words have no objective meaning. For the sake of our readers, who on the preceding pages have discerned meaning where others might just see strings of letters, or black points on white paper, we will nevertheless continue to speak of false certificates and ambiguous meanings.

Quite to the contrary, we should rather expect such legislation to have some deflationary effect. The reason is that the production of debased coins, even though it is now legal, takes time. It is impossible for the government (or for that matter, for any other private agency) to replace the entire existing stock of coins in one stroke. It follows that the gradual introduction of the new debased coins makes the supply of these coins heterogeneous. Old sound coins circulate side by side with new debased coins. When the market participants realize what is happening, they will spend much more time distinguishing between old and new coins; or they might just as well hoard the old coins, or sell them abroad, and use only new coins for payments. But this means a more or less drastic reduction of the coin supply available for exchanges— fiat deflation. Again, this effect is likely to be dampened through the remaining liberty of action. As long as the competitive production of money certificates is still possible, the fiat deflation can be contained within fairly narrow limits.

One thing is sure, however: The legalization of false certificates permanently increases the risk of being cheated in monetary exchanges. Nicholas Oresme wrote: "And so there is no certainty in a thing in which certainty is of the highest importance, but rather uncertain and disordered confusion, to the prince's reproach."[2] Substitute the word government for the word prince, and we have an accurate description of the fact.[3] Oresme also noted that official debasement would invite foreign counterfeiters to seize the opportunity presented by

---

[2]Nicholas Oresme, "Treatise on the Origin, Nature, Law, and Alterations of Money," in Charles Johnson, ed., *The De Moneta of Nicholas Oresme and English Mint Documents* (London: Thomas Nelson and Sons, 1956), p. 31.

[3]Buridan argued that the word "prince" is to be understood in such context, not in the sense of a single ruler, but as referring to all those who have the power to govern. See John Buridan, "Extrait des 'Questions sur la Politique d'Aristote'," book 1, question 11 in Claude Dupuy, ed., *Traité des monnaies et autres écrits monétaires du XIVe siècle* (Lyon: La manufacture, 1989), p. 138.

the general confusion over the debased coinage "and thus rob the king of the profit which he thinks he is making."[4]

2. THE ETHICS OF LEGALIZING FALSIFICATIONS

We have emphasized that the legalization of false money certificates, though harmful, is virtually insignificant from a quantitative point of view, at least in comparison to the inflationary impact of legal monopolies and legal tender laws. Nevertheless this privilege is fundamental because it is the foundation of all other monetary privileges. It would seem impossible, for example, to establish legal tender laws in favor of some debased coin, or of some fractional-reserve banknote, if the latter are *per se* illegal. And thus it follows that the moral case for all other monetary privileges depends on the morality of legalized falsifications.

Nicholas Oresme described the moral character of this practice in no uncertain terms. It was for him a matter of course that imprints on a coin should be truthful (according to the Ninth Commandment). To provide a justification for the practice of falsifying money certificates was impossible. The government could claim no exception. Quite to the contrary, Oresme thought that the falsification of money certificates was particularly offensive in this case. He said:

> ... it is exceedingly detestable and disgraceful in a prince to commit fraud, to debase his money, to call what is not gold, gold, and what is not a pound, a pound, and so forth. . . . Besides, it is his duty to condemn false coiners. How can he blush deep enough, if that be found in him which in another he ought to punish by a disgraceful death?[5]

As a confessor of the powerful, Oresme knew only too well the temptation of inflation. He therefore did not limit his admonition to the case of falsification, but condemned any alteration of existing monies whatsoever. More precisely,

---

[4]Oresme, "Treatise," p. 32.

[5]Ibid., p. 30.

Oresme charged that the government should never alter money, because the legitimacy of the alteration of money made a tyrannous government perfect. To be licit, alterations of coins needed the consent of the entire community of money users, and even in this case consent would not automatically provide legitimacy to the policy (for example, he argued that money should never be debased for regular revenue purposes). Only if the alteration provided the only means to deal with an emergency situation, such as a sudden attack by an overwhelming enemy, could it be licit, provided it had the consent of the entire community. Oresme also observed that the pope will never grant the privilege of altering money; and that, even if it were granted as an exception, it could always be revoked.[6]

---

[6]See ibid., chaps. 14, 15, and 24. On the essentially identical position of the late-scholastic authors Tomás de Mercado and Juan de Mariana, see Alejandro Chafuen, A., *Faith and Liberty: The Economic Thought of the Late Scholastics*, 2nd ed. (New York: Lexington Books, 2003), pp. 65–68.

9

Legal Monopolies

1. Economic Monopolies versus Legal Monopolies

Before we deal with the impact of monopolies on the production of monetary services, let us emphasize that our argument concerns only legal monopolies. It does not concern economic monopolies—market situations in which products and services have just one provider. Such economic monopolies are fairly common on the free market, and they are *per se* perfectly harmless. Typically, the economic monopolist is big enough to serve the entire market and can offer better conditions than any competitor. But this is not writ in stone. The characteristic feature of economic monopolies is that they are contestable. Everybody is free to cater to the same market and thus to "test" whether the current monopolist is really so good that nobody can withstand his competition. By contrast, legal monopolies prevent such testing because violations of the law are suppressed through the courts and police forces.[1]

In monetary affairs, we may speak of a legal monopoly whenever only *some* monetary products (possibly just one product) may be produced, but not any other similar products.

---

[1]See especially Murray Rothbard, *Man, Economy, and State*, 3rd ed. (Auburn, Ala.: Ludwig von Mises Institute, 1993), chap. 10. See also Pascal Salin, *La concurrence* (Paris: Presses Universitaires de France, 1991).

For example, the legal monopoly might provide that only silver may be used as money, or that only the bank X may offer checking accounts, or that only banknotes of the bank Y or coins of the mint Z may be used in payments.

Legal monopolies—which we will call for brevity's sake "monopolies"—entail inflation by the very fact that they shield the privileged products from competition. The monopoly makes the privileged products relatively less costly to acquire (in comparison to competing products) than they otherwise would have been. The market participants therefore tend to use more of them than they otherwise would have used; and as a consequence they also tend to produce more of them than would otherwise have been produced. This inflation works out to the benefit of the producers and first recipients of additional units of the monopoly product, and to the detriment of producers and users of alternative products, which would have been fabricated and used in the absence of those legal privileges. Thus we encounter again the phenomenon that fiat inflation (of the privileged monies or money certificates) goes hand in hand with fiat deflation of other monetary products.

Monetary monopolies are especially harmful when combined with legal tender laws. But even in the absence of such combinations, monopoly has certain baneful effects that are relevant for our present analysis of money and banking from a moral point of view. Let us first deal with monopoly bullion and then turn to monopoly certificates.

2. MONOPOLY BULLION

The government can decree that only one type of precious metal may be used in monetary exchanges and punish the use of all other metals. Or it might simply be the monopoly owner of all mints, and then decide to mint coins only in one metal.[2]

---

[2]The same effect can be brought about through legal tender laws, when they apply only to one metal. We will deal with this case in the next chapter.

Such monopolies have for example been created in Germany and France after the war of 1870–71, when both countries adopted a gold standard and prevented the minting of silver coins (except as tokens for gold). It is true that the bullion monopoly in these cases went hand in hand with a coin monopoly. Still a pure bullion monopoly is conceivable. It creates a greater demand for the privileged metal and crushes the demand for all other metals. Thus we have here again the familiar double phenomenon of fiat inflation and fiat deflation.

Historically, the establishment of monopoly bullion has been an important step in the consolidation and centralization of national monetary systems under government control. The outlawing of silver paved the way to an inflation of fractional-reserve certificates backed by gold. The reason is twofold.

On the one hand, fractional-reserve certificates can be a vehicle for *short-run adjustment* to the fiat deflation of silver. With silver disappearing from circulation the market participants turn to the remaining alternatives such as gold. Because the gold supply cannot be easily extended, the increased demand would entail a drop of gold prices or, in other words, an increase of the purchasing power of gold. But this is a problem for those who operate on debts and who were not shrewd enough to anticipate the drop in prices. These people therefore turn to substitutes for gold that *can* be easily multiplied, such as the notes issued by fractional-reserve banks.

On the other hand, and quite apart from this short-run problem, silver is no longer available as a competitor for gold and thus money users have less possibilities to protect themselves against the inflation of gold-backed money substitutes. Moreover, it is for technical reasons impossible to replace silver coins with gold coins of the same purchasing power because in general the latter would have to be so small as to be impracticable. A case in point is the British quarter guinea, which was minted in the years 1718 and 1762 and each time failed to be generally accepted for monetary service. In such circumstances the silver currency is therefore not in fact replaced by a gold currency, but by a currency of gold *substitutes*. These substitutes might initially be fully backed by gold. However, as we have already argued, it is much easier to turn fully backed money substitutes into fractional-reserve substitutes than it is to debase coins. Hence, the doors are now wide open for inflation.

3. MONOPOLY CERTIFICATES

Virtually all the coins that have circulated have enjoyed a monopoly and were legal tender. Private coinage existed at a few times and places, but even then the definition of the proper coin sizes usually lay in the hands of government. An example is the early United States. Here coinage was largely private, but the U.S. Constitution nevertheless reserved the privilege of defining weights and measures to Congress. It authorized Congress to send in the police against anyone producing or using coins other than the official ones. Thus there was no completely free choice in producing and using alternative coins. Certain coins enjoyed a legal monopoly—monopoly coins.

Notice that monopoly coinage *per se* cannot entail inflation on any quantitatively significant level. This is most certainly so in the case of sound coins. But even in the case of debased coins, inflation is likely to be very limited. The reason is that monopoly privileges "merely" outlaw alternative monies or money certificates. They cut down the menu from which money users may choose, but they do not prevent them from *evaluating* the monopoly monies as they see fit. In the case of debased coins, this means that monopoly laws leave the people at liberty to distinguish between old coins (which contain more fine metal) and the new debased coins. There might then be two price systems or, if it proves to be too cumbersome to distinguish old and new coins in daily trade, the market participants might just as well decide to melt down the old coins or sell them abroad. It follows that there is no inflationary effect whatever (if anything, a slight deflationary effect is more probable).

From the point of view of the debaser—the government—the entire exercise is therefore more or less pointless. He might for some time manage to cheat his customers into thinking that no debasement is going on. But this deception cannot last for any considerable length of time. As soon as the market participants realize what is going on, they will buy and sell the new coins at different nominal prices, so as to leave the *real* exchange ratios (in precious metal weights) unchanged. No additional revenue can thus be gained for the debaser. This is of course the reason why debasement has never been orchestrated under the mere protection of monopoly privileges. In practice, debased government coins have always been protected by the additional privilege of legal tender laws.

Things are very similar in the case of certificates that are not physically connected to the monetary metal (in particular banknotes and demand deposits). They too can be produced on a free market. And in distinct contrast to coins, they actually have been produced under competitive conditions at many times and places in history. In the nineteenth century, most Western governments established banknote monopolies, which were granted to banks with especially close ties to the government. These banks operated on a fractional-reserve basis and created a considerable amount of banknote inflation. But just as in the case of debased coins, the monopoly alone was not the enabler of that inflation. The simple reason is, again, that the monopoly privilege merely suppresses competing products, but does not prevent people from evaluating the monopoly banknotes as they see fit. A banknote monopoly does not therefore prevent the market participants from rejecting these banknotes altogether and conducting their business only in coins (cash). Thus as in the case of coins, we must conclude that monopoly privileges for banknotes are inherently harmful and socially disruptive, but that their quantitative impact is likely to be rather small.

4 . THE ETHICS OF MONETARY MONOPOLY

Our foregoing discussion did not shed any positive light on legal monopolies in money. Why, then, has monopoly been so widespread and longstanding in this field? One standard argument is that the control of the money supply is one of the prerogatives of secular government.[3] But this is of course not

---

[3]See the classic exposition of the argument in Jean Bodin, *Les six livres de la République* (Paris: Jacques du Puys, 1576), bk. 1, chap. 11. See also

an argument at all, unless we equate government omnipotence with the welfare of the commonwealth. The question is why the certification of weights should be entrusted to government, and to government alone. One plausible answer to this question is that it is natural to trust government. Oresme argued quite succinctly that the princes were the natural leaders of society. It seemed only natural to confide the certification of gold and silver weights to the men who were trusted to make life-and-death decisions on behalf of all members of society. If they could not be trusted, who else could?

Even if we grant this deduction for the sake of argument, it is by no means clear that it can be readily applied to our times. The princes of the High Middle Ages personally led their armies into battle. There were therefore much better reasons to trust one's prince, who constantly pledged his own blood, than to trust the members of modern parliaments, who seldom are required to walk their talk.

But even if we concede, again for the sake of argument, that Oresme's deduction could be applied to the modern context, the deduction itself does not hold water. The only conclusion one could infer from the premise that governments are inherently trustworthy is that governments would tend to be successful in the money certification business. But it does not follow at all that *only* the governments should be allowed to enter this business. There is no reason why other people than the princes should not acquire a reputation of trustworthiness equal to, or even superior to theirs. It might be true that in medieval Europe the princes were the most widely trusted members of society. Other people might be most widely trusted at other times and other places. The point is that there is no reason at all to grant such people a monopoly and thus to shield them from competition. Few things are better known in economic theory than the baneful effects of monopoly. Coinage is no exception. As long as a minter lives up to his reputation of being honest and trustworthy, the monopoly is

Arnold Luschin von Ebengreuth, *Allgemeine Münzkunde und Geldgeschichte*, reprint of the 2nd ed. (Darmstadt: Wissenschaftliche Buchgesellschaft, [1926] 1976), pp. 235–44.

simply pointless, because people will use his coins anyway. But as soon as a formerly honest minter gives in to temptation and starts to cheat, his monopoly prevents other people from switching to the better services of other minters. Oresme acknowledged that such cheating was highly unworthy of public authority:

> Also it is absurd and repugnant to the royal dignity to pro-hibit the currency of the true and good money of the realm, and from motives of greed to command, or rather compel, subjects to use less good money; which amounts to saying that good is evil and vice versa, whereas it was said to such from the Lord, by his prophet: *Woe unto them that call evil good and good evil.* [Isaiah 5:20][4]

Notice that this consideration not only applies to the case of a formerly honest monopoly minter who has fallen from grace. It applies to monopoly minting itself, because it necessarily involves "commanding, or rather compelling, subjects to use less good money" than they might be able to use if competition were free.[5]

---

[4]Nicholas Oresme, "Treatise on the Origin, Nature, Law, and Alterations of Money," in Charles Johnson, ed., *The De Moneta of Nicholas Oresme and English Mint Documents* (London: Thomas Nelson and Sons, 1956), p. 31.

[5]What we see here is that any advocacy of monopoly contradicts one of the most cherished principles of Catholic social doctrine, namely, the principle of freedom of association. It is true that twentieth century popes and the Second Vatican Council have defended this principle mainly in the context of the legitimacy of labor associations. But the principle itself extends far beyond that realm. Pope John Paul II made this crystal clear in a passage of *Centesimus Annus* (§7) in which he discussed Leo XIII's *Rerum Novarum*, where the same point had been made:

> In close connection with the right to private property, Pope Leo XIII's Encyclical also affirms other rights as inalienable and proper to the human person. Prominent among these, because of the space which the Pope devotes to it and the importance which he attaches to it, is the "natural human right" to form private associations. This means above all the right to establish professional associations of employers and workers, or of workers alone. Here we find the reason for the

Monopoly prevents people from using what is rightfully their property and thus prevents them from competing with privileged market participants. This is partial theft. If the government allows me to drive my car on all days of the week except for Sunday (for example, because the government itself wants to preserve the monopoly of transport services for that day) then it deprives me of the full use of my property. And I am similarly deprived of the full use of my legitimate property if I may not use it to produce money.

In light of these considerations, it should not be surprising that monopoly's bad press is hardly a fabrication of the classical economist and their followers, who stressed various utilitarian considerations against monopoly.[6] These authors could in fact build on the traditional ethical rejection of monopoly. From a biblical point of view, legal monopolies are condemnable because they violate the Eighth Commandment ("You shall not steal"). The ethical case against legal monopolies is simply an elaboration of this insight. As one historian of

---

Church's defence and approval of the establishment of what are commonly called trade unions: certainly not because of ideological prejudices or in order to surrender to a class mentality, but because the right of association is a natural right of the human being, which therefore precedes his or her incorporation into political society. Indeed, the formation of unions "cannot . . . be prohibited by the State," because "the State is bound to protect natural rights, not to destroy them; and if it forbids its citizens to form associations, it contradicts the very principle of its own existence."

As Leo XIII had pointed out, this right is so primordial that it may only be qualified in the case of associations that are "evidently bad, unlawful, or dangerous to the State." (Leo XIII, *Rerum Novarum*, §52.) But the State has no right whatever to prevent or dissolve any legitimate association. It follows that there is no moral basis, at any rate from a Catholic point of view, to prevent or dissolve associations of persons who wish to produce and use a specific kind of money.

[6]See for example, Adam Smith, *The Wealth of Nations* (New York: Modern Library, [1776] 1994, pp. 680–82, 700, 814; Etienne de Condillac, *Le commerce et le gouvernement*, 2nd ed. (Paris: Letellier, 1795), part 2, chap. 7, pp. 273–76.

thought summed up twentieth century scholarship on medieval views:

> . . . the Scholastics did not oppose the free operation of the marketplace. On the contrary, the Scholastics . . . related the just price to competitive market condition, castigated cartels and the activities of guilds to restrain trade, and had no intention of stigmatizing profits legitimately earned.[7]

According to a subtler argument for government monopoly in money, the government has the right to do to the money of the country whatever it wishes because at all times it owns the entire money supply. Thus the money that the citizens keep in their wallets and their bank accounts is not really their money. They are just stewards for the true owner: the government. The standard justification for this argument is the famous verse in Matthew 22:21. Here the Pharisees show Jesus a coin with Caesar's image and he commends them to "repay to Caesar what belongs to Caesar and to God what belongs to God." Some advocates of monopoly in money take this to mean that all coins belong to the government, in the present case to Caesar.

But this opinion is untenable, as the passage in which the verse appears clearly shows.[8] The passage reads:

> ". . . Tell us, then, what is your opinion: Is it lawful to pay the census tax to Caesar or not?" Knowing their malice, Jesus said, "Why are you testing me, you hypocrites? Show me the coin that pays the census tax." Then they handed

---

[7]Julius Kirshner, "Raymond de Roover on Scholastic Economic Thought," introduction to R. de Roover, *Business, Banking, and Economic Thought in Late Medieval and Early Modern Europe* (Chicago: University of Chicago Press, 1974), p. 19. Before Raymond de Roover, this point had been stressed by Armando Sapori, Albert Sandoz, Josef Höffner, and Joseph Schumpeter. For a recent restatement see Cardinal Josef Höffner, *Christliche Gesellschaftslehre* (Kevelaer: Butzon & Bercker, 1997), pp. 246–47.

[8]See in detail Gary North, *Honest Money* (Ft. Worth, Texas: Dominion Press, 1986), chap. 6.

him the Roman coin. He said to them, "Whose image is this and whose inscription?" They replied, "Caesar's." At that he said to them, "Then repay to Caesar what belongs to Caesar and to God what belongs to God." (Matthew 22:17–21)

Thus it was not just any coin that the Pharisees presented to Jesus, but a coin that was specifically used for the payment of taxes to the Roman Empire. Moreover, Jesus did not even say that the coin itself belonged to the government (Caesar); but only that those sums of money that were owed to the government (if any) were to be paid to it. Oresme too explicitly rejected the opinion that governments somehow are the inherent owners of the entire money supply. He placed great emphasis on this point:

> But if anyone should say that . . . certain commodities are the private property of the prince for which he may set his own prices, as some say is the case with salt and a fortiori with money, we answer that a monopoly or gabelle of salt, or any other necessity, is unjust. And that princes who have made laws to give themselves this privilege are the men of whom the Lord says, in the words of the prophet Isaiah: "Woe unto them that decree unrighteous decrees, and write grievousness which they have prescribed." [Isaiah 10:1] . . . money is the property of the commonwealth.[9]

Is it licit to apply this argument in our modern context? Are democratically elected governments really quite on equal footing with the princes of the Middle Ages? As far as the present question is concerned, there is indeed no essential difference and Oresme's point applies today as it did in the fourteenth century. Democratic governments do not own their citizens. They do not own their citizens' money either.

---

[9]Oresme, "Treatise," p. 16.

10

Legal-Tender Laws

1. FIAT EQUIVALENCE AND GRESHAM'S LAW

A legal tender is money or a money certificate that may be used to make payments *against the will of one of the exchange partners*. Thus the law overrides private contract and provides that the legal tender shall be accepted as payment, rather than the money (or money certificate) promised to the seller or creditor.

Suppose, for example, that Paul gives a credit of 1,000 ounces of silver to John. They agree that after one year John has to pay back 1,050 ounces of silver to Paul. Now legal-tender laws might stipulate that all silver debts may be discharged in gold; or that debtors such as John can fulfill their obligations by paying with silver-denominated banknotes of the FR Bank; or that all payments may be made with copper tokens issued by the public mint, rather than with the type of money desired by the seller.[1] As a consequence, Paul might

---

[1]There is a continuum of possible scopes of legal tender laws. Historically, legal tender privileges have often been limited to certain denominations such as £1 or £2 coins, to special types of payments such as taxes or clearing between commercial banks, or to certain amounts of payment. They have been applied both to debt and spot payments. In our present discussion we will neglect most of these particular forms of legal tender laws and focus on the broad categories. A slightly different version of this chapter has been published under the title "Legal Tender Laws and Fractional-Reserve Banking," *Journal of Libertarian Studies* 18,

not receive the 1,050 ounces of silver that John agreed to pay; most importantly, he would not be able to enforce his original contract with John.

Legal-tender laws would be a mere complication of exchanges were it not for an additional stipulation that is virtually always combined with them. Indeed, legal-tender laws typically establish a legal or "fiat" equivalence between the privileged money (the privileged money certificate) and other monies and money certificates. The point of this scheme is to allow debtors, usually the government among them, to gain at the expense of their creditors. Let us see how this works.

The aforesaid fiat equivalence works like a price control that establishes a legal or fiat price. As long as the fiat price coincides with the market price, everything is good and fine. But as soon as the two prices differ, people stop using the metal that in reality is more valuable than it is according to the letter of the law.

Suppose for example that both gold and silver are legal tender in Prussia, at a fiat exchange rate of 1/20. Suppose further that the market rate is 1/15. This means that people who owe 20 ounces of silver may discharge their obligation by paying only 1 ounce of gold, even though they thereby pay 33 percent less than they would have had to pay on the free market. Prussians will therefore stop making any further contracts that stipulate silver payments to protect themselves from the possibility of being paid in gold; rather they will begin to stipulate gold payments right away in all further contracts. And another mechanism operates to the same effect. People will sell their silver to the residents of other countries, say England, where the Prussian fiat exchange rate is not enforced and where they can therefore get more gold for their silver. The bottom-line is that silver vanishes from circulation in Prussia; and only gold continues to be used in domestic payments. The overvalued money

---

no. 3 (2004). Besides the literature quoted in this article, see also John Zube, *Stop the Legal Tender Crime* (Berrima, Australia: Research Centre for Monetary and Financial Freedom, n.d.).

(here: gold) drives the undervalued money (here: silver) out of the market. This phenomenon is called "Gresham's Law."[2]

Thus we see how legal-tender laws entail an inflation of the legally privileged money, because this money is produced and held in greater quantities than would be the case in the absence of the price control. But legal-tender laws also entail a simultaneous deflation of the other monies and money certificates. In the above example, they entailed an inflation of gold and a deflation of silver.

What are the economic implications? First of all, notice that gold has a much higher purchasing power per weight unit than silver. As a consequence, the new currency cannot be conveniently used to purchase books or groceries; and it is entirely unsuitable to pay for a cup of coffee or for an ice cream. The typical solution for this sort of problem is the use of money substitutes. The market participants will abandon the use of the precious metals and resort to token coins or banknotes in their daily exchanges.

This tendency is reinforced by the fact that the currency substitution process takes time. The passage of a legal-tender law has immediate repercussions on the way people *evaluate* the monies that are concerned, while it takes time to substitute one of them for the other. In our example, while it takes time to export silver, people will immediately stop using it in daily exchanges; in other words, the passage of the legal-tender law increases the demand for silver at the given supply. This will entail a precipitous drop of silver prices being paid for other goods (a tremendous increase of silver's purchasing power). Hence, such legal-tender laws force the market participants to adjust to a more or less severe decline of the price level.

---

[2]After Thomas Gresham, a sixteenth century financial agent of the English Crown in the city of Antwerp. Gresham's Law had however been described long before its namesake, for example, in Aristophanes's poem "The Frogs" and in Nicholas Oresme, "Treatise on the Origin, Nature, Law, and Alterations of Money," in Charles Johnson, ed., *The De Moneta of Nicholas Oresme and English Mint Documents* (London: Thomas Nelson and Sons, 1956), p. 32. Oresme also noticed the deflationary impact.

A lower price level does not have any inconveniences *per se*. However, the process that leads to the lower price level entails ruin and hardship for debtors and businessmen who have not anticipated the event. Most debtors will not be able to pay back nominal debt contracted at a higher price level out of income that can be obtained at the new lower price level. The usual result is bankruptcy. And entrepreneurs who lack foreknowledge will find themselves in very similar circumstances. They have bought factors of production at the old higher price level based on the assumption that they would be able to sell at such higher prices. But the currency substitution forces them to sell their products at the new lower price level. The result is reduced profits, or even losses and bankruptcy.

Under such circumstances, businessmen will be more inclined than ever to use media of exchange that can be immediately substituted for the silver that is now suddenly held back. One solution is the importation of gold. But when the quantities involved are large, such imports will require a considerable logistical effort that cannot be organized at short notice. Gold imports could therefore be a short-term remedy only under circumstances that are so special that we need not deal with them. In fact, the only known technical device for the immediate replacement of the vanishing silver circulation in our example is credit money and fractional-reserve banking. Demand deposits and banknotes can be produced overnight in almost unlimited quantities, and this at virtually zero costs. This is precisely what businessmen are looking for in a situation of a large decline of the price level. They therefore start using fractional-reserve banking to a greater extent than before.

Given these gruesome consequences, the question arises why legal-tender laws have been tried so frequently in the history of monetary institutions. There are two possible answers: ignorance of the political leadership or shameless iniquity. Many economic historians have opted for the first alternative. They have portrayed kings, princes, and democratic parliaments from the Renaissance to the nineteenth century as well-intentioned reformers who were unenlightened about monetary affairs, and about the workings of legal-tender laws in particular. But this seems to be an implausible answer. Virtually all the political leaders of the Western world enjoyed the services of knowledgeable counselors. There was certainly no great lack of enlightenment in these matters after the fourteenth century. It is therefore more probable that past political leaders intentionally established legal-tender laws in order to reap personal profit from the export of the undervalued money and from the possibility of reducing debts contracted in this money. Nicholas Oresme spelled out this very possibility in his discussion of the legal exchange ratio between gold and silver. He argued that this ratio should always follow the market price. Otherwise the government could exploit the difference between legal and market price to its own advantage. This would be unfair and even tyrannical.[3]

2. BIMETALLISM

When legal-tender laws establish fiat exchange ratios between coins made out of different precious metals, the resulting monetary system is called bimetallism.[4] Usually bimetallism is implicit in the set-up of coin systems that comprise coins made out of different precious metals. This was the case, for example, in ancient Rome since the second century B.C., in the Byzantine Empire, and in Western Europe starting in the Renaissance. The operation of Gresham's Law was not often visible in these ancient systems because the undervalued monies were not actually used in the first place. For example, when ancient Rome introduced (undervalued) gold and silver coins into its coin system, it had already a bronze currency, and the (overvalued) bronze coins continued to circulate after the reform. This was of course in accordance with Gresham's Law, but the operation of the Law was invisible because nothing changed.

---

[3]See Oresme, "Treatise," pp. 15–16.

[4]Bimetallism needs to be distinguished from the case in which coins made out of an inferior metal such as copper are used as tokens for gold or silver. Tokens *per se* have nothing to do with legal tender laws.

By contrast, modern history knows a number of spectacular manifestations of Gresham's Law. A famous case in which bimetallism has entailed fiat inflation-deflation was the British currency reform of 1717, when Isaac Newton was Master of the Mint. Newton proposed a fiat exchange rate between the guinea (gold coin) and the shilling (silver coin) very much equal to the going market rate. Yet parliament, ostensibly to "round up" the exchange rate of gold, decreed a fiat exchange rate that was significantly higher than the market rate.[5] And then some well-positioned men helped the British citizens to replace their silver currency with a gold currency.

But this was not all. The resulting deflation was a major factor in stimulating the use of fractional-reserve banknotes in the United Kingdom. It forced businessmen to cut down their prices rather drastically, to adjust to the reduced quantity of money. Many of them found themselves on the verge of bankruptcy, and thus looked out for all sorts of remedies. Accepting banknotes was a convenient solution. Initially businessmen might have believed this to be just a short-term expediency, to bridge the time until more metallic money would become available again in the country. But the bimetallist regime remained, curtailing the money supply below the level it would otherwise have reached, and thus the use of banknotes turned into an ever-more widespread institution.

Events were very similar in the U.S. In 1792, the U.S. Congress voted a bimetallist scheme into existence that decreed the exchange rate between gold and silver to be 1 to 15. The market rate was 1 to 15.5, however, and after a few years the artificially undervalued gold had all but disappeared from circulation. As in the United Kingdom, some people derived great profits from helping Americans exchanging gold for silver, and fractional-reserve banking flourished from the artificial deflation. This operation must have been so profitable that a few decades later it had to be repeated, only this time in the other direction. The U.S. Coin Act of 1834 fixed the legal

---

[5]The market rate was about 1 guinea = 20½ shillings; King George I decreed the rate to be 1 guinea = 21 shillings.

exchange ratio between gold and silver at 1 to 16, and now the entire silver currency of the country was replaced with a gold currency. Again, there were eager helpers, and fractional-reserve banking received another shot in the arm.

In the second half of the nineteenth century, bimetallism found a number of advocates among well-intentioned men who sought to combat the great monetary movement of the time, namely, the trend toward making gold the monopoly money in all countries. The coercive demonetization of silver was bound to curtail the money supply very substantially—another case of fiat deflation. Opposition against these schemes was therefore quite reasonable and legitimate. But the appropriate remedy was not to establish a fiat exchange rate between gold and silver (bimetallism), but to allow both gold and silver to be produced and used at freely fluctuating exchange rates (parallel standards).

3. LEGAL-TENDER PRIVILEGES FOR MONEY CERTIFICATES

Legal-tender laws for money certificates establish a legal equivalence between the certificates and the underlying money, along with an obligation for creditors to accept the certificates up to their full nominal amount.[6] Suppose Brown sells his house for 1,000 ounces of gold to Black. If the notes of the Yellow Bank have legal-tender status, then Black can discharge his obligation by paying with Yellow Bank money certificates of a corresponding amount, even if his contract with Brown stipulates cash payment.

This seems to be unproblematic as far as genuine money certificates are concerned. What difference could it make to a man whether he owns 1 ounce of gold bullion or a genuine certificate for 1 ounce of gold? But it does make a difference. In our above example the demand for Yellow Bank certificates is higher than it otherwise would have been. The least we can say, therefore, is that legal-tender laws inflate one type of

---

[6]We will for now assume that the law grants legal-tender status to all money certificates. Below, we will deal with the more important case of a monopoly legal tender.

monetary service (banknotes) at the expense of other ones. Banknotes are in higher demand than they would have been on the free market.

People usually have a good reason when they use bullion rather than coins, or coins rather than banknotes, or the notes of the A-Bank rather than notes of the B-Bank. There was a reason why Brown stipulated payment in gold, rather than in Yellow Bank notes. Certificates are a matter of trust, and trust cannot be ordained. Where trust is lacking or unequal, there is no true equality between the different monetary objects. It follows that privileging a certificate through legal-tender laws disrupts the balance that would have been established on the market. There is then an inflation of certificates and a deflation of bullion. Certificates enjoy a wider circulation than they would have had in the intrinsic light of the trust that the market participants put into them. If the law compels Brown to accept banknotes that he does not desire, he might at some point decline certain exchanges that he would have made on a free market. Legal-tender laws therefore tend to reduce social cooperation and to impoverish society.

It is true that in the case of genuine money certificates, the quantitative dimension of these effects is negligible. But they do exist, and from a moral point of view this case is not categorically different from other cases in which the quantitative impact of legal-tender laws is incomparably greater.

Legal-tender privileges do have a significant quantitative impact when they are given to *false* certificates. Above we have noticed that the mere legalization of false money certificates could not *per se* lead to large-scale inflation as long as the market participants were free to abandon the use of the false certificates and switch to better ones, or demand payments in bullion. Even the introduction of monopoly privileges does not open the floodgates for inflation, because the monopoly does not impair the ability of the market participants to evaluate them as they see fit. Yet all these barriers to inflation collapse when false money certificates benefit from legal-tender laws.

Consider the following example. Before the institution of legal-tender laws, the Red Bank had operated on a 20 percent reserve ratio. Now the government makes its notes legal tender and thus artificially increases the demand for Red Bank notes; in other words, the owners of these notes redeem them less frequently. Suppose that as a consequence of the reduced demand for redemption, the cash reserves of the Red Bank increase by 2,000 ounces of gold. At the reserve ratio of 20 percent, this means that the Red Bank can issue additional banknotes for 10,000 ounces of gold.

The operation of the market process is perverted. Whereas on a free market there is a tendency for the best available products to be used, legal-tender laws combined with false certificates incite a race to the bottom. Since all money certificates are equal before the law, and because the legal-tender provision overrules private contract, no money user has an interest in paying the higher price for a genuine certificate. And as a consequence no producer has an interest in fabricating such certificates; each one of them now tries to operate at the lowest possible costs. Sooner or later everybody pays with debased coins and fractional-reserve notes. Bullion disappears altogether from public use; it is held back—"hoarded"—or sold abroad.

These are the general effects that result when legal-tender privileges are given to false money certificates. But there are also specific effects that depend on the type of certificate. Legal-tender laws have different consequences when applied to certificates that are physically integrated with the monetary metal (typical case: debased coins) than when applied to those that are not (typical case: fractional-reserve banknote). To these particular effects we now turn.

The Case of Debased Coins

There is no evidence that private minters have been unable to withstand the competition of princes and other governments in truly free markets. But there is a solid historical record documenting how governments have abused the trust that the citizens put into them. There was in fact hardly a dynasty that did not in this way abuse its monopoly of

133

coinage. Ancient Greeks and Romans, medieval princes, dukes and emperors, as well as democratic parliaments have recklessly debased the coins of their country, knowing that the law imposed the bad coins on their subjects at a nominal value determined by the government.[7]

Legal-tender laws eliminate all technical obstacles to an infinite debasement of coins. Any coin, however much it is debased, must be accepted in payment of its full nominal amount. It is therefore possible to debase coins to such an extent that they contain not a trace of precious metal anymore. They can then be made out of inexpensive metal, which allows the fabrication of great quantities before production ceases to be profitable. Consider the case of the Spanish *maravedi* coins. Originally, in the High Middle Ages, they were silver coins, but then the Spanish kings debased them to such an extent that by the end of the sixteenth century they were pure copper coins without a trace of silver. The example shows that legal-tender privileges for debased coins represent a significant source of revenue for the government. Nevertheless they have three great disadvantages from the government's point of view.

---

[7]The fall of the Roman Empire during the fifth and sixth centuries went hand in hand with the disappearance in western Europe of the Roman fiat money system, which had combined gold, silver, and copper coins. The first western ruler to arrogate to himself the monopoly of coinage was the eighh century Carolingian king, Pippin the Short. When the dynasty started to decline in the ninth century, his successors eventually sold monopoly coinage licenses (*ius cudendae monetae*) to a great number of local rulers, such as town governments, abbots, and bishops. Many of these people were in turn no more scrupulous about keeping money sound than the kings. Western European coinage thus continued to deteriorate under the decentralized coin production of the High Middle Ages. See Arthur Suhle, *Deutsche Münz- und Geldgeschichte von den Anfängen bis zum 15. Jahrhundert*, 8th ed. (Berlin: Deutscher Verlag der Wissenschaften, 1975). This highlights the crucial point that the simple multiplication of coin producers is no substitute for true competition. In a way, the decentralized license system was even worse than the old centralized monopoly, because it created constant conflicts between the different coin issuing authorities.

First, as we have pointed out above, the production of debased coins takes time. It is impossible for the government to replace the entire existing stock of coins in one stroke. It follows that the gradual introduction of the new debased coins makes the money supply heterogeneous. Old sound coins circulate side by side with new debased coins. When the market participants realize what is happening, they will hoard the old coins and use only new coins for payments. But this means a more or less drastic reduction of the money supply available for exchanges—a sudden big fiat deflation that entails at least temporary trouble, not only for private fortunes, but also for public finance. The problem vanishes only when the coins are so much debased that they are entirely nominal (zero content of precious metal). This is one of the reasons why government mints, even when their coins enjoyed legal-tender privileges, have traditionally been as secretive about debasement as private counterfeiters.

Second, legal-tender privileges for debased coins may benefit debtors at the expense of creditors.[8] This is of course one of the reasons why governments establish such privileges in the first place. They allow them to rid themselves of a more or less big chunk of their debts, by defrauding their creditors. The problem is that such tricks backfire. First, the fixed revenues of the government are henceforth paid in debased coin too. And second, when the government establishes a reputation as a bad debtor, it becomes very difficult, if not outright impossible, for it to obtain any further credit.

Third, legal-tender privileges for debased coins disrupt the international exchanges and thus jeopardize long-term investments in the country where the privileges are enforced. Nicholas Oresme observed that foreign merchants and capitalists avoid such a country, because "merchants, other things being equal, prefer to pass over to those places in which they

---

[8]As we have pointed out above, this holds true, strictly speaking, only in case when debasement has not been anticipated. But in practice this is very often the case.

receive sound and good money."[9] But even patriotic local entrepreneurs cannot, under such circumstances, maintain their operations if they have to buy their supplies abroad. Oresme emphasized this point:

> Furthermore, in such a kingdom internal trade is disturbed and hindered in many ways by such changes, and while they last, money rents, yearly pensions, rates of hire, cesses and the like, cannot be well and justly taxed or valued, as is well known. Neither can money safely be lent or credit given. Indeed many refuse to give that charitable help on account of such alterations.[10]

There is also a fourth implication of granting legal-tender privileges for debased coins, if these privileges, as we have so far assumed, are granted indiscriminately. This implication is that coins can no longer be produced on a competitive basis without destroying the currency. When a coin producer can debase his product indefinitely and dump it on the other market participants, the race to the bottom has no stopping point short of the resolute rejection of any further indirect exchange by the citizens, that is, short of the total disintegration of the market. This is, again, the reason why legal-tender privileges have rarely been granted under such conditions.[11]

The Case of Fractional-Reserve Banknotes

None of the aforementioned disadvantages exists when legal-tender laws protect fractional-reserve certificates, most

---

[9]Oresme, "Treatise," p. 33.

[10]Ibid., p. 33. He also pointed out that debasement encourages the practice known as money changing.

[11]In 1458, Emperor Friedrich III granted coinage licenses to several of his creditors. It took only one year to run the currency to the bottom and reach total monetary disintegration. See Richard Gaettens, *Inflationen: Das Drama der Geldentwertungen vom Altertum bis zur Gegenwart*, 2nd ed. (Munich: Pflaum, 1955), chap. 2.

notably fractional-reserve banknotes.[12] The reason is that banknotes are not physically integrated with the monetary metal.

If the monetary authorities of a dukedom decide to debase the coinage by one third, then the new coins contain 33 percent less fine metal than the old coins. As we have pointed out, this makes the dukedom's currency heterogeneous and thus entails a deflation. But if the *bank reserves* of that dukedom are reduced by one third, then this affects all banknotes in the same way. The currency does not become heterogeneous and, equally important, the power of any individual banknote to provide its owner with the certified amount of bullion is not necessarily impaired. Indeed, if the banknotes are inflated with sufficient restraint, it may very well be possible to redeem them at any time for as much bullion as before.[13] Nothing disrupts the smooth operation of the market as long as the reserves of the fractional-reserve banks are large enough to satisfy any ongoing demands for redemption.

It follows that, when legal-tender privileges are applied to banknotes (or any other money certificates that are not physically integrated with the monetary metal), they do not produce the deflationary tendencies that arise in the case of debased coins. They do not diminish the government's *other* sources of income; they do not jeopardize international exchanges; they do not hurt the government's creditors; and they do not stand in the way of a competitive production of banknotes.

---

[12]Much of what we say below is also applicable to demand deposits. The differences between banknotes and demand deposits will not be dealt with in the present work. Interested readers should consult the economic literature mentioned in the introduction.

[13]Fractional-reserve banknotes are therefore inherently superior to debased coins. It follows that, if legal-tender privileges are granted to both debasers and fractional-reserve bankers, Gresham's Law will operate to drive the banknotes out of the market. They will be used only in foreign countries, where they circulate without legal-tender protection, whereas the debased coins will be the only currency of the domestic market.

It is true that fractional-reserve banking protected by legal-tender laws is a race to the bottom. Every banker has an incentive to reduce his reserves—to inflate the quantity of his notes—as far as possible. But there *is* a logical stopping point before the total dissolution of monetary exchanges. Every single banker can stay in business only as long as he is able to redeem his notes. Because his customers have the right to demand redemption of his notes into bullion, and because some of them exercise this right, he must keep his note issues within more or less prudent narrow limits. The monetary system as a whole is therefore highly inflationary, but inflation is still limited.

These facts are crucial to understand the last three hundred years of monetary history in the West. The reason why governments have abandoned debasement and started cooperating with fractional-reserve banks was the technical superiority of this type of fiat inflation. It allowed the governments to obtain additional revenue that they could not get from their citizens through taxation, yet without diminishing their other revenues, without hurting their creditors, without disrupting the inclusion of their countries in the international division of labor, and without abolishing competition in banking altogether.

These were great advantages from the point of view of the government. From the ordinary citizens' point of view, the matter looked somewhat less glorious. The inflation of banknotes sucked as many resources out of the rest of the economy as debasement would have, if not more. And it established a permanent partnership between governments and banks. Fractional-reserve banking leverages the inflationary impact of legal-tender laws quite substantially. And inversely, legal-tender laws are a boon for fractional-reserve banking.

4. Legal-Tender Privileges for Credit Money

Very similar considerations come into play when legal-tender privileges are granted to credit money. We have seen that, on a free market, credit money would play a rather insignificant role because of its default risk. But if the market participants *have to* accept it by law in lieu of natural money, it can gain widespread circulation, precisely because it is inferior (but also less costly) to its natural competitors. Again the operation of the market process is perverted; a race to the bottom sets in, though without the inconveniences of debasement.

5. BUSINESS CYCLES

As with all forms of inflation, fractional-reserve banking (and credit money) backed by legal-tender privileges brings about an illegitimate redistribution of income; and since it creates far more inflation than any other institutional set-up, the quantitative impact can be very considerable. The market economy can be understood as a great organism that caters to the needs of consumers—as expressed in money payments. When the economy is flooded with legal-tender fractional-reserve notes, the whole economic body of society begins to cater excessively for the needs of those who control the banking industry. The American economist Frank Fetter once observed that the unhampered market economy resembles a grass-roots democratic process. One penny, one market vote.[14] From this point of view, the imposition of fractional-reserve notes through legal-tender laws creates market votes out of nothing. The bankers and their clients (usually the government in the first place) have many more votes than they would have had in a free society.[15]

---

[14]"The market is a democracy where every penny gives a right of vote." Frank Fetter, *The Principles of Economics* (New York: The Century Co., 1905), p. 395. A few pages later he states: "So each is measuring the services of all others, and all are valuing each. It is the democracy of valuation" (p. 410).

[15]The following hypothetical example gives an idea of the orders of magnitude that are possible under favorable (for the banks) conditions: "A banker starts with $25,000. He issues credit of $250,000. He can take the notes of his customers . . . to the Federal Reserve Bank for discount. He will get something like $245,000 (the balance being the charge for discounting) in Federal Reserve Credit. This he can use as a reserve for further loans. He can extend credit to ten times that amount. That is, $2,450,000. 'Yes, he collects a mere 6 percent, $147,000 in interest' annually. That on a capital of $25,000." Michel Virgil, ed., *The Social Problem,*

139

But legal-tender privileges for fractional-reserve banking also create another very harmful effect: the business cycle. The fundamental practical problem of fractional-reserve banking is that the bank can redeem only as many of its notes as it has money in its vaults. Suppose the FR Bank has issued 1,000 "one-ounce silver FR notes" promising to pay to the bearer of each note the sum of one ounce of silver on demand. Suppose further that the Bank has just 300 ounces of silver ready for redemption. Then it cannot possibly comply with redemption demands from all owners of its notes. In fact it cannot comply with any redemption demand exceeding the sum of 300 ounces of silver. Thus the entire practice of fractional-reserve banking is premised on the assumption that the market participants will not rush to redeem notes once they receive them in payment; but that at least some people will hold them, at least for some time. This assumption very often holds true, especially when such notes are not only legal, but also protected by legal-tender laws. However, because fractional-reserve banks profit from inflation, they have a great economic incentive to extend their note issues; and with each such extension the probability of redemption failure increases. Even if a banker is himself rather prudent, the competition emanating from other bankers pushes him to inflate his note supply, lest he lose market share to these competitors. And thus comes the situation in which the redemption demands for money exceeds the money available in the bank vaults. The bank is unable to meet these demands. It goes bankrupt.

Because of the manifold interconnections amongst banks and between the banks and other businesses, the bankruptcy of one bank is likely to trigger the collapse of the entire fractional-reserve banking industry. This has been observed many times in the history of fractional-reserve banking. Most banking crises of the nineteenth century were of this sort. Similarly, the international banking system that is commonly referred to

---

vol. 2, *Economics and Finance* (Collegeville, Minn.: St. John's Abbey, n.d.), pp. 92–93; quoted from Anthony Hulme, *Morals and Money* (London: St. Paul Publications, 1957), pp. 154–55. Hulme raises the obvious question: "What, we ask, is the justification for this interest?"

as "the system of Bretton Woods" collapsed in 1971 when the U.S. Fed, which redeemed dollar notes held by other central banks into gold, refused further redemption. It goes without saying that a general bank crisis entails hardship for all people who have invested their savings in bank deposits. The collapse of the banking industry also goes hand in hand with a sharp decline of the money supply, because people now refuse to use banknotes, even legal-tender notes, for any length of time, but rush to redeem them into specie. As a consequence, there is a strong downward pressure on money prices (such as wage rates) that forces the market participants through a more or less painful adjustment process. Production is likely to be temporarily interrupted; people are likely to become temporarily unemployed.

The damage can be even greater if the inflation deludes entrepreneurs about the overall resources that are available for investment projects. Every prudent entrepreneur has to make sure that he will have enough resources to bring his production plan to completion, lest he would not only forgo any operating revenues, but also lose all the initial investment. This fundamental fact is emphasized by Jesus as quoted by St. Luke:

> Which of you wishing to construct a tower does not first sit down and calculate the cost to see if there is enough for its completion? Otherwise, after laying the foundation and finding himself unable to finish the work the onlookers should laugh at him and say, "This one began to build but did not have the resources to finish." (Luke 14: 28–30)

The way to find out whether available resources are sufficient to complete a project (such as constructing a tower) is cost calculation. Now fractional-reserve banking has the power to *delude* cost calculations, and thus to induce businessmen into laying foundations that are too large to be completed with the resources available in society. If the fractional-reserve banks make their banknotes available through the credit market, and if credit-taking entrepreneurs do not realize that the additional credit does not come from additional savings, but from inflation, then the interest rate is likely to be lower than it would be in market equilibrium. And because the interest rate is a major component in calculating the prospects of business projects, there are now suddenly many more investment projects that seem to be profitable even though this is not really the case. When the entrepreneurs start investing in such projects, *en masse*, the crisis is programmed in advance. Bringing all these projects to completion would require resources that simply do not exist. The necessary resources exist only in the imagination of businessmen who have mistaken more credit for more savings. What is more, a more or less great part of the resources that really do exist is now actually wasted on projects that cannot be completed. When the crisis sets in, there are then not just temporary interruptions of production. Rather, many projects have to be completely abandoned, and the materials and time sunk into these projects are likely to be lost forever.[16]

6. Moral Hazard, Cartelization, and Central Banks

Above we have stated that the bankruptcy of one fractional-reserve bank is likely to trigger the bankruptcy of many other such banks. The reason is that, in times of severe drain on one bank's cash reserves, the bank turns for short-run credit to other banks. It needs cash to comply with the

---

[16]The foregoing scenario was first analyzed by Ludwig von Mises in his *Theory of Money and Credit* (Indianapolis: Liberty Fund, 1980), chap. 19. See also our discussion in chap. 4, section 6, above. Oresme sensed these things even though his experience was limited to the case of debasement. He observed that inflation of a legal tender was harmful because the money users did not perceive that they lost wealth:

> . . . the prince could thus draw to himself almost all the money of the community and unduly impoverish his subjects. And as some chronic sicknesses are more dangerous than others because they are less perceptible, so such an exaction is the more dangerous the less obvious it is, because its oppression is less quickly felt by the people than it would be in any other form of contribution. And yet no tallage can be heavier, more general or more severe. (Oresme, "Treatise," p. 32)

redemption demands. If the other banks can accommodate its request, no systemic crisis develops. But if the other banks need their cash themselves for the daily redemption demands of *their* customers, they cannot grant any further credit to the other bank. Then the first-mentioned bank goes bankrupt and this launches a chain reaction: bankruptcy of some of its corporate partners, bankruptcy of some of their partners, and finally bankruptcy of other banks who have placed their money in these businesses.

It follows that, under fractional-reserve banking, the bankers have a particularly great personal incentive to support fellow-bankers in times of a redemption crisis. If they cannot extinguish the fire right where it shows up first, it risks spilling over to their own establishment. Thus they are likely to help out fellow-bankers in difficulties. And they are the more likely to be so inclined, the more they themselves operate with low cash reserves.[17] Yet this incentive for mutual support is much less beneficial from a wider social perspective than one might imagine. For the less responsible bankers *know* that this incentive exists on the part of their colleagues. They know that the other bankers will pay part of the bill if they, the imprudent ones, make bad decisions. There is therefore a special temptation for them to inflate their note issues in an especially reckless manner. This is exactly what happened in many periods of unregulated fractional-reserve banking. Economists

---

[17]One striking historic example: when in the summer of 1839 the Bank of England suffered a liquidity crisis, it received credits from the Banque de France (£2,000,000) and from the Hamburger Bank (£900,000); see Ralph Hawtrey, *A Century of Bank Rate*, 2nd ed. (New York: Kelley, 1962), p. 19. For an analysis of cooperation among fractional-reserve banks (central banks and commercial banks) in the era of the classical gold standard, see Giulio Gallarotti, *The Anatomy of an International Monetary Regime: the Classical Gold Standard, 1880–1914* (Oxford: Oxford University Press, 1995), pp. 78–85. In our day, the cooperation between fractional-reserve banks is enshrined into banking legislation such as the French banking law of 1984, presumably to overcome free-rider problems. The law stipulates a *solidarité de place* among French financial institutions.

call such temptation to make others pay for our own projects "moral hazard."[18]

We cannot at this place provide an exhaustive account of the problems of fractional-reserve banking under legal-tender laws. Let us therefore mention only a few organizational devices that, historically, have played an important role in coping with the problems we have just pointed out:

(1) The banks can set up voluntary cartels that regulate the note issues of each cartel member. An essential element of such a cartel would be that only members have access to the inter-bank clearing system.[19]

(2) The clearing institution of the cartel can then be turned into a common cash pool out of which all member banks can draw in times of redemption difficulties. It should be obvious that, due to this essential function, the owners of the pool have great bargaining power and political leverage over the other banks. Thus there is here a tendency for the spontaneous creation of a "central bank" and of a hierarchical banking system.[20]

(3) Wherever it proved to be impossible to establish voluntary cartels, governments have cartelized the banking industry by more or less stringent laws, often at the behest of the most powerful banks.[21]

---

[18]For an Austrian perspective on the theory of moral hazard, see Jörg Guido Hülsmann, "The Political Economy of Moral Hazard," *Politická ekonomie* (February 2006).

[19]See Pascal Salin, *La vérité sur la monnaie* (Paris: Odile Jacob, 1990).

[20]See Jesús Huerta de Soto, *Money, Bank Credit, and Economic Cycles* (Auburn, Ala.: Ludwig von Mises Institute, 2006), pp. 636–39; Lawrence H. White, *The Theory of Monetary Institutions* (Oxford: Blackwell, 1999), pp. 70–80.

[21]For the case of the U.S. see Murray N. Rothbard, *A History of Money and Banking in the United States* (Auburn, Ala.: Ludwig von Mises Institute, 2002). As a matter of fact, legal cartelization and regulation was the next to unexceptional rule. The only known voluntary banking cartel

Again, we cannot afford to dwell at great length on these questions of theory and history, which have been analyzed rather painstakingly in other works. The point we wish to emphasize is that the characteristic institutional features of present-day banking systems—they are national, hierarchical, and regulated by law—are anything but accidental. The cartelization, centralization, and regulation of the banking industry are but organizational techniques (however misguided) to cope with problems of fractional-reserve banking under legal-tender laws.

7. Monopoly Legal Tender

So far we have analyzed the economic impact of legal-tender laws on the assumption that these laws are applied nondiscriminatorily to several money certificates. But this case plays virtually no practical role.[22] Our assumption merely helped us to prepare the analysis of the most relevant case, in which only one type of money certificate is legal tender. To this case we now turn.

Suppose that three different coins are produced in the fair country of Oz: the ducat, the thaler, and the guinea. Now the government makes the ducat alone legal tender, but it does not outlaw the use and production of thalers and guineas. If all three coins are genuine money certificates, the impact of this law is virtually zero. It is true that people who do not trust

---

that operated for any significant period of time was the Suffolk system, named after the Boston-based Suffolk Bank, which organized a clearing system involving a network of New England banks. The Suffolk system went out of business when a competing cartel, led by the Bank for Mutual Redemption started offering much less stringent regulation terms (see ibid., pp. 115–22). This episode seems to highlight a basic problem of any voluntary cartel trying to curb the expansionary power of fractional-reserve banks.

[22]The only significant historical instance was the nineteenth century Italian banking system, which for more than three decades after the unification of Italy featured five different banks issuing legal-tender notes. See M. Fratianni and F. Spinelli, *A Monetary History of Italy* (Cambridge: Cambridge University Press, 1997), chap. 3.

ducats, or do not like them for some other reason, can now be coerced into accepting them; and that the threat of this coercion will in some rare cases diminish the readiness of such people to take part in the division of labor. But such cases are truly rare.

Suppose now that debasement is legal in Oz. If all three coins were legal tender, their producers would set out for a race to the bottom, as we have seen above. But since only the ducat is legal tender, there is no race to the bottom. Rather, the ducat now comes to play the role of a standard of debasement—it sets a pace of debasement that the other two coins must slavishly follow. Assume for example that the ducat is debased to such an extent that it only contains 30 percent of its nominal content of fine silver. Then it makes no sense for the other producers to debase the thalers and guineas even further, say, to 20 percent, because everybody would refuse to accept these inferior coins as payment in the full nominal amount. But neither would it make sense for thalers and guineas to contain *more* silver, say, 40 percent of the nominal amount, because debtors could still pay with ducats. Nobody would then use thalers and guineas either; they would be hoarded as soon as they left the mint, or be exported abroad.

Thus we see how monopoly makes legal-tender privileges workable when applied to debased coins. This is why, historically, legal-tender laws were applied to debased coins by and large only as a monopoly—of course, as a monopoly of the government's mint. But notice that the other disadvantages of legal-tender privileges for debased coins still remain: heterogeneity of the coin supply and fiat deflation, reduction of government revenues, economic destruction of the creditors, and disruption of the international division of labor. We have seen that these problems did not exist when legal-tender laws benefited fractional-reserve notes (and other debased money certificates that were not physically integrated with the bullion). Let us therefore now turn to see how monopoly affects the workings of a fractional-reserve banking system.

Suppose again that we find ourselves in the country of Oz. Only this time nobody in Oz makes coins, but there are three banks issuing notes that are called the pound, the mark, and the franc. Now the government makes the pound alone legal tender, but it does not outlaw the use and production of marks and francs. If all three banknotes are genuine money certificates, the impact of this law is, again, very insubstantial. By contrast, if the practice of fractional-reserve banking were legal in Oz, a legal-tender monopoly for the pound would bring about a pound-inflation, very much as in the above case there was an inflation of debased ducats.

Yet the similarities stop here. Whereas the ducat in our above example played the role of a standard of inflation, the pound in our present example does not play any such role. Legal-tender privileges for the banknotes of one bank do not prevent a race to the bottom, in the course of which each of the other banks attempts to reduce its reserves as far as possible. Assume for example that the pound bank reduces its reserves to 30 percent of its nominal issues. This in no way prevents the mark bank and the franc bank from reducing their reserves even further, say, to 20 percent. Quite to the contrary, there are very powerful incentives for the banks to do precisely that. We have noticed further that fractional-reserve banking systems labor under moral hazard. Each bank has an incentive to be especially reckless in diminishing its reserves (issuing further notes without coverage) because it can rely on the other banks as some sort of a safety net. This incentive is just as present if only one bank enjoys legal-tender privileges. All the other banks then have the tendency to use the notes of this bank, which all market participants are obliged to accept in lieu of specie, to cover their own note issues. Thus we see that, when legal-tender privileges are accorded to just one bank, the cartelization and centralization of the banking industry crystallizes quite naturally around the privileged bank, thus turning it into the central bank.

Notice that the privileged bank then comes into the awkward position that, due to its very privilege, it has to keep larger reserves than all other banks, and is therefore likely to operate less profitably, at least on that account. This was in fact the constant complaint of the Bank of England during most of the nineteenth century. It was the only bank to enjoy legal-tender privileges for its notes; yet all the other banks relied on it for cash and thus forced it to keep much larger reserves than it would have wished to keep.

Although a central bank is in many respects more powerful than the other banks, its fortunes are not independent of the latter. There is still the ultimate reality of moral hazard, inherent in the fractional-reserve principle. And it is easy to see that moral hazard has a tendency to explode the entire banking system. If the other banks are just reckless enough in reducing their reserve ratios, the central bank sooner or later must follow suit, lest it provoke a general banking crisis right away. And on the other hand, the central bank cannot indefinitely go on reducing its reserves without sooner or later jeopardizing its own liquidity, and thus also the liquidity of the entire banking system.

Thus, even if the central bank remains legally independent of the commercial banks, it is in fact their handmaiden. Even if it has no intention to spur inflation, it must play cat and mouse with the commercial banks. The fractional-reserve principle sets the banking system on an expansion path. Smart managers might be able to prevent all too many crises along the way; but such managers are rare, and even they cannot ultimately prevent that redemption demands finally exceed available money reserves. The history of nineteenth century national banking cartels, as well as the history of international banking cartels up to 1971, is very much the history of smart managers inventing ever-new institutions to delay the final bankruptcy. We will give the outline of that history in the third part of the present work.

8. The Ethics of Legal Tender

Legal-tender privileges are even more difficult to justify than the simple monopoly privileges we dealt with in the last chapter. Legal monopoly, as we defined it, diminishes the full use of one's property. It deprives the citizens of options they would otherwise have had. It reduces the menu open for choice. However, it does not attack choice *per se*. The acting person is still free to choose among the remaining alternatives.

By contrast, legal-tender privileges attack individual choice at its very root. They overrule any contractual agreement that a person might make in respect to money. The government imposes the use of some privileged money or money certificate. It coerces the citizens into using these means of payments, even though they might have other contractual obligations and contractual rights. This is why Nicholas Oresme said that alterations of legal-tender money (he took it for granted that money was always legal tender) were "quite specially against nature."[23] They are far worse than usury, because usury, at least, springs from the voluntary agreement between a debtor and a creditor, whereas alterations are done without such an agreement and entail the interdiction of the previous money. Said Oresme:

> The usurer has lent his money to one who takes it of his own free will, and can then enjoy the use of it and relieve his own necessity with it, and what he repays in excess of the principal is determined by free contract between the parties. But a prince, by unnecessary change in the coinage, plainly takes the money of his subjects against their will, because he forbids the older money to pass current, though it is better, and anyone would prefer it to the bad; and then unnecessarily and without any possible advantage to his subjects, he will give them back worse money. . . . In so far then as he receives more money than he gives, against and beyond the natural use of money, such gain is equivalent to usury; but is worse than usury because it is less voluntary and more against the will of his subjects, incapable of profiting them, and utterly unnecessary. And since the usurer's interest is not so excessive, or so generally injurious to the many, as this impost, levied tyrannically and fraudulently, against the interest and against the will of the whole community, I doubt whether it should not rather be termed robbery with violence or fraudulent extortion.[24]

---

[23]Oresme, "Treatise," chap. 16.

[24]Ibid., chap. 17, p. 28.

Thus it is impossible to justify legal-tender laws, especially when they are applied to protect debased coins and fractional-reserve money certificates. Inflation is here at its worst. The floodgates are open and the citizens are denied any protection. Not even self-defense is allowed any more. The masters of the mint and of the banking industry have a free way to enrich themselves—and of course the government, which provides legal coverage for the entire scheme—at the expense of the citizenry. Here this passage comes to mind:

> Your silver is turned to dross, your wine is mixed with water. Your princes are rebels and comrades of thieves; Each one of them loves a bribe and looks for gifts. The fatherless they defend not, and the widow's plea does not reach them. Now, therefore, says the Lord, the LORD of hosts, the Mighty One of Israel: Ah! I will take vengeance on my foes and fully repay my enemies! I will turn my hand against you, and refine your dross in the furnace, removing all your alloy. (Isaiah 1:22–25)

Long before the age of banking, Oresme stressed the scandalous quantitative aspect of inflation protected by legal-tender laws:

> . . . Again, if the prince has the right to make a simple alteration in the coinage and draw some profit from it, he must also have the right to make a greater alteration and draw more profit, and to do this more than once and make still more. . . . And it is probable that he or his successors would go on doing this either of their own motion or by the advice of their council as soon as this was permitted, because human nature is inclined and prone to heap up riches when it can do so with ease. And so the prince would be at length able to draw to himself almost all the money or riches of his subjects and reduce them to slavery. And this would be tyrannical, indeed true and absolute tyranny, as it is represented by philosophers and in ancient history.[25]

---

[25]Ibid., chap. 15, pp. 24f.

One wonders what this great mind might have said about the monetary institutions of our time. Already in his day, Oresme stated that institutionalized inflation—as it can only exist under the protection of government—turns such a government into a tyrant. And this tyranny becomes perfect if the government can enshrine inflation into law.

11

Legalized Suspensions
of Payments

1. The Social Function of Bankruptcy

The fundamental problem of fractional-reserve money tokens is redemption. If a sufficiently large number of the customers choose to demand redemption at the same time, the issuer cannot possibly comply. He goes bankrupt.

Most people tend to regard bankruptcy as a negative event that should be prevented if possible. As far as a bankrupt person and his business partners are concerned, this opinion is understandable. But it is erroneous to assume that bankruptcy is detrimental from any larger social point of view. Bankruptcy fulfills the crucially important social function of preserving the available stock of capital. And it plays this role in all conceivable scenarios: when it results from fraud, when it results from insolvency, and when it results from illiquidity. Let us briefly consider these three cases in turn.

(1) The characteristic feature of a fraudulent company is that from the very outset its promoter never conceived it to generate revenue from real products. Its only purpose was to channel funds from beguiled investors into the pockets of the promoter. The damage done to the investors is patent. Yet such fraud is also socially destructive, because it consumes capital without reproducing it, thus diminishing future wages and the productivity of human efforts. Fraudulent fractional-reserve

153

banking is a case in point. Bankruptcy is its natural death, with the follow-up of criminal persecution of the banker.

(2) In contrast to a fraudulent company, an insolvent company rather unintentionally consumes more resources than it produces. It too impoverishes society, even though in the short run it benefits certain stakeholders of the insolvent company, such as employees and suppliers. The only way an insolvent company can operate for any length of time at all is when it can consume the capital of another entity. Usually this someone is the owner, but sometimes also the creditors. As soon as these people refuse to invest additional funds into it, the insolvent company comes to a standstill. The employees are fired and then work for other firms at lower wage rates; and the machines and other capital goods are sold to other firms for less than their previous book value. This is bankruptcy. It puts an end to wasteful—and therefore socially undesirable—firms, and it forces their stakeholders (laborers, capitalists) to invest their human and material resources in other firms, where the rewards are lower, but which produce more than they consume.

(3) An illiquid company differs from an insolvent company in that it does not suffer from a fundamental mismatch between selling proceeds and cost expenditure. There is "just" a problem of temporary financial mismanagement. A case in point is legalized fractional-reserve banking. Suppose a banker, say, Smith is unable to comply with large-scale redemption demands, for example, during a run on his bank. Smith claims that the fundamental economic data of his firm are excellent. There is just a temporary mismatch between payments and receipts. If his customers only gave him five more hours (days, weeks, months), he could sell his assets for cash and thus comply with the redemption demands. Would it not be bad if he went bankrupt, just because right now he was temporarily unable to honor his promise?

Most people are tempted to agree. As a consequence, legislators have often granted the legal privilege of suspended payments to fractional-reserve banks. But as so often in politics, "suspended payments" is a rather shameless euphemism. It sounds warm-hearted and generous, but the reality is very different. The government no longer enforces payments that the privileged banks have promised to make to their creditors, whereas it continues to enforce payments that these banks receive from their debtors. This is the meaning of suspended payments.

Before we discuss this privilege in more detail, notice that its very premises are questionable. It is usually not possible for fractional-reserve banks to sell their assets at the book value in a reasonably short time, especially if the run is not limited to their bank, but spreads to other banks. In an economy-wide run—historically a frequent phenomenon—the money prices of all assets decline more or less drastically below their book values. No bank can then sell its assets at book value. Hence, the entire (artificial) distinction between insolvency and illiquidity evaporates.

Moreover, even if we grant for the sake of argument that the bank's assets could be sold in a fairly reasonable time at or above book value, the economic case for the rigorous application of bankruptcy law still holds water. Consider that Smith in our above example has not, in fact, complied with the contractual obligation to redeem his notes on demand. At the very least, therefore, he must be considered a bad steward of his customers' money, and the function of bankruptcy would be to drive him out of a leadership position for which he is obviously unfit.

Furthermore, consider that competitors might have anticipated his difficulties and prepared themselves for buying the assets of the Smith Bank. Why should these people be punished for exercising foresight and restraint? After all, they have held back the money necessary to buy the bankrupt company, thus providing to its creditors the very cash that the present owner Smith could not provide. If they had known that fractional-reserve banking was exempt from bankruptcy law, they would probably have set up a fractional-reserve bank too. Rather than preparing to repair the damage done by Smith, they would have created more of that same damage, which enjoys the sanction of the law.

2 . THE ECONOMICS OF LEGALIZED SUSPENSIONS

As long as fractional-reserve banking enjoys no other privilege than being legally recognized, the additional privilege of suspended payments cannot have any large-scale repercussions. The reason is, as we have argued above, that under such conditions fractional-reserve banking would not play any great role in the first place.

Moreover, on a free market, a bankrupt bank would collapse very soon anyway, despite the additional privilege of suspended payments. The use of that privilege is a double-edged sword. It helps the bank out of a momentary calamity, but it also shows the bank to be unreliable—not a great starting point for keeping current customers and attracting new ones. Banks have survived suspensions only when their primary customer was the government itself. The Bank of England went bankrupt after two years of operation, in 1696, and survived only because of government help. The English Crown, which had helped set it up, remained its main customer and granted additional privileges, such as suspension of payments, and legal protection against the competition of other banks.

Things are completely different when fractional-reserve banknotes are legal tender. Here it is sufficient that we concentrate on the most relevant case, namely, on the case of a fractional-reserve bank that enjoys a monopoly legal tender privilege. As we have pointed out before, such a regime entails the tendency to make the privileged banknotes the only currency of the country. If the bank goes bankrupt in such a situation, and if the government then grants it the additional privilege of suspended payments, then this legal act transforms the banknotes from (false) money certificates into paper money.

If a bank can count on the government to authorize suspension of payments, moral hazard comes into play. The bank has less reason to be cautious and keep high reserves. And the bank customers will be encouraged into debt with a bank that they know has the government's blessing. The result is more frequent bankruptcies.

3. The Ethics of Legalized Suspensions

It is probably not necessary to dwell at any length on the ethical inadmissibility of suspended payments. We have said already that the very term "suspended payments" is a shameless euphemism designed to cover up the reality of breach of contract. The bank that suspends payments adopts the absurd position of asserting the legal principle that valid contracts be executed, but only when it insists on receiving payments in fulfillment of its contractual rights; while at the very same time, quite literally in one breath, it rejects the same principle when it denies making payments in fulfillment of its contractual obligations.[1] We mention this only for the sake of completeness in our exposition. No serious attempt at justifying suspended payments has ever been undertaken, at least not on grounds of common law. And no tenable case for legalizing suspensions can be made on grounds of public expediency, as we have argued at length.

---

[1] On the legal implications of this contradiction see Stephan Kinsella, "Punishment and Proportionality: The Estoppel Approach," *Journal of Libertarian Studies* 12, no. 1 (1996).

12

Paper Money

1. THE ORIGINS AND NATURE OF PAPER MONEY

The foregoing discussion has prepared us to deal with the most important case of fiat inflation, namely, with the production of paper money. We have already mentioned that paper money never spontaneously emerged on the free market. It was always a pet child of the government and protected by special legal privileges. We have moreover pointed out the typical sequence of events through which it is established: In a first step, the government establishes a monopoly specie system, either directly by outlawing the monetary use of the other precious metals, or indirectly through the imposition of a bimetallist system. Then it grants a monopoly legal-tender status to the notes of a privileged fractional-reserve bank. Finally, when the privileged notes have driven the other remaining means of exchange out of the market, the government allows its pet bank to decline the (contractually agreed-upon) redemption of these notes. This suspension of payments then turns the former banknotes into paper money.

This scheme fits the sequence of events in all major western countries. Fractional-reserve banknotes had emerged in the seventeenth century and experienced exponential growth rates during the eighteenth century, invariably as a form of government finance and sustained by various privileges. During the nineteenth century, the issues of several privileged banks—the later central banks—acquired monopoly

159

legal-tender status, while the monetary use of silver was out-lawed either directly (Germany, France) or indirectly through bimetallist systems (England, U.S.). To finance the unheard-of destructions of World War I, then, the central banks of France, Germany, and Great Britain suspended the redemption of their notes. Needless to say, this happened with the approval and in fact at the behest of their national governments. Only the Fed did not suspend its payments in World War I, and only the Fed redeemed its notes after World War II under the so-called Bretton Woods system, which lasted until the redemption of U.S. dollar notes was suspended in 1971 (other central banks resumed the redemption of their notes into gold in 1925–31). Since 1971, the entire world is "off the gold standard"—all countries use fiat paper monies.

It is certainly possible to imagine other feasible ways through which paper money could be introduced, but these shall not concern us here. Our point is that, as a matter of fact, paper monies have been introduced in each single case through various progressive infringements on private property, and through massive breaches of contract perpetrated by the central banks. These facts are certainly relevant for a moral evaluation of paper money. In light of them, paper money appears to be tainted by more than a fair share of original sin.

But then there is also another consideration, even more crucial for a proper economic and moral assessment of paper money. The fundamental fact is that, even now, every single paper money continues to exist only because of special legal privilege, which shields it from the competition of other paper monies as well as from the natural monies gold and silver. In particular, paper money is still legal tender and it still enjoys a monopoly on payments that have to be made to governments.[1] This leads us to the important conclusion that paper

---

[1]One of the few weaknesses in Ludwig von Mises's theory of money concerns this point. Mises states: "It can hardly be contested that fiat money in the strict sense of the word is theoretically conceivable. The theory of value proves the possibility of its existence" (*Theory of Money and Credit*, [Indianapolis: Liberty Fund, 1980], p. 75, see also p. 125). Notice that the expression "fiat money" in Mises's book is a translation

money is by its very nature a form of (fiat) inflation. It exists only because of continued legal privileges.[2] It is always and everywhere in greater supply than it would be on the free market, for the simple reason that on the market it could not sustain itself at all.

This is the *only* sense in which paper money can be considered to be a form of inflation. We have to emphasize this point because much ambiguity has been introduced into the debate by a number of opponents of paper money, who have criticized it with the argument that producing paper money was a form of counterfeiting.[3] But this is not the case. A

---

of the original expression "Zeichengeld" which translates literally as "sign money." In fact, the essence of fiat money according to Mises is special legal earmarking to facilitate evaluation by money users. It has nothing to do with the invasion of the property rights of these money users. Fiat money "comprises things with a special legal qualification" (ibid., p. 74). All that the government does here is "to single out certain pieces of metal or paper from all the other things of the same kind so that they can be subjected to a process of valuation independent of that of the rest" (ibid.). In the light of the fact that Mises was wrong on this issue, it is certainly excusable that other writers have let themselves be drawn into certain excesses that derive from that same error. A case in point is Michael Novak, who celebrates the nonmaterial character of modern paper monies in his *Spirit of Democratic Capitalism* (New York: Simon & Schuster, 1982), pp. 348–49. But to really make this point, one would have to prove (1) that the use of gold and silver coins inherently precludes moral and spiritual virtues, and (2) that the lack of a "material" dimension in paper money is inherently praiseworthy from a moral and spiritual point of view. No such proof has been delivered, and it is safe to predict that it will never be delivered. As we have argued, the case is exactly the reverse of what Novak and others assume. The very materiality of gold, silver, and other precious metals makes them especially suitable as money in free society; whereas it is the very nonmateriality of paper money that requires constant coercion to keep them in circulation.

[2]The point has apparently been stressed already in the nineteenth century by the German legal scholar Thöl. See Karl Heinrich Rau, *Grundsätze der Volkswirtschaftslehre*, 7th ed. (Leipzig & Heidelberg, 1863), §295, annotation (d), p. 373.

[3]See in particular Murray N. Rothbard, *The Mystery of Banking* (New York: Richardson & Snyder, 1983), pp. 51–52 and passim; Gary North,

monetary authority that produces its own paper money does not engage in counterfeiting. It does not claim to do or to represent anything other than what it does and represents.

It could be argued that the current notes of the Bank of England provide a counterexample. These banknotes not only feature a portrait of Queen Elizabeth, but also the imprint "I promise to pay the bearer on demand the sum of £20" (on £20 notes). Is this not a fraudulent promise? Is it not a case of counterfeiting? It is not. In actual fact the promise to pay £20 is not more than a deferential bow before the British mind, which worships the preservation of forms that have long outlived their former content. Until 1914, and then between 1925 and 1931, the Bank of England redeemed its £20 notes into a quantity of gold that was called "the sum of £20." Today it redeems these notes into other notes of the same kind. The point is that in the old days the expression "the sum of £20" had a different legal meaning than it has today. At the time it designated some five ounces of gold.[4] Today it means something different. The suspension of payments has turned the expression "the sum of £20" into a self-referential tautology—it now designates £20 paper notes. The notes that promise payment of "the sum of £20" do no more than promise payment in like notes. This sheds of course a somewhat unflattering light on the Queen of England, who appears to make empty promises. But it is an oddity, not a lie.

2. Reverse Transubstantiations

We need to extend the foregoing consideration somewhat further. It is indeed a characteristic problem of paper money that it combines traditional forms with a radically new content.

Honest Money (Ft. Worth, Texas: Dominion Press, 1986), chap. 9; Thomas Woods, *The Church and the Market* (Lanham, Md.: Lexington Books, 2005), p. 97; Friedrich Beutter, *Zur sittlichen Beurteilung von Inflationen* (Freiburg: Herder, 1965), pp. 157, 173. Beutter also qualifies inflation as theft; see ibid., 91, 154.

[4]1 ounce of gold was defined as 3 pounds, 17 shillings, 10.5 pence, or £3.89.

The suspension of payments that turns banknotes into paper money entails various "reverse transubstantiations"—an expression we use because the phenomenon at issue bears a certain resemblance with the central liturgical event of the Catholic mass. We have to speak of a *reverse* transubstantiation, however, because the transubstantiation that results from human hands in the economic sphere cannot be said to sanctify things or otherwise improve them in any sense.[5]

Suppose there is a central bank that issues legal-tender banknotes, and that its notes have a wide circulation. One day the government authorizes the bank to suspend redemption forever. The notes continue to enjoy legal-tender privileges, and the bank declares that it has no intention whatever to resume redemption at any point in the future. This transforms the former banknotes into paper money and the former central bank into a paper money producer. The former banknotes and the former bank preserve all of their external characteristics—the notes still look and smell and feel exactly as before, the buildings of the former bank still displays the inscription "Bank," and so on—but their natures have changed. The notes are no longer certificates.[6] They just *are* what they are: legal tender paper slips. And the former bank is no longer a bank even though it might still call itself "XY Bank" or "Bank of Ruritania." A bank *deals with* money—it offers financial intermediation, safeguarding of deposits, issuing money certificates, and so on. Some banks actually fake money certificates—fractional-reserve banks. But no bank in the proper meaning of the word ever *makes* money. By contrast, the producer of irredeemable legal-tender notes *does* make money. He

---

[5]I owe the expression "reverse transubstantiation" to Professor Jeffrey Herbener. For a number of years, I have used in classroom the expression "economic transubstantiation." But this is a euphemism.

[6]The imprints on coins and banknotes no longer certify ownership of a certain amount of precious metal. Rather, they certify the legitimate origin of these coins and banknotes. Also, present-day coins are no longer certificates; they are not even token money as they were in previous times.

is not a banker, but a money producer, in quite the same sense in which gold miners or silver miners are money producers on the free market.

Thus we see in which sense reverse transubstantiation occurs through legal acts that authorize the suspension of payments of legal-tender notes. Such acts leave all *physical appearances* intact; but they change the essence of the notes and of the issuer of these notes.

Our present-day world is a paper-money world. On August 15, 1971, the central bank of the world, the U.S. Federal Reserve System, suspended the redemption of its notes; and there is presently no intention whatever to ever resume their redemption into specie. The legal act that authorized the suspension of August 1971 transformed the U.S. dollar into a paper money, and by the same token it transformed the banknotes issued by all other central banks into paper money too. It is true that we still *call* our paper money "banknotes," that we *call* the Fed a "Bank," that the Bank of Japan has preserved its name, and that a new "bank" of the same type has been established, namely, the European Central Bank. But as a matter of fact our present day paper-money notes are no longer banknotes, and the aforementioned "banks" are not banks.[7] We stress these facts in some detail because the entire matter poses great difficulties even to experienced observers, and is one of the most widespread sources of confusion for students of monetary affairs. Of course we cannot explore at this point the interesting philosophical questions related to the phenomenon of reverse transubstantiation. We need to focus on the practical implications of paper-money production.

3. THE LIMITS OF PAPER MONEY

One important aspect of this new reality is that institutions like the Fed cannot go bankrupt. They can print any amount

---

[7]More precisely, we would have to say that the nature of present-day "banknotes" is different from the nature of pre-suspension banknotes; and that the nature of present-day central banks is different from the nature these institutions had before the suspension.

of money that they might need for themselves at virtually zero cost. Consider that it takes just a drop of ink to add one or two zeros to a $100 bill! Here is the great difference between the production of paper money and the production of natural monies such as gold and silver. Miners can go bankrupt. They cannot increase their production *ad libitum*, because profitable gold and silver production is possible only within fairly narrow limits. As we have just seen, no such limits exist for the production of paper money.[8]

What imposes certain constraints on paper-money producers is not the danger of bankruptcy, but the danger of hyperinflation. If the purchasing power of their notes declines at such a rapid pace that it becomes ruinous to hold them in one's purse for any length of time, then the citizens would at some point rather forgo the benefits of monetary exchange altogether than go on using these notes. That point is usually reached when the notes lose the bulk of their purchasing power by the hour—a typical phenomenon in the terminal phase of historical hyperinflations. People then stop using the currency ("flight from money") and the economy disintegrates, especially if the government does not lift the

---

[8]A few years ago, the present chairman of the U.S. central bank emphasized this possibility, and the willingness of the authorities to make use of it, if need be, to dispel deflation fears. He said:

> Like gold, U.S. dollars have value only to the extent that they are strictly limited in supply. But the U.S. government has a technology, called a printing press (or, today, its electronic equivalent), that allows it to produce as many U.S. dollars as it wishes at essentially no cost. By increasing the number of U.S. dollars in circulation, or even by credibly threatening to do so, the U.S. government can also reduce the value of a dollar in terms of goods and services, which is equivalent to raising the prices in dollars of those goods and services. We conclude that, under a paper-money system, a determined government can always generate higher spending and hence positive inflation. (Ben Bernanke, "Deflation: Making Sure 'It' Doesn't Happen Here" [Remarks before the National Economists Club, Washington, D.C., 21 November 2002])

legal-tender privilege or adopt some other emergency measure, for example, an all-round monetary reform.[9]

Hyperinflation is a rather loose limitation. In the last thirty years, national and international paper monies have been produced in extraordinary quantities, surpassing any inflationary experience of the past that did not produce a collapse. But although some minor currencies have collapsed in hyperinflations, none of the major currencies (dollar, yen, and euro) has thus far shared this fate.

4. MORAL HAZARD AND PUBLIC DEBTS

The most visible consequence of the global paper-money inflation of the past thirty years is the explosion of public debt. To be true, the debts of private individuals and organizations have increased as well, and this was also as a consequence of inflation. But their growth has been insignificant compared to the growth of public debt.

Consider the situation of a private debtor. The amount of money he can borrow from other people is essentially limited by his present assets and by his expected revenue. He simply could not pay back any sum exceeding this limit. (From the economic point of view, any money "lent" to him in excess of this limit would not be a credit at all, but some form of assistance.) Private debts therefore by and large tend to grow under inflation to the extent that the growing monetary revenues warrant ever higher credits. But however strong the inflation may be, the amount of private credit granted is still limited by present assets and expected revenue.

Now contrast this state of affairs with the situation of a government. The amount of money it can borrow also depends on its present resources and expected revenue from taxation. However, its potential *monetary* resources are *unlimited* because it enjoys unlimited credit from its central bank,

---

[9]Notice again that all historical hyperinflations have been inflations of paper money. See Peter Bernholz, *Monetary Regimes and Inflation* (Cheltenham, U.K.: Edward Elgar, 2003).

the national paper money producer. Central banks are public institutions with special loyalties and obligations toward their governments. As we have seen, they cannot go bankrupt, because they can create *ex nihilo* any amount of money without any technical or economic limitation. It follows that governments too cannot go bankrupt as long as they have the full loyalty of their central banks. Moreover, they can obtain credit far in excess of their current assets and expected revenue from taxation. Investors know that the paper money producer stands behind its government. They therefore know that government will always be able to meet any financial obligation that is denominated in the money of its central bank. As a consequence investors will be willing to buy ever more government bonds even if there is no hope that the public debt could ever be repaid out of tax revenue.

As a tendency, therefore, public debt under a paper-money system does not simply grow at the same pace as the money supply, but at a much faster rhythm. For example, in the case of the U.S., since 1971 the money supply has been increased by the factor 6, whereas the federal debt has grown by the factor 20 (see Table 1).

Those who entertain doubts about the loyalty of today's central banks toward their governments should consider that

Table 1 : Evolution of M1 and Public Debt in the U.S.

	M1 billion U.S. dollars on January 1	Federal debt billion U.S. dollars yearly data
1960	140	290
1970	206	389
1980	386	930
1990	795	3,233
2000	1,121	5,674
2005	1,367	7,933

Source: Federal Reserve Bank of Saint Louis;
  Bureau of the Public Debt

the leadership of these institutions consists entirely of political appointees and that their much-vaunted "independence" can be abrogated by simple majorities in parliament.

One might object that the central banks do not in fact have the legal authorization to replenish the public purse with the printing press. But this objection misses the mark even though it is correct in a narrow technical sense. To be sure, the central banks may generally not engage in any *direct* manner to refinance their governments. However, they cannot be prevented from doing this in a more roundabout way, with the help of their partners in the banking sector and the financial markets. As a matter of fact, central banks increase the money supply mainly through the purchase of short-term financial titles (this is called "open-market policy"). No law prevents—or could conceivably prevent—that such purchases be tied up with an explicit or implicit obligation for the seller to give new credits to the government. In current practice it is not even necessary to impose any such obligation. Banks and investment funds are very eager buyers of government bonds.

5. MORAL HAZARD, HYPERINFLATION, AND REGULATION

Many economists have speculated about the feasibility of pure paper-money systems. Some argue that paper-money producers *could* fabricate money of better quality—more stable purchasing power—than the traditional monies, gold and silver. And they add that this *would* happen if paper-money producers were forced to operate on a free market.

All such considerations are intellectual moonshine. The idea of stable paper money is at odds with all historical experience. And the theoretical case for that idea has no better foundation. We have already pointed out that the ideal of a stable purchasing power is a chimera, and that there are good reasons to believe that no paper money could sustain itself in a truly free competition with gold and silver. Now let us bring a further consideration into play. It is indeed very doubtful that paper-money producers, even if they thoroughly wished to stabilize the purchasing power of their product, could prevent a general economic crisis. The reason is, again, that the mere possibility of inflating the money supply creates moral hazard.

The production of gold and silver does not depend on the good will of miners and minters; and the users of gold and silver coins, as well as creditors and debtors, *know this*. Therefore they do not speculate on the sudden availability of additional gold and silver supplies that miraculously emerge from the depths of the mines. They make all kinds of other errors in their speculations, but not this one. Under a paper-money standard, by contrast, people do speculate on the good will of paper-money producers; and they do not do this in vain. Such speculation occurs on a large scale, because people know that paper money can be produced in virtually any quantity. It is really just a matter of good will on the side of the producers. It follows that more or less *all* market participants will tend to be more reckless in their speculations than they otherwise would have been—a sure recipe for wasteful use of resources and possibly also for macroeconomic collapse.

If just a few persons speculate on the assistance of the paper-money producer, they can be helped with the printing press at the expense of all other owners of money. Suppose that the money supply of an economy is three billion thalers. If one entrepreneur goes bankrupt and is helped by his friends from the central bank with three million thalers fresh from the printing press, the impact on prices might hardly be noticeable. But now suppose one thousand entrepreneurs do the same thing. The owner of the printing press then faces a hard choice. *Either* he helps them too, but in this case he would have to double the money supply, which could hardly fail to have dramatic negative repercussions. *Or* he declines the requests for assistance; then it would come to mass bankruptcy.[10]

---

[10]We can neglect at this point all considerations about the intertemporal misallocation of resources that such mass speculation might entail. See Jörg Guido Hülsmann, "Toward a General Theory of Error Cycles," *Quarterly Journal of Austrian Economics* 1, no. 4 (1998).

The second alternative is of course not really an option. Political pressure on the paper-money producer to comply with the requests would be so great that he could hardly resist this pressure and hope for the continuation of peaceful business relations with the government and others. It is naïve to believe that he could impress people with his case for stable money while their businesses collapse *en masse*. And apart from that, the second alternative also carries great commercial risks for him. Large-scale bankruptcy is usually incompatible with a stable price level, and it is likely to reduce the exchange rate *vis-à-vis* other currencies.

But assume that the producer of the paper money announces with a stern voice and steely eyes that he will be steadfast in his determination to never ever ("read my lips") issue more notes than necessary for the stabilization of purchasing power. Would this be quite as convincing as the implicit guarantees of a gold or silver standard? The answer is patent. Hence, the inescapable dilemma of a paper-money producer is that his *mere presence* creates moral hazard on the side of all other market participants. This in turn will make it impossible for him to avoid increasing rates of inflation in the long run, with the ultimate prospect of a runaway hyperinflation.

The West is still at the beginning of its great experiment with paper money—thirty years is not a long time for a monetary institution. But already the foregoing considerations find a ready confirmation in the economic statistics of the past thirty years, which witnessed an exponential growth of the money supply, as well as of debts private and public, in all major western countries.

Evidence for moral hazard on a mass scale could be found in the last ten years or so in the stock-exchange mania, as well as in the real-estate boom in the United Kingdom and the U.S. Here the market participants have invariably displayed the same characteristic behavior. They have evaluated the assets *without regard for the price-earnings ratio*, speculating entirely on finding, at some point in the future, a buyer who is even more bullish than they are now, and who will therefore consent to pay an even higher price.

Consider the current (2006) U.S. real-estate boom. Many Americans are utterly convinced that American real estate is the one sure bet in economic life. No matter what happens on the stock market or in other strata of the economy, real estate will rise. They believe themselves to have found a bonanza, and the historical figures confirm this. Of course this belief is an illusion, but the characteristic feature of a boom is precisely that people throw any critical considerations overboard. They do not realize that their money producer—the Fed—has possibly already entered the early stages of hyperinflation, and that the only reason why this has been largely invisible was that most of the new money has been exported outside of the U.S.[11] Money prices have increased tremendously above the level they would have reached without the relentless production of greenbacks, but the absolute increase of the domestic price level (as measured by CPI figures) has been relatively moderate so far. However, as soon as foreigners slow down their purchases of U.S. dollars domestic prices will start soaring, and then hyperinflation looms around the corner.

In the past, governments have tried to counter this trend through regulations. Moral hazard first became visible in the banking industry, and today this industry is indeed very strongly regulated.[12] The banks must keep certain minimum amounts of equity and reserves, they must observe a great number of rules in granting credit, their executives must have certain qualifications, and so on. Yet these stipulations trim

---

[11]According to the Federal Reserve Board, between 1995 and 2005 the Fed increased its note issues at an annual pace of 6.6 percent (compare: under a gold standard, annual production has hardly ever added more than 2 percent to the existing gold stock). The Board estimates that between one-half and two-thirds of all U.S. dollar notes are held abroad. See http://www.federalreserve.gov/paymentsystems/coin/default. htm (update of March 14, 2006).

[12]The same thing holds true for financial markets and labor markets. Other markets that are also strongly affected by moral hazard springing from paper money have so far escaped heavy regulation. Notable cases in point are real estate markets.

the branches without attacking the root. They seek to curb certain known excesses that spring from moral hazard, but they do not eradicate moral hazard itself. As we have seen, moral hazard is implied in the very existence of paper money. Because a paper-money producer can bail out virtually anybody, the citizens become reckless in their speculations; they count on him to bail them out, especially when many other people do the same thing. To fight such behavior effectively, one must abolish paper money. Regulations merely drive the reckless behavior into new channels.

One might advocate the pragmatic stance of fighting moral hazard on an *ad-hoc* basis wherever it shows up. Thus one would regulate one industry after another, until the entire economy is caught up in a web of micro-regulations. This would of course provide some sort of order, but it would be the order of a cemetery. Nobody could make any (potentially reckless!) investment decisions anymore. Everything would have to follow rules set up by the legislature. In short, the only way to fight moral hazard without destroying its source, fiat inflation, is to subject the economy to a Soviet-style central plan.

Central planning or hyperinflation (or some mix between the two)—this is what the future holds for an economy under paper money. The only third way is to abolish paper money altogether and to return to a sound monetary order.

6. The Ethics of Paper Money

We need not dwell much on the ethics of paper money. In the light of our foregoing discussion, the case should be clear. Notice first of all that a good moral case against paper money can be made on the mere ground of its illegitimate origins. Paper money has never been introduced through voluntary cooperation. In all known cases it *has been* introduced through coercion and compulsion, sometimes with the threat of the death penalty.

And as we have seen, there are good reasons to believe that paper money by its very nature involves the violation of property rights through monopoly and legal-tender privileges. But at any rate it is a matter of fact that, at present, all paper monies of the world *continue to be protected through such legal privileges* in their countries of origin. We have argued that these privileges cannot be justified, certainly not in the case of money, because there is no need for fiat inflation. It follows that our present-day paper monies, which thrive on these privileges, are morally inadmissible.

The production of paper money has posed formidable obstacles to appropriate ethical judgement. The opponents of paper money among the economists usually claim that the production of *paper* money is inflation—as though the distinction between money production and inflation could be made along purely physical lines. But this view is problematic because it comes close to condemning the production of money *per se*. The relevant fact about our present-day paper monies is not that they are paper monies, but that they are *fiat* paper monies. Their continued production could possibly be justified, even though they have been introduced by illegitimate means. But their imposition by law cannot be justified, as we have argued in some detail.

13

The Cultural and Spiritual Legacy of Fiat Inflation

1. INFLATION HABITS

The notion that inflation is harmful is a staple of economic science. But most textbooks underrate the extent of the harm, because they define inflation much too narrowly as a lasting decrease of the purchasing power of money (PPM), and also because they pay scant attention to the concrete forms of inflation. To appreciate the disruptive nature of inflation in its full extent we must keep in mind that it springs from a violation of the fundamental rules of society. Inflation is what happens when people increase the money supply by fraud, imposition, and breach of contract. Invariably it produces three characteristic consequences: (1) it benefits the perpetrators at the expense of all other money users; (2) it allows the accumulation of debt beyond the level debts could reach on the free market; and (3) it reduces the PPM below the level it would have reached on the free market.

While these three consequences are bad enough, things get much worse once inflation is encouraged and promoted by the state. The government's fiat makes inflation perennial, and as a result we observe the formation of inflation-specific *institutions* and *habits*. Thus fiat inflation leaves a characteristic cultural and spiritual stain on human society. In the present chapter, we will take a closer look at some aspects of this legacy.

2. Hyper-Centralized Government

Inflation benefits the government that controls it, not only at the expense of the population at large, but also at the expense of all secondary and tertiary governments. It is a well-known fact that the European kings, during the rise of their nation states in the seventeenth and eighteenth centuries, crushed the major vestiges of intermediate power. The democratic nation states of the nineteenth and twentieth centuries completed the centralization of power that had been begun under the kings.[1] The economic driving force of this process was inflation, which at that point was entirely in the hands of the central state apparatus. More than any other economic reason, it made the nation state irresistible. And thus it contributed, indirectly at least, to the popularity of nationalistic ideologies, which in the twentieth century ushered in a frenetic worshipping of the nation-state.

Inflation spurs the growth of central governments. It allows these governments to grow larger than they could become in a free society. And it allows them to monopolize governmental functions to an extent that would not occur under a natural production of money. This comes at the expense of all forms of intermediate government, and of course at the expense of civil society at large. The inflation-sponsored centralization of power turns the average citizen more and more into an isolated social atom. All of his social bonds are controlled by the central state, which also provides most of the services that formerly were provided by other social entities such as family and local government. At the same time, the central direction of the state apparatus is removed from the daily life of its wards.

It is difficult to reconcile these trends with the goal of a well-ordered society. In the nineteenth century, the French sociologist Frédéric LePlay, an astute and critical observer of

---

[1]See Alexis de Tocqueville, *L'Ancien régime et la Révolution* (Paris: Michel Lévy frères, 1856); Bertrand de Jouvenel, *Du pouvoir* (Geneva: Bourquin, 1945); Hans-Hermann Hoppe, *Democracy—The God That Failed* (New Brunswick, N.J.: Transaction, 2001).

the centralization of state power, established the moral principle of subsidiarity, according to which any problem should be solved by the—in political terms—lowest-ranking person or organization that is able to solve it.[2] Leo XIII then canonized this principle, in a manner of speaking, in *Rerum Novarum* (§§13, 35), without calling it by its name. Only in 1931, Pope Pius XI adopted the expression "subsidiarity," in his encyclical *Quadragesimo Anno*. But moral precepts will not stop a trend that springs from such powerful sources. The evil has to be attacked at the root.

3. FIAT INFLATION AND WAR

Among the most gruesome consequences of fiat money, and of paper money in particular, is its ability to extend the length of wars. The destructions of war have the healthy effect of cooling down initial war frenzies. The more protracted and destructive a war becomes, therefore, the less is the population inclined to support it financially through taxes and the purchase of public bonds. Fiat inflation allows the government to ignore the fiscal resistance of its citizens and to maintain the war effort on its present level, or even to increase that level. The government just prints the notes it needs to buy cannons and boots.[3]

---

[2] On LePlay see Charles Gide and Charles Rist, *Histoire des doctrines économiques*, 6th ed. (Paris: Dalloz, 2000), bk. 5, chap. 2, pp. 582–90. On the principle of subsidiarity in Catholic social doctrine, see Pontifical Council for Justice and Peace, *Compendium of the Social Doctrine of the Church*, §185–88.

[3] According to Kant, world peace presupposed that public debt not be used to finance war since this would unduly facilitate the waging of war. See Immanuel Kant, "Zum Ewigen Frieden—ein philosophischer Entwurf," *Werkausgabe* 11 (Frankfurt: Suhrkamp, 1991), pp. 198–99. However, the prohibition of a particular use of public debt is unlikely to be effective in practice because it is impossible to tie up a particular type of revenue with a particular type of expenditure. (The government can always claim that it pays for military expenditure with revenue from taxes, whereas the public debt is used for non-military purposes.) It is therefore more effective to attack the problem at its root and to abolish

This is exactly what happened in the two world wars of the twentieth century, at least in the case of the European states. The governments of France, Germany, Italy, Russia, and the United Kingdom covered a large part of their expenses through inflation. It is of course difficult to evaluate any precise quantitative impact, but it is not unreasonable to assume that fiat inflation prolonged both wars by many months or even one or two years. If we consider that the killings reached their climax toward the end of the war, we must assume that many millions of lives could have been saved.

Many people believe that, in war, all means are just. In their eyes, fiat inflation is legitimate as a means to fend off lethal threats to a nation. But this argument is rather defective. It is not the case that all means are just in a war. There is in Catholic theology a theory of just war, which stresses exactly this point. Fiat inflation would certainly be illegitimate if less offensive means were available to attain the same end. And fact is that such means exist and have always been at the disposition of governments, for example, credit money and additional taxation.

Another typical line of defense of fiat money in wartimes is that the government might know better than the citizens just how near victory is at hand. The ignorant population grows weary of the war and tends to resist additional taxation. But the government is perfectly acquainted with the situation. Without fiat money, its hands would be tied, with potentially disastrous consequences. The inflation just gives it the little extra something needed to win.

It is of course conceivable that the government is better informed than its citizens. But it is difficult to see why this should be an obstacle in war finance. The most essential task of political leadership is to rally the masses behind its cause. Why should it be impossible for a government to spread its better information, thus convincing the populace of the need for additional taxes? This brings us to the following consideration.

---

the legal dispositions that impose fractional-reserve banking and paper money. The reduction of the public debt would be a logical consequence.

4. INFLATION AND TYRANNY

War is only the most extreme case in which fiat inflation allows governments to pursue their goals without genuine support from their citizens. The printing press allows the government to tap the property of its people without having obtained their consent, and in fact against their wishes. What kind of government is it that arbitrarily takes the property of its citizens? Aristotle and many other political philosophers have called it tyranny. And monetary theorists from Oresme to Mises have pointed out that fiat inflation, considered as a tool of government finance, is the financial technique characteristic of tyranny.

5. RACE TO THE BOTTOM IN MONETARY ORGANIZATION

As we have seen in some detail, fiat inflation is an inherently unstable way of producing money because it turns moral hazard and irresponsibility into an institution. The results are frequently recurring economic crises. Past efforts to repair these unwelcome effects, yet without questioning the principle of fiat inflation *per se*, have entailed a peculiar evolution of monetary institutions—a kind of institutional "race to the bottom." This does not of course imply a quick process. The devolution of monetary institutions has been underway for centuries, and it has still not quite reached the absolute bottom, even though the process has accelerated considerably in our age of paper money. We have dealt with this phenomenon already at some length and will present it in greater historical context in Part Three.

6. BUSINESS UNDER FIAT INFLATION

Fiat inflation has a profound impact on corporate finance. It makes liabilities (credit) cheaper than they would be on a free market. This prompts entrepreneurs to finance their ventures to a greater extent than otherwise through credit, rather than through equity (the capital brought into the firm by its owners).

In a natural system of money production, banks would grant credit only as financial intermediaries. That is, they could lend out only those sums of money that they had either saved themselves or which other people had saved and then lent to the banks. The bankers would of course be free to grant credit under any terms (interest, securities, duration) they like; but it would be suicidal for them to offer better terms than those that their own creditors had granted them. For example, if a bank receives a credit at 5 percent, it would be suicidal for it to lend this money at 4 percent. It follows that on a free market, profitable banking is constrained within fairly narrow limits, which in turn are determined by the savers. It is not possible for a bank to stay in business *and* to offer better terms than the savers who are most ready to part with their money for some time.

But fractional-reserve banks can do precisely that. Since they can produce additional bank credit at virtually zero cost, they can grant credit at rates that are lower than the rates that would otherwise have prevailed. And the beneficiaries will therefore finance some ventures through debts that they would otherwise have financed with their own money, or which they would not have started at all. Paper money has very much the same effect, but in a far greater magnitude. A paper-money producer can grant credit to virtually any extent and on virtually any terms. In the past few years, the Bank of Japan has offered credit at zero percent interest, and then proceeded in some cases to actually pay people for borrowing its credit.

It is obvious that few firms can afford to resist such offers. Competition is fierce in most industries, and the firms must seek to use the best terms available, lest they lose that "competitive edge" that can be decisive for profits and also for mere survival. It follows that fiat inflation makes business more dependent on banks than they otherwise would be. It creates greater hierarchy and central decision-making power than would exist on the free market. The entrepreneur who operates with 10 percent equity and 90 percent debt is not really an entrepreneur anymore. His creditors (usually bankers) are the true entrepreneurs who make all essential decisions. He is just a more or less well-paid executive—a manager.

Thus fiat inflation reduces the number of true entrepreneurs—independent men who operate with their own money. Such men still exist in astonishing numbers, but they can only survive because their superior talents match the inferior financial terms with which they have to cope. They must be more innovative and work harder than their competitors. They know the price of independence and they are ready to pay it. Usually they are more attached to the family business and care more for their employees than the puppets of bankers.

Because credit springing from fiat inflation provides an easy financial edge, they have the tendency to encourage reckless behavior of the chief executives.[4] This is especially the case with managers of large corporations who have easy access to the capital markets. Their recklessness is often confused with innovativeness. Indeed, the economist Joseph Schumpeter has famously characterized fractional-reserve banks as being some sort of mainspring of economic development.[5] He argued that such banks may use their ability to create credit out of thin air (*ex nihilo*) to provide funding for innovative entrepreneurs. It is conceivable that in some cases they played this role, but the odds are overwhelmingly on the other side. As a general rule, any new product and any thoroughgoing innovation in business organization is a threat for banks, because they are already more or less heavily invested in established companies, which produce the old products and use the old forms of

---

[4]The intimate connection between such recklessness and the prevailing monetary system is usually overlooked, even in penetrating studies of the subject. See for example A. de Salins and F. Villeroy de Galhau, *Le développement moderne des activités financiers au regard des exigencies éthiques du Christianisme* (Vatican: Libreria Editrice Vaticana, 1994), in particular pp. 23–34 where the authors discuss the impact of the "financial sphere" on the economy without even mentioning the problems of moral hazard and of the lender-of-last-resort concept.

[5]See Joseph A. Schumpeter, *Theorie der wirtschaftlichen Entwicklung*, 4th ed. (Berlin: Duncker & Humblot, [1934] 1993), chap. 3.

organization. They have therefore every incentive to either prevent the innovation by declining to finance it, or to communicate the new ideas to their existing partners in the business world. Thus, fractional-reserve banking makes business more conservative than it otherwise would be. It benefits the established firms at the expense of innovative newcomers. Innovation is much more likely to come from independent businessmen, especially if income taxation is low.

7. The Debt Yoke

Some of the foregoing considerations also apply outside of the business world. Fiat inflation provides easy credit not only to governments and firms, but also to private persons. The mere fact that such credit is offered at all incites some people to go into debt who would otherwise have chosen not to do so. But easy credit becomes nearly irresistible in connection with another typical consequence of inflation, namely, the constantly rising price level. Whereas in former times the increase of prices has been barely noticeable, in our day all citizens of the western world perceive the phenomenon. In countries such as Turkey or Brazil, where prices have increased until recently at annual rates of 80 to 100 percent, even younger people have personally experienced it.

Such conditions impose a heavy penalty on cash savings. In the old days, saving was typically done in the form of hoarding gold and silver coins. It is true that such hoards did not provide any return—the metal was "barren"—and that they therefore did not lend themselves to the lifestyle of *rentiers*. But in all other respects money hoards were a reliable and effective form of saving. Their purchasing power did not just evaporate in a few decades, and in times of economic growth they even gained some purchasing power. Most importantly, they were extremely suitable for ordinary people. Carpenters, masons, tailors, and farmers are usually not very astute observers of the international capital markets. Putting some gold coins under their mattress or into a safe deposit box saved them many sleepless nights, and it made them independent of financial intermediaries.

Now compare this old-time scenario with our present situation. The contrast could not be starker. It would be completely pointless in our day to hoard dollar or euro notes to prepare for retirement. A man in his thirties who plans to retire thirty years from today (2008) must calculate with a depreciation factor in the order of 3. That is, he needs to save three dollars today to have the purchasing power of one of these present-day dollars when he retires. And the estimated depreciation factor of 3 is rather on the low side! It follows that the rational saving strategy for him is to go into debt in order to buy assets the price of which will increase with the inflation. This is exactly what happens today in most western countries. As soon as young people have a job and thus a halfway stable source of revenue, they take a mortgage to buy a house—whereas their great-grandfather might still have first accumulated savings for some thirty years and then bought his house with cash.

Things are not much better for those who have already accumulated some wealth. It is true that inflation does not force them into debt, but in any case it deprives them of the possibility of holding their savings in cash. Old people with a pension fund, widows, and the guardians of orphans must invest their money into the financial markets, lest its purchasing power evaporate under their noses. Thus they become dependent on intermediaries and on the vagaries of stock and bond pricing.

It is clear that this state of affairs is very beneficial for those who derive their living from the financial markets. Stockbrokers, bond dealers, banks, mortgage corporations, and other "players" have reason to be thankful for the constant decline of money's purchasing power under fiat inflation. But is this state of affairs also beneficial for the average citizen? In a certain sense, his debts and increased investment in the financial markets is beneficial for him, given our present inflationary regime. When the increase of the price level is perennial, personal debt is for him the best available strategy. But this means of course that without government intervention into the monetary system other strategies would be superior. The presence of central banks and paper money make debt-based financial strategies more attractive than strategies based on prior savings. In the words of Dempsey, we might say that "we have the effect of usury without the personal fault" of the financial agents. "The usury is institutionalized, or systemic."[6]

It is not an exaggeration to say that, through their monetary policy, Western governments have pushed their citizens into a state of financial dependency unknown to any previous generation. Already in 1931, Pius XI stated:

> ... it is obvious that not only is wealth concentrated in our times but an immense power and despotic economic dictatorship is consolidated in the hands of a few, who often are not owners but only the trustees and managing directors of invested funds which they administer according to their own arbitrary will and pleasure.

> This dictatorship is being most forcibly exercised by those who, since they hold the money and completely control it, control credit also and rule the lending of money. Hence they regulate the flow, so to speak, of the life-blood whereby the entire economic system lives, and have so firmly in their grasp the soul, as it were, of economic life that no one can breathe against their will.[7]

One wonders which vocabulary Pius XI would have used to describe our present situation. The usual justification for this state of affairs is that it allegedly stimulates industrial development. The money hoards of former times were not only sterile; they were actually harmful from an economic point of view, because they deprived business of the means of

---

[6]Bernard Dempsey, *Interest and Usury* (Washington, D.C.: American Council of Public Affairs, 1943), p. 207. Dempsey analyzes this phenomenon by distinguishing two forms of "emergent loss" (one of the extrinsic grounds on which interest is licit): "antecedent" and "consequent" emergent loss. See also, pp. 200ff.

[7]Pius XI, *Quadragesimo Anno* (1931), §105, 106. See also Deuteronomy 28: 12, 43–44.

payments they needed for investments. The role of inflation is to provide these means.

We have already exploded this myth in some detail. At this point, let us merely emphasize again that money hoarding does not have any negative macroeconomic implications. It definitely does not stifle industrial investments. Hoarding increases the purchasing power of money and thus gives greater "weight" to the money units that remain in circulation. All goods and services can be bought, and all feasible investments can be made with these remaining units. The fundamental fact is that inflation does not bring into existence any additional resource. It merely changes the allocation of the existing resources. They no longer go to companies that are run by entrepreneurs who operate with their own money, but to business executives who run companies financed with credit.

The net effect of the recent surge in household debt is therefore to throw entire populations into financial dependency. The moral implications are clear. Towering debts are incompatible with financial self-reliance and thus they tend to weaken self-reliance also in all other spheres. The debt-ridden individual eventually adopts the habit of turning to others for help, rather than maturing into an economic and moral anchor of his family, and of his wider community. Wishful thinking and submissiveness replace soberness and independent judgment. And what about the many cases in which families can no longer shoulder the debt load? Then the result is either despair or, alternatively, scorn for all standards of financial sanity.

8. Some Spiritual Casualties of Fiat Inflation

Fiat inflation constantly reduces the purchasing power of money. To some extent, it is possible for people to protect their savings against this trend, but this requires thorough financial knowledge, the time to constantly supervise one's investments, and a good dose of luck. People who lack one of these ingredients are likely to lose a substantial part of their assets. The savings of a lifetime often vanish into thin air during the last few years spent in retirement. The consequence is despair and the eradication of moral and social standards. But it would be wrong to infer that inflation produces this effect mainly among the elderly. As one writer observed:

> These effects are "especially strong among the youth. They learn to live in the present *and scorn those who try to teach them 'old-fashioned' morality and thrift*" [emphasis added]. Inflation thereby encourages a mentality of immediate gratification that is plainly at variance with the discipline and eternal perspective required to exercise principles of biblical stewardship—such as long-term investment for the benefit of future generations.[8]

Even those citizens who are blessed with the knowledge, time, and luck to protect the substance of their savings cannot evade inflation's harmful impact, because they have to adopt habits that are at odds with moral and spiritual health. Inflation forces them to spend much more time thinking about their money than they otherwise would. We have noticed already that the old way for ordinary citizens to make savings was the accumulation of cash. Under fiat inflation this strategy is suicidal. They must invest in assets the value of which grows during the inflation; the most practical way to do this is to buy stocks and bonds. But this entails many hours spent on comparing and selecting appropriate issues. And it compels them to be ever watchful and concerned about their money for the rest of their lives. They need to follow the financial news and monitor the price quotations on the financial markets.

Similarly, people will tend to prolong the phase of their life in which they strive to earn money. And they will place relatively greater emphasis on monetary returns than on any other criterion for choosing their profession. For example, some of those who would rather be inclined to gardening will

---

[8]Thomas Woods, "Money and Morality: The Christian Moral Tradition and the Best Monetary Regime," *Religion & Liberty* 13, no. 5 (September/October 2003). The author quotes Ludwig von Mises. See also William Gouge, *A Short History of Paper Money and Banking in the United States, to which is prefixed an Inquiry into the Principles of the System* (Reprint, New York: Augustus M. Kelley, [1833] 1968), pp. 94–101.

nevertheless seek an industrial employment if the latter offers greater long-run monetary returns. And more people will accept employment far from home, if it allows them to earn a little additional money, than under a natural monetary system.

The spiritual dimension of these inflation-induced habits seems obvious. Money and financial questions come to play an exaggerated role in the life of man. Inflation makes society materialistic. More and more people strive for money income at the expense of other things important for personal happiness. Inflation-induced geographical mobility artificially weakens family bonds and patriotic loyalty. Many of those who tend to be greedy, envious, and niggardly anyway fall prey to sin. Even those who are not so inclined by their natures will be exposed to temptations they would not otherwise have felt. And because the vagaries of the financial markets also provide a ready excuse for an excessively parsimonious use of one's money, donations for charitable institutions decline.

Then there is the fact that perennial inflation tends to deteriorate product quality. Every seller knows that it is difficult to sell the same physical product at higher prices than in previous years. But increasing money prices are unavoidable when the money supply is subject to relentless growth. So what do sellers do? In many cases the rescue comes through technological innovation, which allows a cheaper production of the product, thus neutralizing or even overcompensating the countervailing influence of inflation. This is for example the case with personal computers and other products made with large inputs of information technology. But in other industries, technological progress plays a much smaller role. Here the sellers confront the above-mentioned problem. They then fabricate an inferior product and sell it under the same name, along with the euphemisms that have become customary in commercial marketing. For example, they might offer their customers "light" coffee and "non-spicy" vegetables—which translates into thin coffee and vegetables that have lost any trace of flavor. Similar product deterioration can be observed in the construction business. Countries plagued by perennial inflation seem to have a greater share of houses and streets that are in constant need of repair than other countries.

In such an environment, people develop a more than sloppy attitude toward their language. If everything is whatever it is called, then it is difficult to explain the difference between truth and lie. Inflation tempts people to lie about their products, and perennial inflation encourages the habit of routine lying. We have already pointed out that routine lying plays a great role in fractional-reserve banking, the basic institution of the fiat money system. Fiat inflation seems to spread this habit like a cancer over the rest of the economy.[9]

9. SUFFOCATING THE FLAME

In most countries, the growth of the welfare state has been financed through the accumulation of public debt on a scale that would have been unthinkable without fiat inflation. A cursory glance at the historical record shows that the exponential growth of the welfare state, which in Europe started in the early 1970s, went hand in hand with the explosion of public debt. It is widely known that this development has been a major factor in the decline of the family. But it is commonly overlooked that the ultimate cause of this decline is fiat inflation. Perennial inflation slowly but assuredly destroys the family, thus suffocating the earthly flame of morals.

Indeed, the family is the most important "producer" of a certain type of morals. Family life is possible only if all members endorse norms such as the legitimacy of authority, and the prohibition of incest. And *Christian* families are based on additional precepts such as the heterosexual union between man and woman, love of the spouses for one another and for their offspring, the respect of children for their parents, as well as belief in the reality of the Triune God and of the truth of the

---

[9]The relationship between fiat inflation on the one hand, and misperceptions and misrepresentations of reality on the other hand has been brilliantly discussed in Paul Cantor's case study on "Hyperinflation and Hyperreality: Thomas Mann in Light of Austrian Economics," *Review of Austrian Economics* 7, no. 1 (1994).

Christian faith, etc. Parents constantly repeat, emphasize, and live these norms and precepts. Thus all family members come to accept them as the normal state of affairs. In the wider social sphere, then, these persons act as advocates of the same norms in business associations, clubs, and politics.

Friends and foes of the traditional family agree on these facts. It is among other things because they recognize the family's effectiveness in establishing social norms that Christians seek to protect it. And it is precisely for the same reason that advocates of moral license seek to undermine it. The welfare state has been their preferred tool in the past thirty years. Today, the welfare state provides a great number of services that in former times have been provided by families (and which would, we may assume, still be provided to a large extent by families if the welfare state ceased to exist). Education of the young, care for the elderly and the sick, assistance in times of emergencies—all of these services are today effectively "outsourced" to the state. The families have been degraded into small production units that share utility bills, cars, refrigerators, and of course the tax bill. The tax-financed welfare state then provides them with education and care.[10]

From an economic point of view, this arrangement is a pure waste of money. The fact is that the welfare state is inefficient; it provides comparatively lousy services at comparatively high costs. We need not dwell on the inability of government welfare agencies to provide the emotional and spiritual assistance that only springs from charity. Compassion cannot be bought. But the welfare state is also inefficient in purely economic terms. It operates through large bureaucracies and is therefore liable to lack incentives and economic

---

[10]In many countries it is today possible for families to deduct expenses for private care and private education from the annual tax bill. But ironically (or maybe not quite so ironically) this trend has reinforced the erosion of the family. For example, recent provisions of the U.S. tax code allow family budgets to increase through such deductions—but only if the deductible services are not provided by family members, but bought from other people.

criteria that would prevent wasting money. In the words of Pope John Paul II:

> By intervening directly and depriving society of its responsibility, the Social Assistance State leads to a loss of human energies and an inordinate increase of public agencies, which are dominated more by bureaucratic ways of thinking than by concern for serving their clients, and which are accompanied by an enormous increase in spending. In fact, it would appear that needs are best understood and satisfied by people who are closest to them and who act as neighbors to those in need. It should be added that certain kinds of demands often call for a response which is not simply material but which is capable of perceiving the deeper human need.[11]

Everyone knows this from first-hand experience, and a great number of scientific studies drive home the same point. It is precisely because the welfare state is an inefficient economic arrangement that it must rely on taxes. If it had to compete with families on equal terms, it could not stay in business for any length of time. It has driven the family and private charities out of the "welfare market" because people are forced to pay for it anyway. They are forced to pay taxes, and they cannot prevent the government from floating ever-new loans, which absorb the capital that otherwise would be used for the production of different goods and services.

The excessive welfare state of our day is an all-out direct attack on the producers of morals. But it weakens these morals also in indirect ways, most notably by subsidizing bad moral examples. The fact is that libertine "lifestyles" carry great economic risks. The welfare state socializes the costs of morally reckless behavior and therefore gives it far greater prominence than it would have in a free society. Rather than carrying an economic penalty, licentiousness might then actually go hand in hand with economic advantages, because it frees the protagonists from the costs of family life (for example, the costs associated with raising children). With the backing of the welfare state, these protagonists may mock conservative morals

---

[11]John Paul II, *Centesimus Annus*, §48.

as some sort of superstition that has no real-life impact. The welfare state systematically exposes people to the temptation of believing that there are no time-tested moral precepts at all.

Let us emphasize that the point of the preceding observations was not to attack welfare services, which are in fact an essential component of society. Neither is it here our intention to attack the notion that welfare services should be provided through government. The point is, rather, that fiat inflation destroys the democratic control over the provision of these services; that this invariably leads to excessive growth of the aggregate welfare system and to excessive forms of welfare; and that this in turn is not without consequences for the moral and spiritual character of the population.

The considerations presented in this chapter are by no means an exhaustive account of the cultural and spiritual legacy of fiat inflation. But they should suffice to substantiate the main point: that fiat inflation is a juggernaut of social, economic, cultural, and spiritual destruction.[12] Let us now turn to complement our analysis with a look at the historical evolution of monetary systems.

---

[12]Our study seems to suggest that there is definitely something diabolical in fiat inflation. But we feel incompetent to deal with this question and leave its analysis for another time, or for other scholars. It is certainly significant that a great poet such as Goethe would portray paper money as a creation of the devil. See *Faust*, part II, *Lustgartenszene*.

Part 3

Monetary Order and Monetary Systems

14

Monetary Order

1. The Natural Order of Money Production

The first two parts of this book were devoted to a discussion of the two basic modes of money production: the natural production of money on the free market, and inflation. We studied their general characteristics, but also went into a more detailed study of the subcategories that come into play. Money and money certificates, credit money, paper money, counterfeiting, legal tender, monopoly, and suspension of payments are such subcategories of the production of money. Our theoretical analysis had to dissect them in isolation from one another; and even when we analyzed their interrelations we had to abstract it from any concrete historical context. It is true that we frequently referred to historical events, but these references merely served as illustrations of insights that were in fact obtained through theory. This is standard scientific procedure. It provided us with all we can ever hope to obtain from theory: information about causes and effects, and information about relevant moral aspects of the production of money. Our basic mission has therefore been completed.

In the present third part, we will apply our findings to the analysis of monetary orders. We can define a monetary order as the total network of persons, firms, and other organizations involved in the production of money. Few readers will be surprised to learn that no historical monetary order has been "pure" in the sense of a pure free-market order, or a pure fiat order. A good case could be made that the contemporary paper-money orders are purer than any previous monetary order—which shows that such purity is hardly a virtue *per se*.

Real-life monetary orders combine the categories that we discussed above into a great variety of more or less complicated settings. But it does not follow that it is pointless to deal with pure orders. We have already demonstrated the usefulness of dealing with the pure order—or rather the pure orders—of the free market. The point of the analysis in Part One was not to provide an accurate description of any concrete historical order of the past, but to make us become acquainted with the workings of a monetary order defined by the universal respect of private property. Probably such an order has never existed in a pure form. But for theoretical and practical purposes this is irrelevant. The point is that it could have existed and could be introduced even today, technically at a moment's notice. The importance of this purely hypothetical order is that it presents us with a theoretical benchmark. It is an ideal monetary order, and we will therefore call it by the lofty name of monetary Order.

We have seen in Part Two how this Order provided a meaningful standard of comparison for the analysis of the effects that violations of property rights have on money production. Moreover, it provided us with a meaningful basis for the rational criticism of monetary orders that are based on the violation of private property rights. (Such monetary orders we may call monetary systems.) It makes no sense indeed to criticize existing systems for being different from some idealized scheme. But it does make sense to criticize them for being inferior to known alternatives. It makes sense to reject inflation because there is a well-known and ready alternative to inflation, namely, the production of money on the free market, which is superior to inflation both from an economic and from a moral point of view.

The natural production of money on the free market might be an unrealistic order of things in the sense that abandoning the existing monetary systems presently does not find the necessary political support. But it is unrealistic *only* in that sense.

It is not impossible to establish from any technical point of view, it is not unreasonable, and it is not morally offensive—quite the contrary. It does at present confront a problem of the will. But the human will can change, and it will change under the guidance of truth and courage. The significance of the natural production of money is that it gives us a meaningful goal to strive for.

Notice that the free market is by its very nature a *global* Order of economic relations. Human cooperation in production and trade is beneficial for all parties, not only those within the frontiers of the nation-state. And so are gold and silver—and whatever else free men might discover and develop for monetary service—useful monies not only for the residents of Europe or of North America. There is a natural tendency in the market to spread the use of the most useful monies over the entire world, thus establishing one great network of human cooperation based on indirect exchange.

In the High Middle Ages, when large-scale commerce and the interregional division of labor started to flourish, the great merchants of northern Italy found that no government produced money that was suitable for their new needs. The traditional coin system contained only silver coins, virtually all of which were hopelessly debased and, what is more, were debased to different degrees. The merchants then set out to produce their own money, new and sound gold coins, which at first they used only within their own circles. And because the other governments tolerated this practice—because for once they did not stand in the way—by the thirteenth century the *fiorino d'oro* from Florence became a generally accepted medium of exchange in central and eastern Europe.

A little liberty of this sort could work wonders in our age, which from a technological point of view is so much better endowed than the medieval merchants were.

2. Cartels of Credit-Money Producers

We have already pointed out that the production of credit money is congruent with the principles of a free market. Individual sorts of credit money as well as the cooperation of credit-money producers are therefore legitimate parts of a natural monetary Order in the sense in which we have defined the term above. In particular, we must highlight the possibility of free-market cartels of credit-money producers.[1]

How important would such systems be in a free society? This question can only be answered after the fact. One has to establish a free market for money and see how well credit money fares. It is true that a great success is not very likely because people—and the famous "man on the street" in particular—prefer the tangible security of precious metal, as David Ricardo knew so well. But, again, this is a highly speculative question, and from a moral point of view it does not seem to be very important. The crucial issue is whether the law recognizes the full liberty of the human person within the limits of his own property rights and the like property rights of other persons. Such responsible persons are still free to set up stupid monetary systems, but certainly no inherently evil ones; and there is good hope that they would quickly learn from their errors.

---

[1]Again, we must leave it to the historians to decide whether any such system has already existed. Some historians think that the Suffolk Bank system that existed in the first half of the nineteenth century in the United States was such a system.

15

Fiat Monetary Systems in the Realm of the Nation-State

1. Toward National Paper-Money Producers: European Experiences

The paper-money systems that presently dominate the scene in all countries of the world have developed out of European fractional-reserve banking starting in the seventeenth century. The driving force behind this development was government finance which found in the new institutions a ready source for ever-increasing loans.[1]

The most venerable central bank—or rather: paper money producer—of our time, the Bank of England, was established in 1694 by William Patterson, a Scottish promoter, with the express purpose of providing what was at the time the immense loan of £1,200,000 to the English crown.[2] Its charter authorized the bank to issue notes within certain statutory

---

[1]For an overview see Vera Smith, *The Rationale of Central Banking* (Indianapolis: Liberty Fund, 1990), chaps. 1 to 6; Norbert Olszak, *Histoire des banques centrales* (Paris: Presses Universitaires de France, 1998).

[2]On the history of the Bank of England see John H. Clapham, *The Bank of England: A History, 1694–1914* (Cambridge: Cambridge University Press, [1944] 1970).

limitations, which were subsequently extended to allow for additional loans to the government. The bank was also granted several legal privileges, most notably the privilege of limited liability and the privilege of unilaterally suspending payments to its creditors, which the Bank had to use after a mere two years of operations. Apart from this early incident, however, the bank proved to be reliable and operated without suspending its payments in peacetime. In the following two hundred years, it thrived under the increasing patronage of the government, providing a steady flow of new loans without disrupting the convertibility of its notes.

In the early nineteenth century, Bank of England notes became legal tender, with the consequences that we described in our theoretical analysis: cartelization of the banking system and frequently recurring booms and busts. In 1844, it obtained a monopoly on the issue of banknotes.[3] And in 1914, at the behest of the king, the bank again suspended its payments, to help finance World War I with the printing press.

In other countries such as France and Germany, the development of the national monetary system took somewhat different turns, but the main elements of the British case can be readily identified: monopoly status for one precious metal (gold); privileged fractional-reserve banks in the service of government finance; legal-tender status for the notes of these banks; the consequent cartelization of the entire national banking industry; and the eventual authorization to indefinitely suspend redemption of the notes of the privileged bank, thus turning the latter into national paper-money producers.

In the case of the Bank of England, the conjunction of these elements was brought about by a rather slow process. By contrast, the privileged banks established in other countries were often quite reckless and inflated their currencies at much greater rates than the Bank of England, to still the financial

---

[3]Other note-issuing banks that already existed in 1844 were allowed to continue their business within their statutory limitations. Most of them eventually decided to switch the business model and became checking banks.

Table 2: Milestones in the Development of the Bank of England

Year	Legal action in favor of the Bank	Financial quid pro quo
1694	• First charter	Loan to the government
1696	• Suspension of payments	Maintenance of government credit
1697	• Renewal of charter • Limited liability • Extension of note issue • Monopoly cashier of payments to the government	Loan to the government
1709	• Renewal of charter • Monopoly on joint stock banking with more than six partners	Loan to the government
1713	• Renewal of charter	Loan to the government
1742	• Renewal of charter	Loan to the government (without interest)
1751	• Monopoly administrator of the public debt	
1764	• Renewal of charter	Fee paid to the government
1781	• Renewal of charter	Loan to the government
1793	• Legalization of short-term loans to government beyond statutory limitations	Loan to the government
1795	• Authorization of £5 notes	
1797	• Authorization of £1 and £2 notes • Suspension of payments	Loan to the government
1800	• Renewal of charter	Loan to the government
1812–19	• BoE notes are legal tender	Loans to the government
1833	• BoE notes become legal tender for sums above £5	
1844	• Monopoly of note issue in Great Britain	Loan to the government
1914–25	• BoE notes are legal tender • Suspension of payments	Loans to the government

Source: Vera C. Smith, *The Rationale of Central Banking* (Indianapolis, Liberty Fund, 1990), chap. 2.

appetite of their governments. Not surprisingly, they had to rely much more frequently on the suspension of payments and often experimented with legal-tender paper money. At the end of the eighteenth century, therefore, fractional-reserve banking and paper money had made great inroads in many countries. John Wheatley, a contemporary observer, summarized the events of the preceding century:

> During the first fifty years of the 18th century banks were established, or had already been founded in most of the principal cities of Europe, and the circulation of paper was more or less encouraged by all. . . . But the circulation of paper during this interval was intermissive and irregular; though pushed to an extreme in England and Scotland during the reign of William and part of the reign of Anne, and in France during the regency of the Duke of Orleans, yet its excess was in neither instance of long duration. . . . But from 1750 to 1800 the system of paper currency, however unpropitious in its commencement, was matured and perfected in every part of the civilized world. In England, Scotland, and Ireland, in France, Spain, Portugal, Italy, Austria, Prussia, Denmark, Sweden, and Russia, in America, and even in our Indian provinces, the new medium has been successfully established, and has subjected the intercourse of the world, in all its inferior as well as superior relations, to be carried on in a far greater degree by the intervention of paper than the intervention of specie.[4]

A few pages later, Wheatley characterized the relative market shares of banknotes and specie in the major European countries as of his writing:

> In England, Scotland, and Ireland, in Denmark, and in Austria, scarcely any thing but paper is visible. In Spain, Portugal,

---

[4]Wheatley, *The Theory of Money and Principles of Commerce* (London: Bulmer, 1807), pp. 279–80. Wheatley's statement on the "intercourse of the world" concerns especially international wholesale trade. Things were often quite different in daily retail transactions. On the case of the German lands, see Bernd Sprenger, *Das Geld der Deutschen*, 2nd ed. (Paderborn: Schöningh, 1995), pp. 153–54.

Prussia, Sweden, and European Russia, paper has a decisive superiority. And in France, Italy, and Turkey only, the prevalence of specie is apparent.[5]

This was the situation in 1807. In the following decades, the trend continued. For example, Austria, Russia, and Italy had legal-tender paper monies for many decades in the nineteenth century. These note issues were limited in amount and did not have a full monopoly status; they circulated parallel with coins and banknotes. Eventually, most European countries suspended payments at the onset of Wold War I. From 1914 to 1925, for the first time ever in history, all major nations except for the U.S. used paper monies.

2. TOWARD NATIONAL PAPER-MONEY PRODUCERS: AMERICAN EXPERIENCES

In the history of the North American colonies of the British Empire, the essential features of the European monetary experience can be found as well. But there are two particularities: the American *champions* of paper money had a more direct approach than their European cousins; and the American *opponents* of paper money triumphed, at least for a while, more thoroughly than any of their European friends ever would.[6]

In the seventeenth and eighteenth centuries, the governments of the British colonies more often than not pushed

---

[5]Wheatley, *The Theory of Money and Principles of Commerce*, p. 287.

[6]On the history of American money and banking until the early twentieth century see William Gouge, *A Short History of Paper Money and Banking in the United States* (reprint, New York: Augustus M. Kelley, [1833] 1968), part II; William G. Sumner, *History of Banking in the United States* (New York: Augustus M. Kelley, [1896] 1971); Barton Hepburn, *History of Coinage and Currency in the United States and the Perennial Contest for Sound Money* (London: Macmillan, 1903); Bray Hammond, *Banks and Politics in America* (Princeton, N.J.: Princeton University Press, 1957); Donald Kemmerer and Clyde Jones, *American Economic History* (New York: McGraw-Hill, 1959); Murray N. Rothbard, *A History of Money and Banking in the United States* (Auburn, Ala.: Ludwig von Mises Institute, 2002).

straight for the issue of legal-tender paper notes rather than choosing the more indirect route of promoting privileged fractional-reserve banks. As early as 1690, the colony of Massachusetts issued paper treasury bills that were endowed with legal-tender status. This practice was replicated in five other colonies before 1711, and eventually spread to all British colonies. Among its victims were the creditors of American trade and industry, usually merchants from metropolitan Britain, who were forced to accept the often rapidly depreciating paper notes. They brought their case before Parliament which reacted vigorously starting in the 1720s. It first ordered all New England colonies to seek authorization from Britain before issuing any more legal-tender notes. In 1751, it prohibited the issue of any such notes in New England, and in 1764 prohibited the issue of any legal-tender paper in *all* colonies. This must have been a heavy blow to the political establishment in the British colonies of North America. It is certainly not farfetched here to see one of the roots of the American Revolution.

However, the Revolution did not bring a legal confirmation of the monetary experiments of the colonial period. Quite to the contrary, the American Constitution is, in the modern history of the West, the most radical legal break with a country's inflationary past. The fathers of the new republic did all in their power to prevent legal-tender paper issues of the colonies (now the states) ever to be repeated again. They moreover strove to create a monetary order based on the precious metals. These objectives were deemed so important that they were addressed head-on in the very first article of the Constitution. Section 8 of Article I granted the authority to "coin Money, regulate the Value thereof, and of foreign Coin, and fix the Standard of Weights and Measures" to the *federal* government, not to the states. And Section 10 of Article I specifically prohibited that the states "emit Bills of Credit; make any Thing but gold and silver Coin a Tender in Payment of Debts."

The Constitution proved to be a serious obstacle for the party of inflation, but it ultimately was breached. For the next sixty years, the battle between pro-inflation and anti-inflation forces went back and forth. The champions of inflation pushed through the charters of two "Banks of the United States" (1792–1812, 1816–1836) and their opponents made sure that the charters were not extended. In the war of 1812–14, the federal government issued legal-tender treasury notes—necessary, in the eyes of the government, for the survival of the new republic (and of course for its own survival). In the 1830s, then, the champions of sound money had their last great triumph when President Jackson refused to extend the charter of the Second Bank of the United States, withdrew all public funds from private or state (fractional-reserve) banks, and cut down the public debt from some $60 million at the beginning of his administration to a mere $33,733.05 on January 1, 1835. His successors managed to neutralize these reforms to some extent, especially by bringing the public debt back to more than $60 million within fifteen years of the end of the second Jackson administration.

But the great breakthrough for the inflation party came only with Abraham Lincoln and the War Between the States. Starting in 1862, the federal government again issued a legal-tender paper money, the so-called greenbacks, to finance its war against the seceding Southern states. This experiment ended in 1875, when the government turned the greenbacks into credit money, by announcing that as from 1879 they would be redeemed into gold.[7] Meanwhile, in 1863–65, the Lincoln administration had created a new system of privileged "national banks" that were authorized to issue notes backed by federal government debt, while the notes of all other banks were penalized by a 10 percent federal tax. As a consequence American banking was centralized around the

---

[7]At this point, the U.S. Supreme Court had first ruled against the legality of legal-tender privileges for paper (1870) and then revised its decision in subsequent cases (1871 and 1874). See Donald Kemmerer and C. Clyde Jones, *American Economic History* (New York: McGraw-Hill, 1959), p. 356.

privileged national banks, most notably, the reserve banks of New York City.

In 1913, then, the American banking system finally received a central bank on the European model. The U.S. was the last great nation to introduce central banking. The original interpretation of the Constitution had prevented a quicker procedure for more than a century, but the written word was unable to stem the tide of concentrated financial interests and their pro-inflation public relations campaigns.

The point of the preceding remarks on the early modern monetary history of the West is to highlight the long tradition of our current inflationary regime. It is not the case that monetary affairs were rosy until 1914, when the great inflation of the twentieth century set in. It is true that in our time inflation is incomparably greater than in any previous period, especially due to the current monopoly of paper money. But the roots of our present calamities are much older. This concerns not only the institutional underpinnings, which reach back to the seventeenth century. It also concerns the concrete forms of inflation. Neither paper money, nor today's other major inflationary practices are inventions of the twentieth century. And even the much-vaunted gold standard, which reigned for a few decades before World War I, was not quite as golden as it appears in many narratives.

3. The Problem of the Foreign Exchanges

While national legislation prompted the cartelization of the fractional-reserve banking industry within the boundaries of the nation, no such mechanism existed for a long time in international economic relations. Thus until after World War I, the bulk of international payments were made in specie. But in the four or five decades before the outbreak of that war, the foundations were laid for the later establishment of international monetary systems.

All of these systems until the present day have been essentially cartels among national governments, respectively between national monetary authorities (usually the central banks). Two phases can be distinguished: (1) a phase of banking cartels, which lasted for the century between the end of the Franco-German war in 1871 and the dissolution of the Bretton Woods system in 1971; and (2) a phase of cartels among national paper-money producers, which started in 1971 and is still with us. The next two chapters will deal with them in turn. At this point, let us merely observe that none of these cartels has so far been compulsory. It remains to be seen whether the future development of international political relations will bring about any changes.

16

International Banking Systems, 1871–1971

1. The Classical Gold Standard

By the end of the 1860s, only the U.S. and some major parts of the British Empire had been on the gold standard. In the United Kingdom, gold had been monopoly legal tender since 1821, the United States had a *de facto* gold standard after the Coinage Act of 1834, and Australia and Canada followed suit in the early 1850s. All other states had a silver standard, bimetallic standards, or legal-tender paper monies. Then the German victory over France in the war of 1870–71 ushered in the era known as the classical gold standard.

The new German central government under Bismarck obtained a war indemnity of 5 billion francs in gold. It used the money to set up a fiat gold standard, demonetizing the silver coins that had hitherto been dominant in German lands. Four years later, the financial lackey of Bismarck's Prussian government—the Prussian Bank—was turned into a national central bank (its new name, the Reichsbank, was a marketing coup). Thus the Germans had copied the British model, combining fiat gold with fractional-reserve banking and a central bank, whose notes obtained legal-tender status in 1909.[1]

---

[1]See Herbert Rittmann, *Deutsche Geldgeschichte seit 1914* (Munich: Klinkhardt & Biermann, 1986), chap. 1; Bernd Sprenger, *Das Geld der Deutschen* (Paderborn: Schöningh, 1995), chap. 10.

Why gold? Why did the Germans not set up a silver standard or join a bimetallist system such as the Latin Currency Union?[2] Several factors came into play here. One might mention in particular the influence of "network externalities" that weighed in favor of gold. On the one hand, gold was the money of Great Britain, the country with the world's largest and most sophisticated capital market. On the other hand, several major silver countries including Russia and Austria had suspended payments at the time of the German victory. Thus silver offered no advantages for the international division of labor, whereas gold did.[3] Moreover, one should not neglect that silver, the only serious competitor for gold among the commodity monies, has one grave disadvantage from the point of view of a government bent on inflationary finance. Because of its bulkiness, the use of silver entails higher transportation costs, which makes it less suitable than gold for fractional-reserve banks trying to quash systematic bank runs through cooperation.

Virtually all other Western countries now followed suit. The establishment of international "unity" in monetary affairs required no elaborate justification. It was perfectly congenial to the cosmopolitan spirit of the times, nourished by several decades of free trade and burgeoning international alliances and friendships. Thus it served as the perfect justification for a further massive intervention of national governments into the monetary systems of their countries. Legal privileges were abrogated in all other branches of industry. Monopoly was a

---

[2]The Latin Currency Union had been created in 1865 by the governments of France, Italy, Switzerland, and Belgium. Later members included Greece and Romania. The idea of the Union was to establish a common coin system for all member countries. It lasted, nominally, until 1926. In fact, it was abandoned in 1914 with the near-universal suspension of payments.

[3]See Leland B. Yeager, *International Monetary Relations* (New York: Harper & Row, 1966), pp. 252–58; Barry Eichengreen, *Globalizing Capital*, 2nd ed. (Princeton, N.J.: Princeton University Press, 1998), chap. 2, especially the section on the introduction of the international gold standard.

curse word more than ever before. But it seemed to be tolerable as a means for that noble cosmopolitan end of international monetary union. By the early 1880s, the countries of the West and their colonies all over the world had adopted the British model.[4] This created the great illusion of some profound economic unity of the western world, whereas in fact the movement merely homogenized the national monetary systems. The homogeneity lasted until 1914, when the central banks suspended their payments and prepared to finance World War I by the printing press.

On the positive side, it could be claimed that the classical gold standard eliminated the exchange-rate fluctuations between gold and silver and thus boosted the international division of labor. It is somewhat difficult to evaluate the quantitative impact of this advantage. Let us therefore merely observe that exchange-rate fluctuations between gold and silver are negligible when compared to the fluctuations between our present-day paper monies.

On the negative side, the classical gold standard created a considerable fiat deflation due to the demonetization of silver. From 1873–1896, prices fell more or less sharply in the countries that had adopted the gold standard first (U.K., U.S., Germany) because of the gold exports that resulted when other countries followed their example and established a gold-based currency too.[5] This in turn created pressure to reinforce the practice of fractional-reserve banking, both on the level of the central banks and on the level of the commercial banks (see Table 3). Above we have analyzed the inherent fragility of

---

[4]The only exception was India, which adopted the gold standard in 1898. Russia made the step in 1897. China alone among the major countries remained on a silver standard.

[5]We have emphasized in the present work that there is nothing wrong with falling prices *per se*, and the period under consideration is in fact the best illustration of this claim. Growth rates were very substantial in the countries struck by the deflation. The point is that the fiat deflation brought *forced* hardship for those who would have fared better under a competitive regime that tolerated other types of specie than gold.

Table 3: Evolution of the Money Supply in the German Reich (in Mill. Mark)

End of Year	Money Stock (Precious Metal)	Cash Bank Reserves (incl. note issuing banks)	Bank Deposits of Non-Banks (Current Accounts, Time and Savings Deposits)
1875	2.634	721	3.975
1880	2.400	738	4.757
1885	2.299	883	6.443
1890	2.476	1.094	8.809
1895	2.870	1.224	11.678
1900	3.244	1.195	16.126
1905	4.100	1.356	23.759
1910	4.734	1.616	33.825
1913	5.200	2.170	38.420

Source: Bernd Sprenger, *Das Geld der Deutschen*, table 28, p. 201.

fractional-reserve systems and seen that this fact, because it is known to the bankers, incites them to postpone the crisis through cooperation. Under the classical gold standard, this was the case too.[6] Yet for the reasons we have discussed in some detail, cooperation cannot stop the dynamics of inflation inherent in the system itself. Sooner or later this process finds its limits and the fractional-reserve banking system collapses or is transformed into something else. The classical gold standard was no exception. It was spared collapse or transformation into a gold-exchange standard only because another lethal accident (WWI) killed it before it could die from its own cancer. World War I delivered the pretext for the suspension of payments. But sooner or later suspension would have become inevitable anyway. The system did *not* limit inflation. All of its

---

[6]See Guilo Gallarotti, *The Anatomy of an International Monetary Regime: the Classical Gold Standard, 1880–1914* (Oxford: Oxford University Press, 1995), pp. 78–85.

main protagonists—the national central banks—were fractional-reserve banks, and under their auspices and protection
the commercial banks happily trotted down an inflationary
expansion path.

The glory of the classical gold standard was that it demonstrated, for the last time so far, how a worldwide monetary
system could emerge without political scheming and red tape
between national governments. They adopted it independ-
ently of one another. There was no treaty, no conference, and
no negotiation to bring it about. However, as we have seen,
even in this respect the classical gold standard was rather
imperfect. It did after all not result from the free choice of free
citizens, but from the discretion of national governments. It
gave the world a common monetary standard—gold—but
this standard sprang from the coercive elimination of all alternative monies. Its ultimate effect was, not to give the citizens
of the world an efficient monetary system, but to deliver a pretext for national governments to finally bring the monetary
systems of their countries under their control. The classical
gold standard was therefore hardly a bulwark of liberty. It was
a crucial breakthrough for the societal scourge of our age—
government omnipotence.

We have to stress these facts because many advocates of the
free market believe the classical gold standard was something
like the paradise of monetary systems. This reputation is
undeserved. The classical gold standard differed only in
degree, not in essence, from its successors, all of which have
been widely and deservedly criticized in the literature on our
subject.[7]

---

[7]See for example Yeager, *International Monetary Relations*, pp. 260–65;
Henry Hazlitt, *The Inflation Crisis, and How to Resolve It* (Irvington-on-
Hudson, N.Y.: Foundation for Economic Education, [1978] 1995), pp.
173f.; Rothbard, *A History of Money and Banking in the United States*
(Auburn, Ala.: Ludwig von Mises Institute, 2002), pp. 159–69. See also the
references in Barry Eichengreen, *Globalizing Capital* (Princeton, N.J.:
Princeton University Press), chap. 2.

2. THE GOLD-EXCHANGE STANDARD

The expression "gold-exchange standard" is usually applied to the organizational set-up of the international monetary system that existed between 1925 and 1931. But this organization was thoroughly unoriginal. It had existed before; in fact it had been part and parcel of the classical gold standard. Rather, the new system that was created in the latter half of the 1920s was characterized by the more or less explicit objective of most of its participants to strive for monetary expansion (inflation) through international cooperation.[8]

Under the classical gold standard, each central bank was responsible for making sure that its notes could be redeemed into gold. The central banks of Great Britain, France, Germany, Switzerland, and Belgium (and later of the U.S.) kept their entire reserves in gold. These reserves were supposed to be large enough for them to survive emergency situations. Things were different in the realm of the commercial fractional-reserve banks that operated within the national economies of these countries. The commercial banks usually kept the lion's share of their reserves in the form of central banknotes and only held extremely low gold reserves. The latter were needed only for emergency situations, and in such cases the commercial banks had also learned to rely on the reserves of their central bank. In some countries, this practice predated the classical gold standard by quite a few decades. For example, it was already the practice of the English country banks in the first half of the nineteenth century. They kept Bank of England notes as part of their reserves and, in times of great strain on their gold reserves, often redeemed their own notes, not into gold, but into notes of the Bank.[9]

---

[8]On the gold-exchange standard see Yeager, *International Monetary Relations*, pp. 277–90; Murray N. Rothbard, "The Gold-Exchange Standard in the Interwar Years," Kevin Dowd and Richard H. Timberlak, eds., *Money and the Nation State* (New Brunswick, N.J.: Transaction, 1998), pp. 105–65.

[9]This practice was widespread even before the notes of the Bank of England became legal tender in 1833, mainly due to the introduction of a monopoly status for gold after 1821.

Under the classical gold standard, most central banks adopted exactly the same scheme. The central banks of Russia, Austria-Hungary, Japan, the Netherlands, and of the Scandinavian countries, as well as the central banks of British dominions such as South Africa and Australia redeemed their own notes not only in gold, but also in notes of the more important foreign central banks. Still other countries such as India, the Philippines, and various Latin American countries held their reserves *exclusively* under the form of foreign gold-denominated banknotes.[10] The purpose of the structure is patent. The pooling of gold reserves in a few reliable central banks allows a larger inflation of the worldwide note supply than would otherwise have been possible. The pitfall is that it places the entire responsibility of keeping sufficiently large reserves on a small number of "virtuous" fractional-reserve banks. The latter have a reason to accept this burden, however, because their virtue gives them political power over the other banks, especially in times of crises.

The significance of the gold-exchange standard of 1925–31 was that it elevated this practice of coordinated inflation into a principle of international monetary relations.[11] Only two banks—the American Fed and the Bank of England—were to remain true central banks, but this time they would be the central banks of the entire world. All other national central banks should keep a more or less large part of their reserves in the form of U.S. dollar notes and British pound notes. This would assure the possibility of inflationary expansion for all banks. The expansion rate would be comparatively low in the case of

---

[10]See the overview in Eichengreen, *Globalizing Capital,* chap. 2, section on phases of the gold standard.

[11]Governments agreed on this principle at the Genoa Conference, held from April 10 to May 19, 1922. See Rothbard, "The Gold-Exchange Standard in the Interwar Years," p. 130; Carole Fink, *The Genoa Conference: European Diplomacy, 1921–1922* (Chapel Hill: University of North Carolina Press, 1984).

the central banks of the U.S. and the United Kingdom; but the latter would be repaid in terms of political power.[12]

Thus from the very outset, the gold-exchange standard was meant to encourage irresponsible behavior. *Designed to facilitate inflation*, it was not surprising that it lasted only six years. It collapsed when, in the wake of the 1929 financial crisis on Wall Street, various governments turned to protectionist policies (most notably in the U.S.) or imposed foreign exchange controls (as in Germany, Austria, and a number of Latin American countries), thus choking off international payments and making it impossible for the Bank of England to replenish its reserves. As a consequence, the Bank suspended payments in September 1931. The other central banks followed suit, plunging the world into a regime of fluctuating exchange rates that lasted until the end of World War II.

3. THE BRETTON WOODS SYSTEM

In July 1944, at a conference in Bretton Woods, New Hampshire, the western allies agreed on an international monetary system that should be instituted after their victory in World War II. As one might expect, the point of the new scheme was to make the production of banknotes more "flexible" (that is, expansionary) than ever before. How? The trick was to pool the gold reserves of the entire world into just one large pool. There was to be only one remaining bank that would still redeem its notes into gold—the U.S. Fed—while all the other central banks would keep the bulk of their reserves in U.S. dollars and, accordingly, redeem their own notes only into dollars.

Thus the Bretton Woods system was a gold-exchange standard writ large.[13] It was far more expansionary than its

---

[12]One of the few countries that abstained from participation in this system was France. The main motivation was to avoid political dependency on the Anglo-Saxon countries. The Banque de France had herself for a long time pursued the policy of dependence-creation *vis-à-vis* foreign banks.

[13]On the Bretton Woods system see in particular Jacques Rueff, *The Monetary Sin of the West* (New York: Macmillan, 1972); Henry Hazlitt,

predecessors because it applied the pooling technique to a far greater extent. Under the classical gold standard, there were many gold pools in the world economy, because the different nations kept their gold pools separate from one another (in the national central banks). Under the gold-exchange standard, the number of gold pools had declined very substantially, and the point of the Bretton Woods system was to go the way of pooling almost to the end. It is true that the system did not exhaust its full potential for inflation. When it collapsed in 1971, there were still substantial gold pools in central banks other than the Fed; thus a further centralization of these resources could have kept the system going for a while. In any case, the Bretton Woods system was so far the most ambitious attempt ever to create an international monetary system through a cartel of fractional-reserve banks.

We have repeatedly highlighted the fact that pooling creates political dependency. In the present case, the other central banks and their governments became dependent on the good will of the Fed, which administered the world gold pool and which therefore had the power to allocate the world's banknotes—U.S. dollars—at its own discretion. Thus the crucial question is: Why did the other national central banks consent to the centralization of the gold pool, and thus to the centralization of power? Part of the answer is that it might be useful to have an international monetary system (stable exchange rates among the national currencies) even if this entails some measure of dependency. But there were also other aspects that came into play in the present case.

The historical accident was that during World War I and its long aftermath, the United States became a safe haven for European gold. This predestined the Fed to be one of the two

From Bretton Woods to World Inflation (Chicago: Regnery, 1984); Eichengreen, *Globalizing Capital*, chap. 4; Leland Yeager, "From Gold to the Ecu: The International Monetary System in Retrospect," Kevin Dowd and Richard H. Timberlake, eds., *Money and the Nation State* (New Brunswick, N.J.: Transaction, 1998), pp. 88–92.

great gold pools of the gold-exchange standard in 1925–31. At the end of World War II, then, the Fed controlled the largest gold pool the world had ever seen. Fort Knox was the world's gold pool even before the postwar system saw the light of day. The conference at Bretton Woods merely acknowledged this reality. The great majority of its delegates sought to create a postwar monetary order along the traditional lines—in which fractional-reserve central banks inflated their banknote currencies, backed up with gold reserves. This order was impossible without having the Fed as its pivot. But this meant that henceforth the monetary systems of France and Britain, and of all other member countries would be dependent on the Fed.[14]

To alleviate this dependency, the Bretton Woods conference created two international bureaucracies that have survived until the present day: the International Monetary Fund (IMF) and the World Bank. The function of these institutions was to give the other major governments some impact on the global allocation of inflation. Without them, the Fed alone would have picked the first recipients of new banknotes; it alone would have granted or declined credit in times of runs on the national central bank. Through the IMF and the World Bank, a somewhat more collegial principle was introduced into the direction of the postwar monetary order. The boards of the two bureaucracies included representatives from all major western allies, and they provided short-term (IMF) and long-term (World Bank) loans to "member states in difficulties"—that is, primarily to the board members themselves in case of self-inflicted emergencies.

---

[14]This was one of the reasons why the government of the United Kingdom—under the leadership of Lord Keynes—pushed for a radically different postwar constitution at the Bretton Woods conference. Rather than pushing for more fractional-reserve banking, it proposed the establishment of a fiat paper money for the entire world. It expected to have greater influence on the allocation of the world paper money than it could hope to have on the allocation of U.S. dollars.

These institutions made the Bretton Woods system politically acceptable to the postwar junior partners of the United States government. But they could not of course turn the system itself into a viable operation. Like its predecessors, it was designed to increase the inflationary potential for all cartel members. Restraint was not a part of its mission, and the very anchor of the system—the Fed—was particularly ruthless in its inflation of the dollar supply. It was therefore just a question of time until the gold reserves of the Fed would be exhausted, forcing the Fed to suspend payments. This point was reached on August 15, 1971 when U.S. President Nixon "closed the gold window."

The event concluded a period of one hundred years in which three great cartels of central banks had flooded the western world with their banknotes without nominally abandoning the gold standard. Each new cartel was created in such a way as to allow for more inflation than its predecessor, and the Bretton Woods cartel eventually collapsed because it too did not create enough inflation to satisfy the appetites of its members. There has been no other monetary system since that encompassed the entire world.

4. APPENDIX:
THE IMF AND THE WORLD BANK
AFTER BRETTON WOODS

With the demise of the system of Bretton Woods, it would have been only natural to abolish its institutions: the IMF and the World Bank. But large bureaucracies do not die a quick death, especially if they can manage to adopt a new mission. By the late 1970s, the new mission of those two bureaucracies turned out to be the support of Third World countries through short-term and long-term loans.

Thus the IMF and the World Bank do not have anything to do anymore with global monetary organization. And strictly speaking they do not have anything to do anymore with banking either, at least if we understand banking in the narrow commercial meaning of the word. Both institutions are today, in actual fact, large machines for the mere redistribution of income from the taxpaying citizens of the developed countries to irresponsible governments of undeveloped countries.[15]

Many people let themselves be deluded about the IMF and the World Bank because they tend to evaluate financial institutions in light of their (declared) intentions rather than in light of their true nature. They assimilate the IMF into some sort of collective charity, and chide it for not being generous enough whenever the management insists on granting additional credit only under certain conditions (usually a change of economic policy in the recipient country). But the fact is that both bureaucracies do not obtain their funds on the free market, but out of government budgets. They spend taxpayer money, not money that anybody has entrusted to them. They are therefore not "banks," certainly not in the commercial sense of the word. And they are not charities in the sense in which private organizations administer charity.

Responsible governments can obtain loans on the free market, and in fact do obtain such loans all the time. Poverty of the nation is not an obstacle, as many examples show, especially from Southeast Asia. It is true that certain governments are unable to find creditors—in particular those that do not pay back loans, or that nationalize foreign investments, or that regulate or tax investors to such an extent that profitable production becomes impossible. Such governments can only obtain "political credit" through intergovernmental organizations such as the IMF and the World Bank. Irresponsible governments make life in their countries miserable. As long as they have the backing of the citizens, they can stay in power. But in most cases they have this backing only as long as they can hand out material benefits, which they themselves obtain

15See Roland Vaubel, "The Political Economy of the International Monetary Fund," R. Vaubel and T.D. Willets, eds., *The Political Economy of International Organizations: A Public Choice Approach* (Boulder, Colo.: Westview Press, 1991), pp. 204–44; Alan Walters, *Do We Need the IMF and the World Bank?* (London: Institute of Economic Affairs, 1994); Jörg Guido Hülsmann, "Pourquoi le FMI nuit-il aux Africains?" *Labyrinthe* 16 (Autumn 2003).

through taxation and expropriation. As soon as there is nothing more for them to loot, the population turns against them. This is where the political credit facilities of the IMF and the World Bank come into play. Their effect is to keep corrupt and irresponsible governments in business longer than they otherwise would be. Bokassa, Mobutu, Nkruma, Somoza and other dictators would not have stayed in power as long as they did without the financial support of those institutions.[16] The political price to be paid for these political loans usually consists in cooperative behavior in other fields, for example, when it comes to the establishment of Western military bases in these countries, or to international trade agreements, or to special privileges for a few large "multinational" corporations.

The Catholic Church has avidly endorsed the integration of all countries into the international division of labor, as a condition for economic and social development.[17] But leaders from the Third World have only very recently begun to demand the abolition of the protectionism that is so pervasive in the developed countries. Could it be that the effect of political credit was to mute for a long time any opposition to Northern protectionism in the underdeveloped South?

Free trade and private property are not some sort of legal privilege to the sole benefit of a small number of "haves" and to the exclusion of the great majority of have-nots. The case is exactly the reverse, as many economists have demonstrated: the have-nots stand to benefit most from a social order based on the undiluted respect of property rights. Governments that systematically expropriate investors and oppose free trade—

---

[16]See George Ayittey, *Africa in Chaos* (New York: St. Martin's Press, 1998), pp. 270ff., where the author discusses the cases of Zambia, Rwanda, Somalia, Algeria, and Mozambique.

[17]See in particular the Second Vatican Council on *Gaudium et Spes* (1965); John Paul II, *Sollicitudo Rei Socialis* (1988); idem, *Centesimus Annus* (1991). Paul VI's *Populorum Progression* (1967), which dealt with development economics, focused on the more problematic aspects of international trade.

be it out of ignorance or malice—ruin their citizens, and especially the poor. Organizations that support such governments create misery and death. It follows that political-credit organizations such as the World Bank and the IMF are needless at best—because responsible government would obtain credit anyway—and positively harmful in their actual operation. Support for them is hard to square with concern for the well-being of the poor.

17

International Paper-Money Systems, 1971– ?

1. THE EMERGENCE OF PAPER-MONEY STANDARDS

The Fed's suspension of payments in August 1971 created in one mighty stroke a great number of paper monies. Before that date, all national currencies were basically fractional-reserve certificates for gold (via the U.S. dollar). The suspension "transubstantiated" these certificates into paper monies, with all the concomitant effects we have discussed above.

Many observers believed that the world would remain so fragmented. Advocates of paper money thought this was all well and good, because each government was now at last autonomous in its monetary policy. Others looked with horror on the reality of fluctuating exchange rates, which undermined the international division of labor and thus created misery and death for many millions of people. But the world did not long remain in monetary fragmentation. The events of the past thirty-five years illustrate that there is a tendency for the spontaneous emergence of international paper-money standards. Today the reasons for this development are not difficult to discern.[1]

---

[1]However, they have been overlooked for many years. The standard explanation of this phenomenon is indeed untenable. In this account,

One driving force of this process was of course the presence of private individuals and firms operating in many countries. These persons and organizations constantly look for ways of saving money, for example, by minimizing the costs of holding money. One way to do this is to make the bulk of one's payments in terms of only one kind of money. But this driving force, formidable though it might appear in our present time of multinational corporations, does not go a very long way in explaining the *emergence* of an international paper-money standard. The reason is that multinational corporations do not play a great role in a world of wildly fluctuating exchange rates. They operate profitably and grow to significant size only when the political framework has already stabilized the foreign exchanges. That is, by and large they come into play only once a monetary standard already exists.

This brings us to the main driving force of the emergence of international paper-money monetary standards, namely, the constant appetite of governments for additional revenue. Most governments that obtain income mostly from their own citizens—be it in the form of taxation or in the form of debt—have a rather small revenue base. To increase revenues they have by and large only two strategies: (1) induce foreign citizens to buy its bonds; (2) adopt policies that make their own citizens richer, so that they can pay more taxes and buy more government bonds.

No investor intentionally wastes his money. When he buys the bonds of a foreign government, he seeks to earn interest. He would abstain from the deal altogether if he had good reasons to believe that the money would be wasted. If he must fear, for example, that the debtor-government will simply print the money needed to pay back the credit, thus

---

the different countries of the post-1971 world economy are compared to the participants of a barter economy. The point of an international paper-money standard is then to allow for a greater volume of exchanges as compared with the initial barter situation. But these hypothetical additional exchanges are conceivable only if international money already exists—and the point is to explain how this happens in the first place.

provoking a fall in the exchange rate, he will not buy its bonds at all.[2] Thus the question is what a susceptible debtor-government can do to dispel such fears. The answer is that it must establish institutional safeguards against a falling exchange rate of its currency in terms of the currency used by its creditors.

The same considerations come into play if we turn to the second fundamental strategy for increasing public revenue. The idea is very simple: adopt policies that permit the citizens to make themselves richer so that they can pay more taxes and buy more government bonds. But the crucial point is that the productive capacity of a nation entirely depends on the capital stock it can use. This capital stock could be increased through savings from current income. But the accumulation of capital through savings can take many years and decades until it reaches any significant proportion. And during this time the government must keep the tax load as small as possible. Unfortunately such restraint requires more virtue than most governments have. The only remaining way out is, again, to encourage foreigners to provide capital that they have accumulated in their home countries—in other words, to make "foreign direct investments" in that country. But this reverts back to our previous consideration. In a paper-money world, foreign capital can be attracted only under sufficient institutional safeguards.

Four such institutions have played a significant role in the past thirty years. They go a long way in explaining the emergence of international paper money standards.

First, debtor-governments have floated bonds that were denominated in a foreign paper money, the production of which they cannot directly control; preferably this would be the paper money used in the country of its creditors. In the

---

[2]Many observers have been deluded about this point because in the period between 1948 and 1989 huge amounts of western credit have been given to corrupt governments in the Third World without any financial safeguards whatever. But these were political loans. Their purpose was not to earn monetary interest, but to buy the support of these governments during the Cold War.

past twenty years, this has become a widespread practice. Today many governments issue bonds that are denominated in U.S. dollars or euros.

Second, the government and / or the monetary authority of the country in which the creditors reside could give explicit or implicit guarantees to maintain the market exchange rate. It is widely assumed, for example, that the U.S. Federal Reserve gave such guarantees in the 1990s to the governments of Mexico, Singapore, Malaysia, Thailand, and other countries of the Far East. The great disadvantage of this practice is that it entails moral hazard for the beneficiaries. The receiving governments can set out to inflate their currencies without fearing any negative repercussions on the exchange rate. And thus they are able to expropriate not only their own population, but also the population of the country in which its creditors reside.

In the above-mentioned cases, the exchange-rate policies of the Fed had the effect of making U.S. citizens pay for the monetary abuses of the governments of Mexico and other countries. (They pay by constantly delivering goods and services to Mexico that they could have enjoyed themselves and in payment for which nothing but peso-denominated paper slips are sent to the U.S.) Because no diplomatic solution could be found for this problem, the Fed eventually abolished its policy and thus provoked financial crises in Mexico (1994) and various other countries, especially in Asia (1997). Since then, there have been no new major experiments with exchange-rate stabilization.

Third, debtor-governments have set up currency boards, thus transforming their currency into a substitute for a foreign paper money. This technique too is widely used today, for example, in Hong Kong, Bulgaria, Estonia, Lithuania, Bosnia, and Brunei.

Fourth, debtor-governments have abandoned the use of the national currency altogether and adopted the use of the paper money used by the creditors. Economists call such a policy "dollarization," even when the government adopts not the U.S. dollar, but a different foreign paper money. Among recently dollarized countries are Ecuador, El Salvador, Kosovo, and Montenegro.[3]

We conclude that the driving force for the emergence of an international paper-money standard is the quest of governments for additional funds, which most of them can obtain only from abroad. And our analysis also explains which paper monies will tend to be chosen as international standards: the paper monies that are legal tender in the territories with the largest capital markets. In the period under consideration, these territories happened to be the U.S., Japan, and Europe. It is therefore not surprising that the U.S. dollar and the yen have emerged as regional monetary standards of the world economy.

The operation of the same mechanism could be observed in the case of the German mark, which during the 1990s was used as a (unofficial) parallel currency in many countries of the former East Bloc. And it currently brings about a wider geographical circulation of the euro, which was only created in early 1999, and which did not exist in the form of banknotes before the year 2002. The creation of the euro is of some interest because here an international standard did not emerge through the unilateral adoption of paper money used on foreign capital markets, but through merger. This form of monetary integration could play a role in the future development of the international monetary order. We will therefore take a brief look at it.[4]

---

[3]Dollarization is the most complete way for a government to renounce its control over the production of money. By contrast, the creation of a currency board still leaves open the possibility of a quick return to a national paper money. See Nikolay Gertchev, "The Case against Currency Boards," *Quarterly Journal of Austrian Economics* 5, no. 4 (2002).

[4]We have analyzed the development of the European Monetary System and the emergence of the euro in more detail in Jörg Guido Hülsmann, "Schöne neue Zeichengeldwelt," epilogue to Murray Rothbard, *Das Schein-Geld-System* (Gräfelfing: Resch, 2000), pp. 111–54.

2. Paper-Money Merger: The Case of the Euro

After the demise of the Bretton Woods system in 1971, the countries of Western Europe for a few years fell into monetary disarray and the fiscal anarchy that typically goes in hand with it. Each national government issued its own paper money and started piling up public debts to an unheard-of extent. The newly available funds were used to expand government welfare services. For a while, things looked rosy and only a few fiscal conservatives bemoaned the new laxity. But soon even the champions of the new policy began to understand that the new monetary order affected their interests in very tangible negative ways. Exchange rates fluctuated very widely and effectively prevented the further development of international trade. The division of labor in Europe, one of the most densely populated regions of the world, lagged behind the American economy and even—or so it seemed in those days—the Soviet economy. It was therefore but a question of time until tax revenues would fall far behind the revenues of the great competitors of the European governments: the governments of the U.S. and of the Soviet Union. Something had to be done.

The first attempts at stabilizing the exchange rates between European paper monies had failed miserably. Then, at a December 1978 conference in the German city of Bremen, the core governments of the European Economic Community, as it was called in those days, launched a new attempt at integration: the European Monetary System (EMS). The EMS was a cartel of the national paper-money producers, who agreed to coordinate their policies in order to stabilize exchange rates between their monies at certain levels or "parities." As in the case of the previous international banking cartels, the EMS essentially relied on the self-restraint of its members. "Coordination" meant in practice that the least inflationary money producer set the pace of inflation for all others. If for example the supply of the Italian lira increased by 30 percent, whereas the supply of French francs increased only by 15 percent, it was very likely that the lira would drop on the foreign exchanges *vis-à-vis* the franc. In order to maintain the lira-franc parity, it was necessary either that the Banque de France increase the production of francs, or that the Banco d'Italia reduce its production of lira. As we have said, the EMS essentially relied on self-restraint; thus in our example the Banca d'Italia would be expected to reduce its lira production. If for political reasons it was unwilling to do this, there would be a "realignment" of the parity, and stabilization would henceforth seek to preserve the new parity.

Now by far the least inflationary money producer happened to be the German Bundesbank. Accordingly, for the next twelve years or so, the main problem of European monetary politics was that the Bundesbank did not inflate the supply of the Deutsche mark quite enough to suit the needs of foreign governments. The latter were therefore forced to cut down their money production. It also came to frequent changes or realignments of parities. The problem was settled only in the early 1990s, when the German government sought to take over former communist East Germany and needed the consent of its major western partners. The price for that consent was the abdication of the Deutsche mark.[5] Within a few years, the political and legal foundations were laid for merging the different national paper-money producers into one organization: the European System of Central Banks (ESCB), the coordination of which lay in the hands of the European Central Bank (ECB). The ESCB started its operations in January 1999 and three years later issued its euro notes and coins.

From an economic and ethical point of view, the euro does not bring any new aspects into play. It is just another paper money. In public debate, the introduction of the euro has often been justified by the benefits that spring from monetary integration. It is true that such benefits exist. But, as we have repeatedly emphasized in our study, these benefits can be obtained much more conveniently and assuredly by allowing the citizens to choose the best money they can get. If this had been the policy of the European governments, it would not

---

[5]For an insider view of the conflicts and struggles behind European monetary integration see Bernard Connolly, *The Rotten Heart of Europe* (London: Faber and Faber, 1995).

have prevented European monetary unification. But this would have been a *spontaneous* unification. Gold and silver coins would have been the harbingers of monetary integration under the auspices of liberty and responsibility.

But the European governments never intended to grant their citizens the sovereignty that they have according to the letter of written constitutions. The governments wished above all to stay in control of monetary affairs. It was out of the question to abolish the privileges for paper money. European monetary integration had to be built on paper money, for the sole reason that paper money is the source of virtually unlimited government income, at the expense of the population. This is a point that cannot be emphasized enough. The euro was not introduced out of any economic necessity. All true benefits that it conveys could have been conveyed much better through commodity monies such as gold and silver.

The story of the euro is not a success story, unless the standard of success is to be seen in the expansion of government power. Yet the euro story could be seen as a model for further monetary integration on a global scale.

3. THE DYNAMICS OF MULTIPLE PAPER-MONEY STANDARDS

The international monetary order at the outset of the twentieth-first century is characterized by the presence of several competing paper-money systems. Each of these systems is hierarchical, with standard paper money on the one hand, and a plethora of secondary and tertiary currency on the other hand. The three most important standards are the yen, the dollar, and the euro. Only these standard monies are true *monies*—paper monies or electronic monies. The secondary currencies in each of the three systems are not monies at all; rather they are national certificates for the standard money, issued on a fractional-reserve basis by a national authority (usually called a "central bank" or "currency board"). And then there are tertiary currencies that are also fractional-reserve certificates, in particular, the demand deposits of commercial banks.

We have already discussed the dialectical power relationship between national central banks and commercial banks under the gold standard. Similar considerations apply in the present case. The difference is, of course, that there is no longer any commodity-money standard that could act as a natural restraint on the drive to inflate. Even more to the point, it is at present equally impossible to restrain this drive by *legal* means, because the principle of national sovereignty still holds.[6] As a consequence, the secondary and tertiary layers have, in the present order of things, far greater power to inflate than they ever had before. Let us explain this in more detail.

The producers of international paper money have the privilege of picking those who receive the newly printed notes first, and they have political leverage on the producers of the secondary currencies in times of crises. But this dependency is mutual. Consider that, within each nation, the commercial banks can exploit the moral hazard of the central bank. They can push inflation with the good hope that the central bank will bail them out in times of a liquidity crisis. In an international paper-money system, the same mechanism bears on the

---

[6]In each country the banking industry is regulated to curb some of the excesses of fractional-reserve banking. The strength of these regulations varies from one country to another, and the banks operating from the least regulated countries have therefore a competitive advantage over the other banks. Yet the risks of their enhanced activities are experienced even in the more regulated countries, because international business ties create spill-over effects. More recently, therefore, a number of governments have tried to set up international standards for the regulation of the banking industry. In particular, they seek to impose on fractional-reserve banks a minimum capital-reserve requirement on their loans; and to make this capital-reserve also dependent on the risk of each individual credit, as evaluated according to formulas developed by an international committee. The activities of the regulators are coordinated by the Bank for International Settlements (BIS) in Basel, Switzerland. They have recently published a detailed proposal known as the "Basel II Agreement" (June 2004). Let us emphasize again that, in light of our analysis, it would be more commensurate to simply abolish the legal privileges of the banking industry, rather than to layer additional international regulations atop the manifold national regulations.

relationship between the producer of the standard money and the producers of the secondary and tertiary currencies. The latter have an incentive to push inflation and speculate on bailouts.

If the producer of the standard money gives in to these demands, the exchange rate of his money will drop and the price level will increase. Both events will tend to make his money less attractive as a financial asset. Moreover, both events will tend to make the economies in which his money is used less attractive places to invest in. If he undertakes a major bailout, he even risks a hyperinflation and subsequent destruction of his product.

But our producer of standard money also runs into difficulties if he does *not* give in to any bailout demands. Consider the following scenario. The hypothetical country Ruritania has a currency board issuing Rurs backed up with dollars. The dollar exchange-rate of the Rur has been set at a very low level in order to encourage exports to the U.S. The dollars that stream into Ruritania as payment for these exports are not spent on U.S. products, but stockpiled as reserves in the vaults of the local central bank. Suppose further that the commercial banks of that country have created a huge amount of credit out of thin air (inflation) and are now in a liquidity crisis. The Ruritanian currency board turns for help to the U.S. Fed, but the Fed refuses to bail out the Ruritanian banks. At that point, the currency board could threaten to sell all its dollars for euros, thus putting the country on the euro standard. Depending on the size of Ruritania, this action would have a more or less notable impact on the dollar-euro exchange rate. It would harm the U.S. capital markets and thus provide an incentive for investors to leave Manhattan and Chicago, and to turn to Frankfurt and Paris. Moreover, if we assume that Ruritania is a very large country with substantial dollar reserves even by world standards, then the mere announcement that the Ruritanian government will switch to the euro standard might incite other member countries of the dollar standard to do the same. This could precipitate the dollar into a spiralling hyperinflation. The dollars would sooner or later end up in the United States, the only country where people are forced to accept them because of their legal-tender status. Here all prices would soar, possibly entailing a hyperinflation and collapse of the entire monetary system.

The same considerations apply, *mutatis mutandis*, to all other international paper-money standards. The point is that, in the present regime of virtually unhampered international flows of capital, it is out of the question to prevent the outflow of standard money into foreign countries. And the more of that money that accumulates abroad, the more its producer risks being subject to the sort of blackmail we have already discussed.[7] Notice the irony that the potential for such blackmail is greatest precisely when the institutional safeguards against fluctuating exchange rates are strongest—in the case of currency boards and dollarization.

The leadership of the U.S. Federal Reserve is aware of this situation. To guard itself against the danger of switching, it has developed a program of shared seignorage. That is, U.S. authorities actually pay foreign governments for dollarizing their economies, and especially for maintaining the dollarization.

However, such schemes for the integration of standard monies and secondary currencies have been applied, so far, only in relatively unimportant cases. The only realistic scenario that could curb the expansionary drift of monetary blackmail as analyzed above is cooperation between the producers of standard paper money. For example, if in a dollar crisis the euro producers commit to stabilize the dollar-euro exchange rate on the downside, then the financial incentives for going out of dollar-denominated assets and into euro-denominated assets would largely disappear.

But why should producers of standard money such as the euro be willing to assist a competitor in dire straits? There are

---

[7]The same thing would happen on a national scale if there were competing central banks. In times of strain on the reserves, the commercial banks could then threaten to switch from one central bank to another, dooming in the process the system they leave. This is one of the reasons why no bank has ever assumed the responsibilities of a central bank (lender of last resort) without being compensated through a legal monopoly that prevented such switching. The Bank of England is a case in point.

at least two good reasons for such cooperation. First, they might wish to discourage monetary blackmail by the producers of secondary currencies, because in the next round they themselves could be the victims of such attempts. Second, they themselves would be negatively affected in the event of a currency crisis hitting their competitor. It is true that in the short run they would benefit from investors rushing into euro-denominated assets. However, they could not prevent that the same investors rush out again once the dollar-crisis has been solved, for example, through some monetary reform. Standard paper-money producers would thus be ill-advised to play cat and mouse with international investors, in the hope to profit from a currency crisis hitting one of their competitors.

Now the crucial point is that all relevant parties know all this and that therefore moral hazard comes into play again. Paper-money producers have a strong incentive to expand their production because they know that their competitors, acting in their own interest, would be likely to assist them whenever they are threatened with a currency crisis. Thus we find the same strong incentive for expansionary collusion between paper-money producers that we have already described in earlier sections for the case of domestic fractional-reserve banks. This monetary expansion path results from the very nature of paper-money competition, just as the expansion of fractional-reserve certificates results from the very nature of competitive fractional-reserve banking.

Is there any way out of this monetary quagmire? One solution would be the return to autarky, cutting all ties with the international currency and financial markets; but this would entail misery and starvation, and is therefore not really an option. Another solution would be to merge the standard paper money producers, possibly along the lines of the European System of Central Banks and possibly along with international regulation of capital markets and the banking industry.[8] But is world paper-money union a viable solution?

---

[8]See Stephen F. Frowen, "The Functions of Money and Financial Credit: Their Objectives, Structure and Inbuilt Deficiencies," *Journal of the Association of Christian Economists* 14 (February 1993).

4. Dead End of the World Paper-Money Union

As we have seen, there is a strong tendency for the formation of currency blocks around the paper monies used in the countries with the largest capital markets. The driving force in this process is the quest of foreign governments for additional revenue. The governments that control the large capital markets have little incentive to adopt the currencies controlled by other governments. But governments that control only a small tax base and cannot tame their appetite for more money must at some point turn to international capital markets; and this sooner or later forces them to adopt a foreign paper money, or to merge its paper money with the paper monies controlled by other governments.

We have also seen that the connectivity between international capital markets creates an incentive for competing standard paper-money producers to cooperate and, eventually, to merge. This consolidation and centralization process is at present far from being completed. Today's international monetary order is an order in transition. In the preceding section we have analyzed some of the problems that could manifest themselves in the next few years if political leaders do not take appropriate action. We have pointed out that one way of avoiding a world of spiraling hyperinflations and currency wars is global monetary integration on a paper standard. There would then be just one paper money for the entire world, possibly with a few remaining national paper currencies that serve as money certificates for the global money. The great project that Lord Keynes unsuccessfully promoted at the 1944 Bretton Woods conference would then finally have come true.

We have already pointed out all essential implications of such an event. Even a national paper money is a powerful engine of economic, cultural, and spiritual degradation. How much more would this be the case with a global paper money? Such a monetary regime would provide the economic foundation of a totalitarian nightmare.

It is true that we are still far away from this scenario. Great obstacles stand in its way, because it would require no less

235

than a political unification of mankind. But let us assume for the moment that these problems could be overcome in the near future. And let us also assume that fears of totalitarianism could be dispelled by an appropriate moral education of political leaders, who would then excel in the art of self-restraint. Would this solve the problem of monetary constitution? Would it give the world a true monetary order that did not bear in its very bosom a tendency for self-destruction, a tendency inherent in all fiat monetary systems?

In light of our general discussion of paper money, the answer is patent. All paper-money systems, be they national or international, labor under the presence of moral hazard. In the long run, therefore, a global paper money cannot evade the fate of national paper money. It must either collapse in hyperinflation or force the government to adopt a policy of increasing control, and eventually total control, over all economic resources. Both scenarios entail economic disruptions on a scale that we can barely imagine today. The inevitable result would be death for many hundreds of millions of human beings.

There is hope, however. Mankind is free to return at any time to the natural production of money, which is in fact the only ethically justifiable and economically viable monetary order.

Conclusion

1. Two Concepts of Capitalism

The ancient philosophers generally took a negative attitude toward labor, commerce, and money. The outlook of medieval Christian scholastics was decidedly different. Their more favorable perspective on commerce, entrepreneurship, and market forces made for fertile intellectual soil for the growth of economic science and the application of ethics to economics. It was the scholastic tradition that first saw the grave problems associated with the legal monopolization of money production.

During the twentieth century, the Catholic Church expressed a mixed attitude toward capitalism. Pius XI distinguished between a capitalistic "economic system" that was "not to be condemned in itself" and a "'capitalist' economic regime" that he found in many respects unacceptable.[1] This distinction ran through all subsequent church statements on the question. Pope John Paul II stressed this point when he discussed the question whether capitalism was the economic model to be recommended to the Third World. The answer depends on what we mean by the word "capitalism":

> If by "capitalism" is meant an economic system which recognizes the fundamental and positive role of business, the market, private property and the resulting responsibility for the means of production, as well as free human creativity in the economic sector, then the answer is certainly in the

---

[1]Pius XI, *Quadragesimo Anno*, §§101, 103.

affirmative, even though it would perhaps be more appropriate to speak of a "business economy," "market economy" or simply "free economy." But if by "capitalism" is meant a system in which freedom in the economic sector is not circumscribed within a strong juridical framework which places it at the service of human freedom in its totality, and which sees it as a particular aspect of that freedom, the core of which is ethical and religious, then the reply is certainly negative.[2]

Very similarly, many economists—and most notably the economists of the Austrian School—have portrayed capitalism as the most suitable system to provide the economic underpinnings for the full development of man and society. Yet by capitalism they meant a social system of division of labor that is based on the full and universal respect of the fundamental economic institutions of society: private property and the freedom of association. In this regard, as we have shown, there is no fundamental disagreement between the views of the Austrians and the Catholic moral concerns. The Austrians do not mean to justify the actual economic systems that prevailed in the so-called "capitalist" West in the twentieth century. Quite to the contrary, they have always stressed that these systems deviated from the capitalistic ideal in manifold ways, and they have demonstrated that these deviations were harmful for society and its members.

Thus Austrian economics and the Catholic teaching *do* agree that many aspects of our western economic systems must be criticized. They should also agree that the prevailing monetary system is an important case in point. There is no tenable economic, legal, moral, or spiritual rationale that could be adduced in justification of paper money and fractional-reserve banking. The prevailing ways of money production, relying as they do on a panoply of legal privileges, are alien elements in the capitalist economy. They provide illicit incomes, encourage irresponsibility and dependence, stimulate the artificial centralization of political and economic

---

[2]John Paul II, *Centesimus Annus*, §42.

decision-making, and constantly create fundamental economic disequilibria that threaten the life and welfare of millions of people. In short, paper money and fractional-reserve banking go a long way toward accounting for the excesses for which the capitalist economy is widely chided.

We have argued that these monetary institutions have not come into existence out of any economic necessity. They have been created because they allow an alliance of politicians and bankers to enrich themselves at the expense of all other strata of society. This alliance emerged rather spontaneously in the seventeenth century; it developed in multifarious ways up to the present day, and in the course of its development it created the current monetary institutions.

Let us emphasize that this alliance is, and has always been, an *ad hoc* alliance. We do not claim that our monetary institutions have resulted from a three-hundred-year-old conspiracy between bankers and politicians. It is certainly naïve to assume that no such conspiracy has ever been concocted, or is not presently concocted. But, as our analysis has shown, the conspiracy question is only of secondary importance. The driving force that propelled the development of central banks and paper money was the reckless determination of governments, both aristocratic and democratic, to increase their revenue, if necessary in violation of good faith and of all established rules of commerce.[3] On this point we find, again, fundamental agreement between our economic analysis and the ethical concerns of the Church:

> This concentration of power and might, the characteristic mark, as it were, of contemporary economic life, is the fruit that the *unlimited* freedom of struggle among competitors

---

[3]We do not of course claim that every single government betrayed the public faith; only that several of them in the past three hundred years did this. Their decisions gave us our present-day monetary institutions. The alliance with the banking industry resulted merely from the technical superiority of banknotes and paper money as vehicles of that illicit increase of revenue.

has of its own nature produced, and which lets only the strongest survive; and this is often the same as saying, those who fight the most violently, those who give least heed to their conscience.[4]

Notice again that our present study does not purport to provide a full discussion of all considerations that have been brought up on the subject. We have presented a broad picture and dealt with details only where appropriate. The point was to show that the evidence for our case is sufficiently clear and sufficiently important to warrant closer examination. The serious student must still acquaint himself with the discussions that can be found in other works on our subject.

2. MONETARY REFORM

The monetary institutions of our time are in dire need of reform for many reasons. Present-day discussion of monetary reform, insofar as it takes place at all, however, suffers from an amazing intellectual narrowness. It is of course impossible to provide the antidote in a short study, but our exposition might nevertheless be useful in pointing out the directions where alternatives might be found. One such alternative is the natural production of money, even though it presently plays no practical role.[5] It is a significant fact that one cannot get

---

[4]Pius XI, *Quadragesimo Anno*, §107; emphasis added.

[5]Concrete reform schemes are discussed, for example, in Ludwig von Mises, *Theory of Money and Credit* (Indianapolis: Liberty Fund, 1980), pt. 4; Murray N. Rothbard, *The Case Against the Fed* (Auburn, Ala.: Ludwig von Mises Institute, 1994); Hans Sennholz, *Age of Inflation* (Belmont, Mass.: Western Islands, 1979), chap. 6; idem, *Money and Freedom* (Spring Mills, Penn.: Libertarian Press, 1985), chap. 8; idem., ed., *The Lustre of Gold* (Westport, Conn.: Greenwood Press, 1975), pt. 4; Jesús Huerta de Soto, *Money, Bank Credit, and Economic Cycles* (Auburn, Ala.: Ludwig von Mises Institute, 2006), chap. 9; Gary North, *Honest Money* (Ft. Worth, Texas: Dominion Press, 1986), chaps. 11–13; Edwin Vieira, *Pieces of Eight*, 2nd ed. (Fredericksburg, Va.: Sheridan, 2002); and Pierre Leconte, *La tragédie monétaire*, 2nd ed. (Paris: François-Xavier de Guibert, 2003).

around the natural order even in theory, because it alone provides a solid starting point for any serious analysis of monetary institutions. And in monetary policy too, as we have argued, it is something like the *optimum optimorum*.

Notice that we do not recommend simply turning back the clock. A natural monetary order in our day is certainly not identical with what a natural monetary order would have looked like in the sixteenth century. We do not advocate abolishing credit cards, checking deposits, and whatever other viable financial institutions might originate on the market. The point is to return to a universal respect for property rights. We need not change *instruments* such as banknotes, paper money, and the organization of central banks; but the *legal rules* under which central banks operate and under which paper money is produced. We need to abolish the legal privileges of central banks and monetary authorities. There is no tenable rationale for preventing the citizens from using the best monies and money substitutes. Quite to the contrary, a reform in this direction is necessary for many reasons. Immediate and vigorous action is called for.

Many will object that it is impossible to bring about such a return, now that we have progressed so far on the way toward a global paper money. This is a thoroughly defeatist point of view because it takes the coming disaster (hyperinflation or global tyranny) for granted. Most importantly, however, it is morally wrong. As we have argued, we face a problem of the human will; but this is after all *only* a problem of the will. In 1258, King Louis IX of France began a monetary reform that would eventually restore the currency of his realm on natural metallic bases. He seems to have been the last ruler so far of his country who fulfilled God's promise:

> In place of bronze I will bring gold, instead of iron, silver; In place of wood, bronze, instead of stones, iron; I will appoint peace your governor, and justice your ruler. (Isaiah 60:17)

It might be argued that Saint Louis had a comparatively easy job. After all, he just needed to clean up the mess in what was still basically a metallic monetary system. By contrast, fractional-reserve banking and paper money have been with us for quite a while, and they have changed habits and even our mentality. Yet consider that China ran through various experiments with fractional-reserve banking and paper money for five hundred years (from about 960 to about 1455 of our time) and in this epoch repeatedly suffered from hyper-inflations and other problems that we have analyzed in this volume. Then the country returned to monetary sanity when the political leadership no longer suppressed the circulation of silver and copper coins. And consider that the makers of the American Revolution, the Founding Fathers of the U.S. Constitution gloriously cut the legal ground from under the century-long tradition of colonial paper money. Consider that President Andrew Jackson, against the frantic resistance of vested interests in banking and financial circles, withdrew the legal privileges from all fractional-reserve banks and cut back the public debt to an amount that could have been paid by any individual wealthy citizen. There is no reason why today we should be unable to accomplish such things, or something even better.

References

BOOKS AND ARTICLES

Anderson, Benjamin. *The Value of Money*. Reprint. Grove City, Penn.: Libertarian Press, 1917.

Aquinas, Saint Thomas. *Summa Theologica*. 5 vols. New York: Benziger, 1948.

———. *Commentary on the Nicomachean Ethics*. 2 vols. Chicago: Regnery, 1964.

———. *On Kingship, To the King of Cyprus*. Toronto: Pontifical Institute of Mediaeval Studies, 1949.

Aristotle. *Politics*.

———. *Nicomachean Ethics*.

Atkeson, A., and P.J. Kehoe. "Deflation and Depression: Is There an Empirical Link?" *American Economic Review, Papers and Proceedings* 94 (May 2004).

Ayittey, George. *Africa in Chaos*. New York: St. Martin's Press, 1998.

Azpilcueta, Martín de. "Commentary on the Resolution of Money." *Journal of Markets and Morality* 7, no. 1 (2004).

Baader, Roland. *Geld, Gold und Gottspieler*. Gräfelfing: Resch, 2004.

Baird, Charles W. *Liberating Labor*. Grand Rapids, Mich.: Acton Institute, 2002.

Bastiat, Frédéric. "Maudit Argent." *Journal des économistes* (April 1849); trans. in *Quarterly Journal of Austrian Economics* 5, no. 3 (2002).

———. *Harmonies économiques*. 2nd ed. Paris: Guillaumin, 1851.

Bernanke, Ben. "Deflation: Making Sure 'It' Doesn't Happen Here." Remarks before the National Economists' Club. Washington, D.C., 21 November 2002.

Bernholz, Peter. *Monetary Regimes and Inflation*. Cheltenham, U.K.: Edward Elgar, 2003.

Beutter, Friedrich. *Zur sittlichen Beurteilung von Inflationen.* Freiburg: Herder, 1965.

———. "Geld im Verständnis der christlichen Soziallehre." In W.F. Kasch, ed. *Geld und Glaube.* Paderborn: Schöningh, 1979.

Blessing, Karl. "Geldwertstabilität als gesellschaftspolitisches Problem." In *Kirche und Wirtschaftsgesellschaft.* K. Hoffman, W. Weber, and B. Zimmer, eds. Cologne: Hanstein, 1974.

Block, Walter. "Fractional Reserve Banking: An Interdisciplinary Perspective." In *Man, Economy, and Liberty.* Walter Block and Llewellyn H. Rockwell, Jr., eds. Auburn, Ala.: Ludwig von Mises Institute, 1988.

Bodin, Jean. *Les six livres de la République.* Paris: Jacques du Puys, 1576.

Böhm-Bawerk, Eugen von. *Capital and Interest.* South Holland, Ill.: Libertarian Press, 1959.

Borchert, Manfred. *Geld und Kredit.* Munich: Oldenbourg, 2001.

Bordo, Michael D., and Angela Redish. "Is Deflation Depressing? Evidence from the Classical Gold Standard." NBER Working Paper #9520. Cambridge, Mass.: National Bureau of Economic Research, 2003.

Brants, Victor. *L'économie politique au Moyen-Age: esquisse des théories économiques professées par les écrivains des XIIIe et XIVe siècles.* Reprint. New York: Franklin, 1970.

Braudel, Fernand P., and Frank Spooner. "Prices in Europe from 1450 to 1750." In *The Cambridge Economic History of Europe.* Vol. 4. E.E. Rich and C.H. Wilson, eds. Cambridge: Cambridge University Press, 1967.

Bridrey, Émile. *La théorie de la monnaie au XIVe siècle, Nicolas Oresme.* Paris: Giard & Brière, 1906.

Burdekin, R.C.K., and P.L. Siklos, eds. *Deflation: Current and Historical Perspectives.* Cambridge: Cambridge University Press, 2004.

Buridan, Jean. "Extrait des 'Questions sur la Politique d'Aristote'." In *Traité des monnaies et autres écrits monétaires du XIVe siècle.* C. Dupuy, ed. Lyon: La manufacture, 1989.

Burns, Arthur R. *Money and Monetary Policy in Early Times.* New York: Augustus M. Kelley, [1927] 1965.

Cantillon, Richard. *La nature du commerce en général.* Paris: Institut national d'études démographiques, 1997.

Cantor, Paul. "Hyperinflation and Hyperreality: Thomas Mann in Light of Austrian Economics." *Review of Austrian Economics* 7, no. 1 (1994).

Carrier, Hervé. *Nouveau regard sur la doctrine sociale de l'église.* Vatican: Pontifical Council "Justice and Peace," 1990.

Chafuen, Alejandro A. *Faith and Liberty: The Economic Thought of the Late Scholastics*. 2nd ed. New York: Lexington Books, 2003.

Chown, John E. *A History of Money*. London: Routledge, 1994.

Clapham, John Harold. *The Bank of England: A History, 1694–1914*. Cambridge: Cambridge University Press, [1944] 1970.

Condillac, Etienne de. *Le commerce et le gouvernement*. 2nd ed. Paris: Letellier, 1795.

Connolly, Bernard. *The Rotten Heart of Europe*. London: Faber and Faber, 1995.

Copernicus, Nicolas. "Traité de la monnaie." In *Traité de la première invention des monnoies, de Nicole Oresme . . . et Traité de la monnoie, de Copernic*. L. Wolowski, ed. Paris: Guillaumin, 1864.

Coughlin, Charles E. *Money! Questions and Answers*. Royal Oak, Mich.: National Union for Social Justice, 1936.

d'Azeglio, Luigi Taparelli, *Saggio teoretico di diritto naturale appogiato sul fatto*. 5 vols. Palermo: Antonio Muratori, 1840–43.

Dempsey, Bernard W. *Reorganization of Social Economy; The Social Encyclical Developed and Explained*. New York: Bruce Pub., 1936–37.

———. *Interest and Usury*. Washington, D.C.: American Council of Public Affairs, 1943.

———. *The Functional Economy*. Englewood Cliffs, N.J.: Prentice Hall, 1958.

———. *The Frontier Wage*. Chicago: Loyola University Press, 1960.

Dowd, Kevin. "The Emergence of Fiat Money: A Reconsideration." *Cato Journal* 20, no. 3 (2001).

Drinkwater, Francis H. *Money and Social Justice*. London: Burns, Oates & Washbourne, 1934.

Ederer, Rupert J. *The Evolution of Money*. Washington, D.C.: Public Affairs Press, 1964.

Ehrenberg, Richard. *Das Zeitalter der Fugger: Geldkapital und Creditverkehr im 16. Jahrhundert*. Jena: Fischer, 1896.

Eichengreen, Barry. *Globalizing Capital*. 2nd ed. Princeton, N.J.: Princeton University Press, 1998.

Fahey, Denis. *Money Manipulation and Social Order*. Dublin: Browne & Nolan, 1944.

Federal Reserve Bank of Cleveland. *Deflation—2002 Annual Report*. 9 May 2003.

Fetter, Frank A. *The Principles of Economics*. New York: The Century Co., 1905.

Fink, Carole. *The Genoa Conference: European Diplomacy, 1921–1922.* Chapel Hill: University of North Carolina Press, 1984.

Fisher, Irving, *Stabilized Money: A History of the Movement.* London: George Allen and Unwin, 1935.

Fratianni, Michele, and Franco Spinelli. *A Monetary History of Italy.* Cambridge: Cambridge University Press, 1997.

Friedman, Milton. "The Resource Cost of Irredeemable Paper Money." *Journal of Political Economy* 94, no. 3 (June 1986).

Friedman, Milton, and Anna Schwarz. *A Monetary History of the United States.* Chicago: University of Chicago Press, 1963.

Frowen, Stephen F. "The Functions of Money and Financial Credit: Their Objectives, Structure and Inbuilt Deficiencies." *Journal of the Association of Christian Economists* 14. February 1993).

Gaettens, Richard. *Inflationen: Das Drama der Geldentwertungen vom Altertum bis zur Gegenwart.* 2nd ed. Munich: Pflaum, 1955.

Gallarotti, Giulio M. *The Anatomy of an International Monetary Regime: The Classical Gold Standard, 1880–1914.* Oxford: Oxford University Press, 1995.

Garrison, Roger W. "The Costs of a Gold Standard." In *The Gold Standard.* Llewellyn H. Rockwell, Jr., ed. Auburn, Ala.: Ludwig von Mises Institute, 1992.

Gertchev, Nikolay. "The Case against Currency Boards." *Quarterly Journal of Austrian Economics* 5, no. 4 (2002).

Gide, Charles, and Charles Rist. *Histoire des doctrines économiques.* 6th ed. Paris: Dalloz, [1944] 2000.

Gillard, Lucien. "Nicole Oresme, économiste." *Revue historique* 279 (1988).

Goethe, Wolfgang. *Faust.*

Gouge, William M. *A Short History of Paper Money and Banking in the United States, to which is prefixed an Inquiry into the Principles of the System.* Reprint. New York: Augustus M. Kelley, [1833] 1968.

Grauwe, Paul de, and Theo Peeters. *The ECU and European Monetary Integration.* Basingstoke, Macmillan, 1989.

Grice-Hutchinson, Marjorie. *The School of Salamanca.* Oxford: Clarendon Press, 1952.

———. *Economic Thought in Spain.* L. Moss and C. Ryan, eds. Aldershot: Edward Elgar, 1993.

Groseclose, Elgin. *Money and Man: A Survey of Monetary Experience.* New York: Frederick Ungar, 1961.

Guynn, Jack. "Ethical Challenges in a Market Economy." Speech delivered at Bridgewater College, Bridgewater, Va. 11 April 2005.

Haberler, Gottfried von. *Der Sinn der Indexzahlen.* Tübingen: Mohr, 1927.

Habiger, Matthew. *Papal Teaching on Private Property, 1891 to 1991.* Lanham, Md.: University Press of America, 1990.

Hammond, Bray. *Banks and Politics in America.* Princeton, N.J.: Princeton University Press, 1957.

Hawtrey, Ralph G. *A Century of Bank Rate.* 2nd ed. New York: Augustus M. Kelley, 1962.

Hayek, Friedrich August. *Monetary Nationalism and International Stability.* New York: Augustus M. Kelley, [1937] 1964.

———. *Free Choice in Currency.* London: Institute of Economic Affairs, 1976.

Hazlitt, Henry. *The Inflation Crisis, and How to Resolve It.* Irvington-on-Hudson, N.Y.: Foundation for Economic Education, [1978] 1995.

———. *From Bretton Woods to World Inflation.* Chicago: Regnery, 1984.

Henning, Friedrich-Wilhelm. *Handbuch der Wirtschafts- und Sozialgeschichte Deutschlands.* Vol. 1. Paderborn: Schöningh, 1991.

Hepburn, A. Barton. *History of Coinage and Currency in the United States and the Perennial Contest for Sound Money.* London: Macmillan, 1903.

Hesse, Helmut and Otmar Issing eds., *Geld und Moral* (Munich: Vahlen, 1994).

Hodge, Ian. *Baptized Inflation.* Tyler, Texas: Institute for Christian Economics, 1986.

Höffner, Josef. *Christliche Gesellschaftslehre.* Kevelaer: Butzon & Bercker, 1997.

Holzbauer, Georg. *Barzahlung und Zahlungsmittelversorgung in militärisch besetzten Gebieten.* Jena: Fischer, 1939.

Hoppe, Hans-Hermann. *A Theory of Socialism and Capitalism.* Boston: Kluwer, 1989.

———. *The Economics and Ethics of Private Property.* Boston: Kluwer, 1993.

———. "How Is Fiat Money Possible?—or, The Devolution of Money and Credit." *Review of Austrian Economics* 7, no. 2 (1994).

———. *Democracy—The God That Failed.* New Brunswick, N.J.: Transaction, 2001.

Hoppe, Hans-Hermann, Jörg G. Hülsmann, and Walter Block. "Against Fiduciary Media," *Quarterly Journal of Austrian Economics* 1, no. 1 (1998).

Huber, Joseph, and James Robertson. *Creating New Money*. London: New Economics Foundation, 2000.

Huerta de Soto, Jesús. "New Light on the Prehistory of the Theory of Banking and the School of Salamanca." *Review of Austrian Economics* 9, no. 2 (1996).

———. "Juan de Mariana: The Influence of the Spanish Scholastics." In *15 Great Austrian Economists*. Randall Holcombe, ed. Auburn, Ala.: Ludwig von Mises Institute, 1999.

———. *Money, Bank Credit, and Economic Cycles*. Auburn, Ala.: Ludwig von Mises Institute, 2006.

Hulme, Anthony. *Morals and Money*. London: St. Paul Publications, 1957.

Hume, David. *Essays*. Indianapolis: Liberty Fund, 1987.

Humphrey, Thomas. "John Wheatley's Theory of International Monetary Adjustment." *Federal Reserve Bank of Richmond Economic Quarterly* 80, no. 3 (1994).

Hülsmann, Jörg Guido. *Logik der Währungskonkurrenz*. Essen: Management Akademie Verlag, 1996.

———. "Toward a General Theory of Error Cycles." *Quarterly Journal of Austrian Economics* 1, no. 4 (1998).

———. "Schöne neue Zeichengeldwelt." Postface to Murray Rothbard, *Das Schein-Geld-System*. Gräfelfing: Resch, 2000.

———. "Has Fractional-Reserve Banking Really Passed the Market Test?" *Independent Review* 7, no. 3 (2003).

———. "Pourquoi le FMI nuit-il aux Africains ?" *Labyrinthe* 16 (Autumn 2003).

———. "Optimal Monetary Policy." *Quarterly Journal of Austrian Economics* 6, no. 4 (2003).

———. "Legal Tender Laws and Fractional-Reserve Banking." *Journal of Libertarian Studies* 18, no. 3 (2004).

———. "The Political Economy of Moral Hazard." *Politická ekonomie* (February 2006).

Jouvenel, Bertrand de. *Du pouvoir*. Geneva: Bourquin, 1945.

Kant, Immanuel. "Zum Ewigen Frieden—ein philosophischer Entwurf." *Werkausgabe*. Vol. 11. Frankfurt: Suhrkamp, 1991.

Kasch, Wilhelm F. "Geld und Glaube. Problemaufriß einer defizitären Beziehung." In *Geld und Glaube*. W. Kasch, ed. Paderborn: Schöningh, 1979.

Kaspers, Wolfgang. "The Liberal Idea and Populist Statism in Economic Policy: A Personal Perspective." In *Do Ideas Matter? Essays in Honour of Gerard Radnitzky.* Hardy Bouillon, ed. Brussels: Centre for the New Europe, 2001.

Kemmerer, Donald L., and C. Clyde Jones. *American Economic History.* New York: McGraw-Hill, 1959.

Kershner, Howard. *God, Gold, and Government.* Englewood Cliffs, N.J.: Prentice-Hall, 1957.

Kimball, James. "The Gold Standard in Contemporary Economic Principles Textbooks: A Survey." *Quarterly Journal of Austrian Economics* 8, no. 3 (2005).

Kinsella, Stephan. "Punishment and Proportionality: The Estoppel Approach." *Journal of Libertarian Studies* 12, no. 1 (1996).

———. "A Libertarian Theory of Contract." *Journal of Libertarian Studies* 17, no. 2 (2003).

Kirshner, Julius. "Raymond de Roover on Scholastic Economic Thought." Introduction to R. de Roover, *Business, Banking, and Economic Thought in Late Medieval and Early Modern Europe.* Chicago: University of Chicago Press, 1974.

Kuznetsov, Yuri. "Fiat Money as an Administrative Good." *Review of Austrian Economics* 10, no. 2 (1997).

Langholm, Odd. *Economics in the Medieval Schools: Wealth, Exchange, Value, Money and Usury According to the Paris Theological Tradition, 1200–1350.* Leiden: Brill, 1992.

Lapidus, André. "Une introduction à la pensée économique médiévale." In *Nouvelle histoire de la pensée économique* 1. A. Béraud and G. Faccarello, eds. Paris: La Découverte, 1992.

———. "Metal, Money, and the Prince: John Buridan and Nicholas Oresme after Thomas Aquinas." *History of Political Economy* 29 (1997).

Law, John. *Money and Trade Considered etc.* Edinburgh: Anderson, 1705.

Leconte, Pierre. *La tragédie monétaire.* 2nd ed. Paris: François-Xavier de Guibert, 2003.

Locke, John. "Some Considerations of the Consequences of the Lowering of Interest and Raising the Value of Money" (1691). In P.H. Kelly, ed. *Locke on Money.* Oxford: Clarendon Press, 1991).

Long, Stephen D. "Bernard Dempsey's Theological Economics: Usury, Profit, and Human Fulfillment." *Theological Studies* 12, no. 1 (1996).

———. *Divine Economy: Theology and the Market.* London: Routledge, 2000.

Lottieri, Carlo. *Denaro e comunità.* Naples: Alfredo Guida, 2000.

Luschin von Ebengreuth, Arnold. *Allgemeine Münzkunde und Geldgeschichte*. Reprint of the 2nd ed. Darmstadt: Wissenschaftliche Buchgesellschaft, [1926] 1976.

Machlup, Fritz. *Die Goldkernwährung*. Halberstadt: Meyer, 1925.

Mäkeler, Hendrik. "Nicolas Oresme und Gabriel Biel: Zur Geldtheorie im späten Mittelalter." *Scripta Mercaturae* 37, no. 1 (2003).

Mariana, Juan de. (1609) "A Treatise on the Alteration of Money." *Journal of Markets and Morality* 5, no. 2 (2002).

Menger, Carl. *Grundsätze der Volkswirtschaftslehre*. Vienna: Braumüller, 1871.

————. *Untersuchungen über die Methode der Socialwissenschaften und der politischen Oekonomie insbesondere*. Leipzig: Duncker & Humblot, 1883.

————. "Geld." *Handwörterbuch der Staatswissenschaften* 4 (1909). Reprinted in Carl Menger, *Gesammelte Werke*. Vol. 4. 2nd ed., Tübingen: Mohr, 1970.

Messner, Johannes. *Das Naturrecht*. 6th ed. Innsbruck: Tyrolia, 1966.

Meyer, Matthias. *Kirchen und soziale Marktwirtschaft—eine ordnungspolitische Perspektive*. Berlin: Stiftung Marktwirtschaft, 2003.

Mises, Ludwig von. *Theorie des Geldes und der Umlaufsmittel*. Leipzig: Duncker & Humblot, 1912; trans. *The Theory of Money and Credit*. Indianapolis: Liberty Fund, 1980.

————. *Geldwertstabilisierung und Konjunkturpolitik*. Jena: Fischer, 1928.

————. *Socialism*. Indianapolis: Liberty Fund, 1981.

————. *Nationalökonomie*. Geneva: Union, 1940.

————. *Human Action*. Scholar's edition, Auburn, Ala.: Ludwig von Mises Institute, 1998.

Mishkin, Frederic S. *The Economics of Money, Banking, and Financial Markets*. 7th ed. New York: Addison Wesley, 2003.

Montesquieu, Charles de. *De l'esprit des lois*. Paris: Gallimard/Pléiade, 1951.

Mote, Frederick W. *Imperial China: 900–1800*. Cambridge, Mass.: Harvard University Press, 2000.

Nederman, C.J. "Community and the Rise of Commercial Society: Political Economy and Political Theory in Nicholas Oresme's De Moneta." *History of Political Thought* 21, no. 1 (2000).

Nell-Breuning, Oswald von. "Geldwesen und Währung im Streit der Zeit." *Stimmen der Zeit* 63, no. 10. (July 1933).

————. *Reorganization of Social Economy: The Social Encyclical Developed and Explained*. Milwaukee: Bruce, 1936.

————. "Geld." *Lexikon für Theologie und Kirche.* Vol. 4. 2nd ed. Freiburg: Herder, 1960.

Nell-Breuning, Oswald von, and J. Heinz Müller. *Vom Geld und vom Kapital.* Freiburg: Herder, 1962.

Nocken, Ulrich. "Die Große Deflation: Goldstandard, Geldmenge und Preise in den USA und Deutschland 1870–1896." In *Geld und Währung vom 16. Jahrhundert bis zur Gegenwart.* A. Béraud and G. Faccarello, eds. Stuttgart: Franz Steiner, 1993.

Noonan, John T. *The Scholastic Analysis of Usury.* Cambridge, Mass.: Harvard University Press, 1957.

North, Gary. *Honest Money.* Ft. Worth, Texas: Dominion Press, 1986.

————. *An Introduction to Christian Economics.* Dallas, Texas: The Craig Press, 1973.

Novak, Michael. *Catholic Ethics and the Spirit of Capitalism.* New York: Simon & Schuster, 1982.

————. *Spirit of Democratic Capitalism.* New York: Simon & Schuster, 1982.

Olszak, Norbert. *Histoire des banques centrales.* Paris: Presses Universitaires de France, 1998.

Oresme, Nicholas. "Treatise on the Origin, Nature, Law, and Alterations of Money." In *The De Moneta of Nicholas Oresme and English Mint Documents.* Charles Johnson, ed. London: Thomas Nelson and Sons, 1956.

Ottavj, Christian. *Monnaie et financement de l'économie.* 2nd ed. Paris: Hachette, 1999.

Parker, Geoffrey. "Die Entstehung des modernen Geld- und Finanzwesens in Europa 1500–1730." In C.M. Cipolla and K. Borchardt, eds. *Europäische Wirtschaftsgeschichte.* Vol. 2, *Sechzehntes und siebzehntes Jahrhundert.* Stuttgart: Gustav Fischer, 1983.

Passage, H. du. "Usure." *Dictionnaire de Théologie Catholique* 15. Paris: Letouzey et Ane, 1909–1950.

Perrot, Étienne. *Le chrétien et l'argent—Entre Dieu et Mammon.* Paris: Assas éditions/Cahiers pour croire aujourd'hui. Supplement no. 13 (1994).

Pesch, Heinrich. *Lehrbuch der Nationalökonomie* 5. Freiburg i.Br.: Herder, 1923.

Plato. *The Laws.*

Poughon, Jean-Michel. "Les fondements juridiques de l'économie politique." *Journal des Économistes et des Études Humaines* 1, no. 4 (1990).

Ptolemy of Lucca. *On the Government of Rulers*. Philadelphia: University of Pennsylvania Press, 1997.

Quillet, Jeanne, ed. *Autour de Nicole Oresme. Actes du Colloque Oresme organisé à l'Université de Paris 12*. Paris: Bibliothèque de l'histoire de la philosophie, 1990.

Rau, Karl Heinrich. *Grundsätze der Volkswirtschaftslehre*. 7th ed. Leipzig & Heidelberg: 1863.

Redish, Angela. *Bimetallism—An Economic and Historical Analysis*. Cambridge: Cambridge University Press, 2000.

Reisman, George. *Capitalism*. Ottawa, Ill.: Jameson Books, 1996.

Ricardo, David. "Proposals for an Economical and Secure Currency." *Works and Correspondence*. Piero Sraffa, ed. Vol. 4. Cambridge: Cambridge University Press, 1951–73.

———. *Principles of Political Economy and Taxation*. London: Penguin, 1980.

Rittmann, Herbert. *Deutsche Geldgeschichte seit 1914*. Munich: Klinkhardt & Biermann, 1986.

Roover, Raymond de. *Business, Banking, and Economic Thought in Late Medieval and Early Modern Europe*. Chicago: University of Chicago Press, 1974.

Rose, Tom. *God, Gold, and Civil Government*. Mercer, Penn.: American Enterprise Publications, 2002.

Rothbard, Murray N. "New Light on the Prehistory of the Austrian School." In *The Foundations of Modern Austrian Economics*. Edwin G. Dolan, ed. Kansas City: Sheed & Ward, 1976.

———. *What Has Government Done to Our Money?* 4th ed. Auburn, Ala.: Ludwig von Mises Institute, 1990.

———. *The Mystery of Banking*. New York: Richardson & Snyder, 1983.

———. *Man, Economy, and State*. 3rd ed. Auburn, Ala.: Ludwig von Mises Institute, 1993.

———. *The Case against the Fed*. Auburn, Ala.: Ludwig von Mises Institute, 1994.

———. *Economic Science before Adam Smith*. Cheltenham, U.K.: Edward Elgar, 1995.

———. *The Ethics of Liberty*. 2nd ed. New York: New York University Press, 1998.

———. "The Gold-Exchange Standard in the Interwar Years." In *Money and the Nation State*. Kevin Dowd and Richard H. Timberlake, eds. New Brunswick, N.J.: Transaction, 1998.

———. *America's Great Depression*. 5th ed. Auburn, Ala.: Ludwig von Mises Institute, 2000.

———. *A History of Money and Banking in the United States*. Auburn, Ala.: Ludwig von Mises Institute, 2002.

Rueff, Jacques. *The Monetary Sin of the West*. New York: Macmillan, 1972.

Rugina, Angel. *Geldtypen und Geldordnungen*. Stuttgart: Kohlhammer 1949.

Rushdoony, Rousas John. *The Institutes of Biblical Law*. New York: The Craig Press, 1973.

———. *The Roots of Inflation*. Vallecito, Calif.: Ross House Books, 1982.

———. "Hard Money and Society in the Bible." In *Gold Is Money*. Hans Sennholz, ed. Westport, Conn.: Greenwood, 1975.

Salin, Pascal. *La vérité sur la monnaie*. Paris: Odile Jacob, 1990.

———. *La concurrence*. Paris: Presses Universitaires de France, 1991.

Salins, Antoine de, and François Villeroy de Galhau. *Le développement moderne des activités financiers au regard des exigencies éthiques du Christianisme*. Vatican: Libreria Editrice Vaticana, 1994.

Sargent, T.J., and F.R. Velde. *The Big Problem of Small Change*. Princeton, N.J.: Princeton University Press, 2002.

Say, Jean-Baptiste. *Traité d'économie politique*. 6th ed. Paris: Guillaumin, 1841.

Schefold, Bertram, ed. *Vademecum zu einem Klassiker der mittelalterlichen Geldlehre*. Düsseldorf: Wirtschaft & Finanzen, 1995.

Schneider, Jakob Hans Josef. "Oresme, Nicolas." *Biographisch-Bibliographisches Kirchenlexikon*. Vol. 6. Nordhausen: Bautz, 1993.

Schumpeter, Joseph A. *A History of Economic Analysis*. New York: Oxford University Press, 1954.

———. *Capitalism, Socialism, and Democracy*. London: Allen & Unwin, 1944.

———. *Theorie der wirtschaftlichen Entwicklung*. 4th ed. Berlin: Duncker & Humblot, [1934] 1993.

Selgin, George. "On Ensuring the Acceptability of a New Fiat Money." *Journal of Money, Credit, and Banking* 26 (1994).

———. *Less Than Zero*. London: IEA, 1997.

Selgin, George, and Lawrence White. "How Would the Invisible Hand Handle Money?" *Journal of Economic Literature* 32, no. 4 (1994).

———. "A Fiscal Theory of Government's Role in Money." *Economic Inquiry* 37 (1999).

Sennholz, Hans, ed. *Gold Is Money*. Westport, Conn.: Greenwood Press, 1975.

———. *Age of Inflation*. Belmont, Mass.: Western Islands, 1979.

———. *Money and Freedom*. Spring Mills, Penn.: Libertarian Press, 1985.

———, ed. *The Lustre of Gold*. Irvington-on-Hudson, N.Y.: Foundation for Economic Education, 1995.

Skousen, Mark. *Economics of a Pure Gold Standard*. 3rd ed. Irvington-on-Hudson, N.Y.: Foundation for Economic Education, 1996.

Smith, Adam. *The Wealth of Nations*. New York: Modern Library, [1776] 1994.

Smith, Vera C. *The Rationale of Central Banking and the Free Banking Alternative*. Indianapolis: Liberty Fund, 1990.

Souffrin, Pierre, and Alain P. Segonds, eds. *Nicolas Oresme. Tradition et innovation chez un intellectuel du XIVe siècle*. Paris: Belles Lettres, 1988.

Sprenger, Bernd. *Das Geld der Deutschen*. 2nd ed. Paderborn: Schöningh, 1995.

Steuart, James. *An Inquiry Into the Principles of Political Economy*. London: Millar & Cadell, 1767.

Strohm, Christoph. "Götze oder Gabe Gottes? Bemerkungen zum Thema 'Geld' in der Kirchengeschichte." *Glaube und Lernen* 14 (1999).

Suhle, Arthur. *Deutsche Münz- und Geldgeschichte von den Anfängen bis zum 15. Jahrhundert*. 8th ed. Berlin: Deutscher Verlag der Wissenschaften, 1975.

Sumner, William G. *History of Banking in the United States*. New York: Augustus M. Kelley, [1896] 1971.

Tocqueville, Alexis de. *L'Ancien régime et la Révolution*. Paris: Michel Lévy frères, 1856.

Tortajada, Ramon. "La renaissance de la scolastique, la Réforme et les théories du droit naturel." In *Nouvelle histoire de la pensée économique* 1. A. Béraud and G. Faccarello, eds. Paris: La Découverte, 1992.

Vaubel, Roland. "The Political Economy of the International Monetary Fund." In *The Political Economy of International Organizations: A Public Choice Approach*. A. Béraud and G. Faccarello, eds. Boulder, Colo.: Westview Press, 1991.

Vermeersh, A. "Interest." *Catholic Encyclopedia* 8 (1910).

———. "Usury." *Catholic Encyclopedia* 15 (1912).

Viner, Jacob. "Religious Thought and Economic Society." *History of Political Economy* 10, no. 1 (Spring 1978).

Virgil, Michel, ed. *The Social Problem.* Vol. 2, *Economics and Finance.* Collegeville, Minn.: St John's Abbey, n.d.

Wagner, Adolf. *Die russische Papierwährung—eine volkswirtschaftliche und finanzpolitische Studie nebst Vorschlägen zur Herstellung der Valuta.* Riga: Kymmel, 1868.

Walters, Alan. *Do We Need the IMF and the World Bank?* London: Institute of Economic Affairs, 1994.

Weber, Wilhelm. *Geld und Zins in der spanischen Spätscholastik.* Münster: Aschendorff, 1962.

Wheatley, John. *The Theory of Money and Principles of Commerce.* London: Bulmer, 1807.

White, Lawrence H. *The Theory of Monetary Institutions.* Oxford: Blackwell, 1999.

———. "The Federal Reserve System's Influence on Research in Monetary Economics." *Econ Journal Watch* 2, no. 2 (2005).

Williams, Jonathan et al. *Money: A History.* London: Palgrave Macmillan, 1998.

Wilson, Rodney. *Economics, Ethics, and Religion.* New York: New York University Press, 1997.

Wittreck, Fabian. *Geld als Instrument der Gerechtigkeit. Die Geldrechtslehre des Hl. Thomas von Aquin in ihrem interkulturellen Kontext.* Paderborn: Schöningh, 2002.

Woods, Thomas. "Money and Morality: The Christian Moral Tradition and the Best Monetary Regime." *Religion & Liberty* 13, no. 5 (September/October 2003).

———. *The Church and the Market.* Lanham, Md.: Lexington Books, 2005.

Yeager, Leland B. *International Monetary Relations.* New York: Harper & Row, 1966.

———. "From Gold to the Ecu: The International Monetary System in Retrospect." In *Money and the Nation State.* Kevin Dowd and Richard H. Timberlake, eds. New Brunswick, N.J.: Transaction, 1998).

———. *Ethics as Social Science: The Moral Philosophy of Social Cooperation.* Cheltenham, U.K.: Edward Elgar, 2001.

Zube, John. *Stop the Legal Tender Crime.* Berrima, Australia: Research Centre for Monetary and Financial Freedom, n.d.

HOLY SCRIPTURE

New American Bible. Washington, D.C.: United States Conference of Catholic Bishops, 2003.

CATHOLIC CHURCH DOCUMENTS

Lagasse, Paul, et al. eds. *Columbia Encyclopedia Britannica.* 6th ed. Gale Group, 2003.

Pontifical Council for Justice and Peace, *Compendium of the Social Doctrine of the Church.* Vatican: Libreria Editrice Vaticana, 2004.

Pope John Paul II. *Veritatis Splendor* (1993).

Pope John Paul II. *Centesimus Annus* (1991).

Pope John Paul II. *Sollicitudo Rei Socialis* (1988).

Pope Paul VI. *Populorum Progression* (1967).

Second Vatican Council. *Gaudium et Spes* (1965).

Pope John XXIII. *Mater et Magistra* (1961).

Pope Pius XI. *Quadragesimo Anno* (1931).

Pope Leo XIII. *Rerum Novarum* (1891).

Pope Leo XIII. *Arcanum Divinae* (1880).

Pope Innocent III. "Quanto." *Decretalium Gregorij Papae Noni Compilatio,* Liber II, Titulus XXIII, Caput XVIII, col. 809–10 [1199].

Index of Names

Africa in Chaos (Ayittey), 221n16
"Against Fiduciary Media" (Hoppe, Hülsmann, Block), 11n17
Age of Inflation (Sennholz), 10n16, 240n5
Allgemeine Münzkunde und Geldgeschichte (Ebengreuth), 120n3
American Economic History (Kemmerer and Jones), 203n6, 205n7
America's Great Depression (Rothbard), 66n15
Anatomy of an International Monetary Regime: The Classical Gold Standard, 1880–1914, The (Gallarotti), 143n17, 212n6
Anderson, Benjamin
   The Value of Money, 32n16
Aquinas, Thomas, x, 8n12, 25n6, 74–75
   Commentary on the Nicomachean Ethics, 75n23
   On Kingship, To the King of Cyprus, 73n20
Aristophane
   "The Frogs," 127n2
Aristotle, 49, 56, 75, 100, 179
   Nicomachean Ethics, 75n24
   Politics, 24n2, 35n1, 49n4, 51n8, 100n14
Atkeson, A.
   "Deflation and Depression: Is There an Empirical Link?," 66n16
Autour de Nicole Oresme, Actes du Colloque Oresme organisé à l'Universuté de Paris XII, 7n11
Ayittey, George
   Africa in Chaos, 221n16

Azpilcueta, Martín
   "Commentary on the Resolution of Money," 47n3

Baader, Roland
   Geld, Gold und Gottspieler, 16n26
Bank of England, The: A History 1694–1914 (Clapham), 199n2
Banks and Politics in America (Hammond), 203n6
Baptized Inflation (Hodge), 16n26
Barzahlung und Zahlungsmittelversorgung in militärisch besetzten Gebieten (Holzbauer), 32n17
Bastiat, Frédéric
   Harmonis économiques, 24n3
   "Maudit Argent," 24n3
Belloc, Hilaire, 15n24
Bernanke, Ben
   "Deflation: Making Sure 'It' Doesn't Happen Here," 165n8
   "Bernard Dempsey's Theological Economics: Usury, Profit, and Human Fulfillment" (Long), 13n21
Bernholz, Peter
   Monetary Regimes and Inflation, 90n1, 166n9
Beutter, Friedrich, 13
   "Geld im Verständnis der christlichen Soziallehre," 87n2
   Zur sittlichen Beurteilung von Inflationen, 14n22, 162n3
Big Problem of Small Change, The (Sargent and Velde), 3n4
Bimetallism—An Economic and Historical Analysis (Redish), 3n4

257

Blessing, Karl
"Geldwerstabilität als gesellschaftspolitisches Problem," 75–76n26
Block, Walter
"Against Fiduciary Media," 11n17
"Fractional Reserve Banking: An Interdisciplinary Perspective," *Man, Economy, and Liberty*, 11n17
Bodin, Jean
Les six livres de la République, 119n3
Böhm-Bawerk, Eugen von
Capital and Interest, 52n10
Borchardt, K.
Europäische Wirtschaftsgeschichte, 74n21
Borchert, Manfred
Geld und Kredit, 105n3
Bordo, Michael D.
"Is Deflation Depressing? Evidence from the Classical Gold Standard," 66n16
Brants, Victor
L'économie politique au Moyen-Age: esquisse des théories économiques professées par les écrivains des XIIIe et XIVe siècles, 8n13, 53n10
Braudel, F.P.
"Prices in Europe from 1450 to 1750," 74n21
Bridrey, Émile
La théorie de la monnaie au XIVe siècle, Nicolas Oresme, 7n11
Buridan, John
"Extrait des 'Questians sur la Politique d' Aristote'," 111n3
Burns, Arthur
Money and Monetary Policy in Early Times, 36n3
Business, Banking, and Economic Thought in Late Medieval and Early Modern Europe (Roover), 12n18, 52n10, 122n7

Cantillon, Richard
La nature du commerce en général, 9n15, 45n1
Cantor, Paul
"Hyperinflation and Hyperreality: Thomas Mann in Light of Austrian Economics," 188n9
Capital and Interest (Böhm-Bawerk), 52n10
Capitalism (Reisman), 11n17
Capitalism, Socialism and Democracy (Schumpeter), 68n18
Carrier, Hervé
Nouveau regard sur la doctrine sociale do l'église, 4n7
"Case against Currency Boards, The" (Gertchev), 227n3
Case Against the Fed, The (Rothbard), 10n16, 240n5
Centesimus Annus (John Paul II), 2n2, 26n8, 76n26, 122n5, 190n11, 221n17, 238n2
Century of Bank Rate, A (Hawtrey), 143n17
Chafuen, Alejandro
Faith and Liberty: The Economic Thought of the Late Scholastics, 11n18, 113n6
Chown, John E.
A History of Money, 30n11
Church and the Market, The (Woods), 14, 15n24, 85n1, 162n3
Cipolla, C.M.
Europäische Wirtschaftsgeschichte, 74n21
Clapham, John H.
The Bank of England: A History 1694–1914, 199n2
Columbia Encyclopedia Britannica, 58n5
Commentary on the Nicomachean Ethics, 75n23
"Commentary on the Resolution of Money" (Azpilcueta), 47n3
"Community and the Rise of Commerical Society: Political Economy and Political Theory in Nicholas

Oresme's De Moneta" (Nederman), 8n11

Compendium of the Social Doctrine of the Church, 2n3, 26n7

Condillac, Étienne
Le commerce et le gouvernement, 9n15, 122n6

Connolly, Bernard
The Return Heart of Europe, 229n5

Copernicus, Nicholas
"Traité de la monnaie," 36n2

Coughlin, Charles
Money! Questions and Answers, 15n24

Creating New Money (Huber and Robertson), 15n24

Das Geld der Deutschen (Sprenger), 202n4, 209n1

Das Schein-Geld-System (Rothbard), 227n4

Das Zeitalter der Fugger: Geldkapital und Creditverkehr im 16. Jahrhundert (Ehrenberg), 93n6

d'Azeglio, Luigi Taparelli
Saggio teoretico di diritto naturale appoggiato sul fatto, 6n8

De l'esprit des lois (Montesquieu), 30n12

De Moneta of Nicholas Oresme and English Mint Documents, The, 4n6, 38n4, 46n2, 56n2, 99n12, 104n2, 111n2, 121n4, 127n2

Deflation—2002 Annual Report (Federal Reserve Bank of Cleveland), 65n14

"Deflation and Depression: Is There an Empirical Link?" (Atkeson and Kehoe), 66n16

Deflation: Current and Historical Perspectives, 65n14

"Deflation: Making Sure 'It' Doesn't Happen Here" (Bernanke), 165n8

Democracy—The God That Failed (Hoppe), 24n4, 176n1

Dempsey, Bernard
Interest and Usury, 13, 53n10, 53n11, 184n6

Der sinn der Indexahlen (Haberler), 77n29

Deutsche Geldgeschichte seit 1914 (Rittmann), 209n1

"Die Entstehung des modernen Geld—und Finanzwesens in Europa 1500–1730" (Parker), 74n21, 93n6

Die Golkernwährung (Machlup), 10n16

"Die Große Deflation: Goldstandard, Geldmenge und Preise in den USA und Deutschland 1870-1896" (Nocken), 62n11

Die russische Papierwährung (Wagner), 31n13, 80n33

Divine Economy: Theology and the Market (Long), 13n21

Do Ideas Matter? Essays in Honour of Gerard Radnitzky, 17n27

Do We need the IMF and the World Bank? (Walters), 220n15

Dowd, Kevin
"The Emergence of Fiat Money: A Reconsideration," 30n11

Drinkwater, Francis
Money and Social Justice, 15n24

Du pouvoir (Jouvenel), 176n1

Ebengreuth, Arnold Luschin von
Allgemeine Münzkunde und Geldgeschichte, 120n3

Economic Thought Before Adam Smith: An Austrian Perspective on the History of Economic Thought (Rothbard), x, 11n18, 53n10

Economic Thought in Spain (Grice-Hutchinson), 75n25

Economics and Ethics of Private Property, The (Hoppe), 11n17, 24n4

Economics in the Medieval Schools: Wealth, Exchange, Value, Money and Usury According to the Paris Theological Tradition, 1200–1350 (Langholm), 8n12

Economics of a Pure Gold Standard (Skousen), 11n17

Economics of Money, Banking and Financial Markets, The (Mishkin), 105n3

Ederer, Rupert J.
  The Evolution of Money, 29n9

Ehrenberg, Richard
  Das Zeitalter der Fugger: Geldkapital und Creditverkehr im 16. Jahrhundert, 93n6

Eichengreen, Barry
  Globalizing Capital, 210n3, 213n7, 215n10, 217n13

"Emergence of Fiat Money: A Reconsideration, The" (Dowd), 30n11

Essays (Hume), 9n15

"Ethical Challenges in a Market Economy" (Guynn), 1n1

Ethics as Social Science: The Moral Philosophy of Social Cooperation (Yeager), 4n7

Ethics of Liberty, The (Rothbard), 24n4

Europäische Wirtschaftsgeschichte (Cipolla and Borchardt), 74n21

Evolution of Money, The (Ederer), 29n9

"Extrait des 'Questians sur la Politique d' Aristote'" (Buridan), 111n3

15 Great Austrian Economists, 11n18

Fahey, Dennis
  Money Manipulation and Social Order, 7n10, 15n24

Faith and Liberty: The Economic Thought of the Late Scholastics (Chafuen), 11n18, 113n6

Faust (Goethe), 191n12

Federal Reserve Bank of Cleveland
  Deflation—2002 Annual Report, 65n14

"Federal Reserve System's Influence on Research in Monetary Economics, The" (White), 17n27

Fetter, Frank
  The Principles of Economics, 139n14

"Fiat Money as an Administrative Good" (Kuznetsov), 32n17

Fink, Carole
  The Genoa Conference: European Diplomacy, 1921–1922, 215n11

"Fiscal Theory of Government's Role in Money, A" (Selgin and White), 103n1

Fisher, Irving, 78n30
  Stabilized Money: A History of the Movement, 76n28

Foundations of Modern Austrian Economics, The, 11n18

"Fractional Reserve Banking: An Interdisciplinary Perspective" (Block), 11n17

Fratianni, M.
  A Monetary History of Italy, 145n22

Free Choice in Currency (Hayek), 10n16

Friedman, Milton, 17n27
  A Monetary History of the United States (with Schwartz), 62n11
  "The Resource Cost of Irredeemable Paper Money," 80n34

"Frogs, The" (Aristophane), 127n2

From Bretton Woods to World Inflation (Hazlitt), 216–17n13

"From Gold to the Ecu: The International Monetary System in Retrospect" (Yeager), 217n13

Frowen, Stephen F.
  "The Functions of Money and Financial Credit: Their Objectives, Structure and Inbuilt Deficiencies," 234n8

Funk and Wagnalls Standard College Dictionary, 85n1

Gaettens, Richard
  Inflationen: Das Drama der Geldentwertungen vom Altertum bis zur Gegenwart, 90n1, 136n11

Galhau, F. Villeroy de
  Le développement moderne des activités financiers au regard des exigencies éthiques du Christianisme, 181n4
Gallarotti, Giulio
  The Anatomy of an International Monetary Regime: The Classical Gold Standard, 1880–1914, 143n17, 212n6
Garrison, Roger W.
  "The Costs of a Gold Standard," 80n34
"Geld" (Menger), 10n16
"Geld" (Nell-Breuning), 22n1
Geld, Gold und Gottspieler (Baader), 16n26
Geld als Instrument der Gerechtigkeit. Die Geldrechtslehre des Hl. Thomas von Aquin in ihrem interkulturellen Kontext (Wittreck), 8n12
"Geld im Verständnis der christlichen Soziallehre" (Beutter), 87n2
"Geld und Glaube. Problemaufriß einer defizitären Beziehung" (Kasch), 13n20
Geld und Kredit (Borchert), 105n3
Geld und Zins in der spanischen Spätscholastik (Weber), 12n18
"Geldwerstabilität als gesellschaftspolitisches Problem" (Blessing), 75–76n26
Geldwertstabilisierung und Konjunkturpolitik (Mises), 78n31
"Geldwesen und Währung im Streite der Zeit" (Nell-Breuning), 40n7
Geltypen und Geldordnungen (Rugina), 24n3
Genoa Conference: European Diplomacy, 1921–1922, The (Fink), 215n11
Gertchev, Nikolay, 65n14
  "The Case against Currency Boards," 227n3
Gide, Charles
  Histoire des doctrines économiques, 177n2

Gillard, Lucien
  "Nicole Oresme, économiste," 7n11
Globalizing Capital (Eichengreen), 210n3, 213n7, 215n10, 217n13
God, Gold, and Civil Government (Rose), 16n26
God, Gold, and Government (Kershner), 16n26
Goethe
  Faust, 191n12
Gold is Money, 3n5
Gold Standard, The, 80n34
"Gold Standard in Contemporary Economic Prinicples Textbooks, The: A Survey," (Kimball), 59n8
"Gold-Exchange Standard in the Interwar Years, The" (Rothbard), 214n8, 215n11
"Götze oder Gabe Gottes? Bemerkungen zum Thema 'Geld' in der Kirchengeschichte" (Strohm), 49n4
Gouge, William
  A Short History of Paper Money and Banking in the United States to which is prefixed an Inquiry into the Principles of the System, 10n15, 24n3, 30n12, 80n34, 186n8, 203n6
  Government of Rulers, On the (Ptolemy of Lucca), 73n20, 99n13
Gresham, Thomas, 127n2
Grice-Hutchinson, Marjorie
  Economic Thought in Spain, 75n25
  The School of Salamanca, 12n18
Groseclose, Elgin
  Money and Man: A Survey of Monetary Experience, 29n9
Grundsätze der Volkswirtschaftslehre (Menger), 10n16, 24n2
Grundsätze der Volkswirtschaftslehre (Rau), 161n2
Guynn, Jack
  "Ethical Challenges in a Market Economy," 1n1

Haberler, Gottfired von
  Der sinn der Indexahlen, 77n29
Habiger, Matthew
  *Papal Teaching on Private Prop-
  erty, 1892 to 1991*, 6n8, 26n7
Hammond, Bray
  Banks and Politics in America,
  203n6
*Handbuch der Wirtschafts- und
  Sozialgeschichte Deutschlands* (Hen-
  ning), 74n22
"Hard Money and Society in the
  Bible" (Rushdoony), 3n5
Harmonis économiques (Bastiat), 24n3
"Has Fractional-Reserve Banking
  Really Passed the Market Test?"
  (Hülsmann), 96n9
Hawtrey, Ralph
  A Century of Bank Rate, 143n17
Hayek, F.A.
  Free Choice in Currency, 10n16
  *Monetary Nationalism and Inter-
  national Stability*, 10n16
Hazlitt, Henry
  *From Bretton Woods to World
  Inflation*, 216–217n13
  *The Inflation Crisis and How to
  Resolve It*, 10n16
Henning, Friedrich-Wilhelm
  *Handbuch der Wirtschafts- und
  Sozialgeschichte Deutschlands*,
  74n22
Hepburn, Barton
  *History of Coinage and Currency
  in the United States and the
  Perennial Contest for Sound
  Money*, 203n6
Herbener, Professor Jeffrey, 163n5
Histoire des banques centrales
  (Olszak), 95n7, 199n1
Histoire des doctrines économiques
  (Gide and Rist), 177n2
*History of Banking in the United
  States* (Sumner), 31n13, 203n6
*History of Coinage and Currency in
  the United States and the Perennial
  Contest for Sound Money* (Hep-
  burn), 203n6

History of Economic Analysis
  (Schumpeter), x
*History of Money and Banking in the
  United States, A* (Rothbard),
  144n21, 203n6, 213n7
History of Money, A (Chown), 30n11
Hodge, Ian
  Baptized Inflation, 16n26
Höffner, Josef
  Christliche Gesellschaftlehre,
  122n7
Holzbauer, Georg
  *Barzahlung und Zahlungsmit-
  telversorgung in militärisch
  besetzten Gebieten*, 32n17
Honest Money (North), 15–16, 122n8,
  161–62n3, 240n5
Hoppe, Hans-Hermann
  "Against Fiduciary Media,"
  11n17
  Democracy—The God That Failed,
  24n4, 176n1
  *Economics and Ethics of Private
  Property, The*, 11n17, 24n4
  "How Is Fiat Money Possible?
  —or, The Devolution of Money
  and Credit," 11n17
  *Theory of Socialism and Capital-
  ism, A*, 24n4
"How Is Fiat Money Possible?—or,
  The Devolution of Money and
  Credit" (Hoppe), 11n17
"How Would the Invisible Hand
  Handle Money?" (Selgin and
  White), 104n1
Huber, Joseph
  Creating New Money, 15n24
Huerta de Soto, Jesús, 105n3
  "Juan de Mariana: The Influence
  of the Spanish Scholastics,"
  15 Great Austrian Economists,
  11n18
  *Money, Bank Credit, and Eco-
  nomic Cycles*, 11n17, 53n10,
  70n19, 92n5, 104n1, 144n20,
  240n5
  "New Light on the Prehistory
  of the Theory of Banking and

the School of Salamanca,"
9n14, 11n18, 96n10
Hulme, Anthony
  Morals and Money, 7n10, 14n23,
  92n5, 140n15
Hülsmann, Jörg Guido
  "Against Fiduciary Media,"
  11n17
  "Has Fractional-Reserve Bank-
  ing Really Passed the Market
  Test?," 96n9
  Logik der Währungskonkurrenz,
  11n17, 32n15
  "Political Economy of Moral
  Hazard, The," 144n18
  "Pourquoi le FMI nuit-il aux
  Africains?," 220n15
  "Schöne neue Zeichengeld-
  welt," 227n4
  "Toward a General Theory of
  Error Cycles," 169n10
Human Action (Mises), 10n16, 22n1,
  24n4, 59n7, 70n19, 78n31
Hume, David
  Essays, 9n15
Humphrey, Thomas
  "John Wheatley's Theory of
  International Monetary
  Adjustment," 58n5
"Hyperinflation and Hyperreality:
  Thomas Mann in Light of Aus-
  trian Economics" (Cantor), 188n9

*Inflation Crisis and How to Resolve It,
  The* (Hazlitt), 10n16
*Inflationen: Das Drama der Gelden-
  twertungen vom Altertum bis zur
  Gegenwart* (Gaettens), 90n1,
  136n11
Innocent III
  Quanto, 4, 72–73n20
*Inquiry Into the Principles of Political
  Economy, An* (Steuart), 30n12
Institutes of Biblical Law (Rush-
  doony), 16n26
"Interest" (Vermeersh), 53n10
Interest and Usury (Dempsey), 13,
  53n10, 53n11, 184n6

International Monetary Relations
  (Yeager), 210n3, 213n7, 214n8
"Is Deflation Depressing? Evidence
  from the Classical Gold Standard"
  (Bordo and Redish), 66n16

Jackson, Andrew, 205, 242
John Paul II, 26n7
  Centesimus Annus, 2n2, 26n8,
  76n26, 122n5, 190n11, 221n17,
  238n2
  Sollicitudo Rei Socialis, 221n17
  Veritatis splendor, 100n15
"John Wheatley's Theory of Inter-
  national Monetary Adjustment"
  (Humphrey), 58n5
John XXIII, 25n5
  Mater et Magistra, 2n3, 76n27
Jones, Clyde
  American Economic History,
  203n6, 205n7
Jouvenel, Betrand de
  Du pouvoir, 176n1
"Juan de Mariana: The Influence of
  the Spanish Scholastics," (Huerta
  de Soto), 11n18

Kant, Immanuel
  "Zum Ewigen Frieden—ein
  philosophischer Entwurf,"
  177n3
Kasch, Wilhelm
  "Geld und Glaube. Proble-
  maufriß einer defizitären
  Beziehung," 13n20
Kaspers, Wolfgang
  "The Liberal Idea and Populist
  Statism in Economic Policy: A
  Personal Perspective," *Do
  Ideas Matter? Essays in Honour
  of Gerard Radnitzky,* 17n27
Kehoe, P.J.
  "Deflation and Depression: Is
  There an Empirical Link?,"
  66n16
Kelly, P.H.
  Locke on Money, 57n3

Kemmerer, Donald
  Amerian Economic History,
    203n6, 205n7
Kershner, Howard
  God, Gold, and Government,
    16n26
Keynes, John Maynard, 235
Kimball, James
  "The Gold Standard in Contemporary Economic Prinicples Textbooks: A Survey," 59n8
Kingship, To the King of Cyprus, On (Aquinas), 73n20
Kinsella, Stephan
  "Libertarian Theory of Contract, A," 88n3
  "Punishment and Proportionality: The Estoppel Approach," 157n1
Kirshner, Julius
  "Raymond de Roover on Scholastic Economic Thought," 122n7
  "Raymond de Roover on Scholastic Economic Thought," *Business, Banking, and Economic Thought in Late Medieval and Early Modern Europe,* 12n18
Kuznetsov, Yuri
  "Fiat Money as an Administrative Good," 32n17

L' Ancien régime et la Révolution (Tocqueville), 176n1
La concurrence (Salin), 115n1
La nature du commerce en général (Cantillon), 9n15, 45n1
"La renaissance de la scolastique, la Réforme et les théories du droit naturel," (Tortajada), 12n18
La théorie de la monnaie au XIVe siècle, Nicolas Oresme (Bridrey), 7n11
La tragédie monétaire (Leconte), 240n5
La vérité sur la monnaie (Salin), 11n17, 144n19

Langholm, Odd
  Economics in the Medieval Schools: Wealth, Exchange, Value, Money and Usury According to the Paris Theological Tradition, 1200–1350, 8n12
Lapidus, André
  "Metal, Money, and the Prince: John Buridan and Nicholas Oresme after Thomas Aquinas," 75n25
  "Une introduction à la pensée économique médiévale," 75n25
Law, John, 60n9
  Money and Trade Considered etc., 24n2
Laws, The (Plato), 56n1
Le chrétien et l'argent—Entre Dieu et Mammon (Perrot), 60n9
Le commerce et le gouvernement (Condillac), 9n15, 122n6
Le développement moderne des activités financiers au regard des exigencies éthiques du Christianisme (Salins and Galhau), 181n4
L'économie politique au Moyen-Age: esquisse des théories économiques professées par les écrivains des XIIIe et XIVe siècles (Brants), 8n13, 53n10
Leconte, Pierre
  La tragédie monétaire, 240n5
  "Legal Tender Laws and Fractional-Reserve Banking," 125n1
Lehrbuch der Nationalökonomie (Pesch), 60n9
Leo XIII, 25n5, 25n6
  Rerum Novarum, 26n7, 104n2, 121–22n5
LePlay, Frédéric, 176–77
  "Les fondements juridiques de l'économie politique" (Poughon), 11n18
Les six livres de la République (Bodin), 119n3
Less Than Zero (Selgin), 66n16
Lexicon für Theologie und Kirche, 24n2

"Liberal Idea and Populist Statism in Economic Policy: A Personal Perspective, The" (Kaspers), 17n27

"Libertarian Theory of Contract, A" (Kinsella), 88n3

Lincoln, Abraham, 205

Locke, John, 50n7, 57n3

Locke on Money (Kelly), 57n3

Logik der Währungskonkurrenz (Hülsmann), 11n17, 32n15

Long, Stephen D.
"Bernard Dempsey's Theological Economics: Usury, Profit, and Human Fulfillment," 13n21
Divine Economy: Theology and the Market, 13n21

Lottieri, Carlo
Denaro e comunitá, 24n3

Louis IX (King), 241

Lustre of God, The (Sennholz), 240n5

Machlup, Fritz, 17n27
Die Golkernwährung, 10n16

Mäkeler, Hendrik
"Nicolas Oresme und Gabriel Biel: Zur Geldtheorie im späten Mittelalter," 8n11

Man, Economy, and Liberty (Block and Rockwell), 11n17

Man, Economy, and State (Rothbard), 10n16, 66n15, 70n19, 77n29, 115n1

Mariana, Juan de, 46–47, 50n7, 113n6
"A Treatise on the Alteration of Money," 9n14, 104n2
Markets and Morality, 104n2

Mater et Magistra (John XXIII), 2n3, 76n27

"Maudit Argent" (Bastiat), 24n3

Menger, Carl
"Geld," 10n16
Grundsätze der Volkswirtschaftslehre, 10n16, 24n2
Untersuchungen über die Methode der Socialwissenschaften und der politischen Oekonomie insbesondere, 10n16

Mercado, Tomás de, 113n6

"Metal, Money, and the Prince: John Buridan and Nicholas Oresme after Thomas Aquinas" (Lapidus), 75n25

Mises, Ludwig von, 11, 21, 30n12, 58, 105n3, 179, 186n8
Geldwertstabilisierung und Konjunkturpolitik, 78n31
Human Action, 10n16, 22n1, 24n4, 70n19, 78n31
Nationalökonomie, 22n1
"Observations on the Causes of the Decline of Ancient Civilization," *Human Action*, 59n7
Socialism, 22n1, 26n7, 53n10
Theorie des Geldes und der Umlaufsmittel, 10n16
Theory of Money and Credit, 24n2, 60n9, 78n31, 100n14, 142n16, 160–61n1, 240n5

Mishkin, Frederic S.
The Economics of Money, Banking and Financial Markets, 105n3

Monetary History of Italy, A (Fratianni and Spinelli), 145n22

Monetary History of the Untied States, A (Friedman and Schwartz), 62n11

Monetary Nationalism and International Stability (Hayek), 10n16

Monetary Regimes and Inflation (Bernholz), 90n1, 166n9

Monetary Sin of the West, The (Rueff), 216n13

Money, Bank Credit, and Economic Cycles (Huerta de Soto), 11n17, 53n10, 70n19, 92n5, 104n1, 144n20, 240n5

Money: A History (Williams), 31n14

Money and Freedom (Sennholz), 10n16, 240n5

Money and Man: A Survey of Monetary Experience (Groseclose), 29n9

Money and Monetary Policy in Early Times (Burns), 36n3

"Money and Morality: The Christian Moral Tradition and the Best Monetary Regime" (Woods), 186n8

Money and Social Justice (Drinkwater), 15n24

Money and the Nation State, 214n8, 217n13

Money and Trade Considered etc. (Law), 24n2

Money Manipulation and Social Order (Fahey), 7n10, 15n24

Money! Questions and Answers (Coughlin), 15n24

Monnaie et financement de l' économie (Ottavj), 105n3

Montesquieu, Charles de, 50n7
De l'esprit des lois, 30n12

Morals and Money (Hulme), 7n10, 14n23, 92n5, 140n15

Müller, J. Heinz
Vom Geld und vom Kapital, 15n24, 75n26

Mystery of Banking, The (Rothbard), 10n16, 161n3

Nationalökonomie (Mises), 22n1

Nederman, C.J.
"Community and the Rise of Commerical Society: Political Economy and Political Theory in Nicholas Oresme's De Moneta," 8n11

Nell-Breuning, Oswald von
"Geld," 22n1
"Geldwesen und Währung im Streite der Zeit," 40n7
Reorganization of Social Economy: The Social Encyclical Developed and Explained, 6n8
Vom Geld und vom Kapital, 15n24, 75n26

"New Light on the Prehistory of the Austrian School" (Rothbard), 11n18

"New Light on the Prehistory of the Theory of Banking and the School of Salamanca" (Huerta de Soto), 9n14, 11n18, 96n10

Newton, Isaac, 130

Nichomachean Ethics, 100n14

Nicolas Oresme, Tradition et innovation chez un intellectuel du XIVe siècle, 7n11

"Nicolas Oresme und Gabriel Biel: Zur Geldtheorie im späten Mittelalter" (Mäkeler), 8n11

"Nicole Oresme, économiste" (Gillard), 7n11

Nicomachean Ethics, 75n24

Nixon, Richard, 219

Nocken, Ulrich
"Die Große Deflation: Goldstandard, Geldmenge und Preise in den USA und Deutschland 1870–1896," 62n11

Noonan, John T.
The Scholastic Analysis of Usury, 13n21, 52n10

North, Gary
Honest Money, 15–16, 122n8, 161–62n3, 240n5

Nouveau regard sur la doctrine sociale do l'église (Carrier), 4n7

Nouvelle histoire de la pensée économique, 12n18

Novak, Michael
The Spirit of Democratic Capitalism, 64n12, 161n1

"Observations on the Causes of the Decline of Ancient Civilization," *Human Action* (Mises), 59n7

Olszak, Norbert
Historie des banques centrales, 95n7, 199n1

"On Ensuring the Acceptability of a New Fiat Money" (Selgin), 30n11

Oresme, Nicholas, ix, x, 7, 73n20
"A Treatise on the Origin, Nature, Law, and Alterations of Money," 4n6, 38n4, 46n2, 50n6, 52n9, 56n2, 59n7, 61n10, 99n12, 100n14, 101n16, 104n2, 111n2, 112–13nn4–6, 121n4, 124n9, 127n2, 129n3, 136n9–10,

142n16, 149–50n23–25
See also subject index
"Oresme, Nicolas" (Schneider),
    8n11
Ottavj, Christian
    Monnaie et financement de l'
    économie, 105n3

Papal Teaching on Private Property,
    1892 to 1991 (Habiger), 6n8, 26n7
Parker, Geoffrey
    "Die Entstehung des modernen
    Geld—und Finanzwesens in
    Europa 1500–1730," 74n21,
    93n6
Passage, H. du
    "Usure," 53n10
Patterson, William, 199–200
Paul VI
    Populorum Progression, 221n17
Perrot, Étienne
    Le chrétien et l'argent—Entre
    Dieu et Mammon, 60n9
Pesch, Heinrich
    Lehrbuch der Nationalökonomie,
    60n9
Pieces of Eight (Vieira), 240n5
Pius XI, 26n7
    Quadragesimo Anno, 6n8, 184n7,
    237n1, 240n4
Plato, 56
    The Laws, 56n1
Political Economy of International
    Organizations, The: A Public Choice
    Approach, 220n15
"Political Economy of Moral Haz-
    ard, The" (Hülsmann), 144n18
"Political Economy of the Interna-
    tional Monetary Fund, The"
    (Vaubel), 220n15
Politics (Aristotle), 24n2, 35n1, 49n4,
    51n8, 100n14
Pontifical Council for Justice and
    Peace
    Compendium of the Social Doc-
    trine of the Church, 2n3, 4–5n7,
    26n7

Pontifical Institute of Mediaeval
    Studies in Toronto, 73n20
Populorum Progression (Paul VI),
    221n17
Poughon, Jean-Michel
    "Les fondements juridiques de
    l'économie politique," 11n18
"Pourquoi le FMI nuit-il aux
    Africains?" (Hülsmann), 220n15
"Prices in Europe from 1450 to
    1750" (Braudel and Spooner),
    74n21
Principles of Economics, The (Fetter),
    139n14
Principles of Political Economy and
    Taxation (Ricardo), 22n1
"Proposals for an Economical and
    Secure Currency," *Works and Cor-*
    respondence (Ricardo), 41n8,
    57–58n3
Ptolemy of Lucca
    On the Government of Rulers,
    73n20, 99n13
"Punishment and Proportionality:
    The Estoppel Approach" (Kin-
    sella), 157n1

Quadragesimo Anno (Pius XI), 6n8,
    184n7, 237n1, 240n4
Quanto (Innocent III), 4, 72–73n20

Rationale of Central Banking, The
    (Smith), 199n1, 201
Rau, Karl Heinrich
    Grundsätze der Volkswirtschaft-
    slehre, 161n2
"Raymond de Roover on Scholastic
    Economic Thought" (Kirshner),
    12n18, 122n7
Redish, Angela
    Bimetallism—An Economic and
    Historical Analysis, 3n4
    "Is Deflation Depressing? Evi-
    dence from the Classical Gold
    Standard," 66n16
Reisman, George, 105n3
    Capitalism, 11n17

"Religious Thought and Economic Society" (Viner), 4n7

Reorganization of Social Economy: The Social Encyclical Developed and Explained (Nell-Breuning), 6n8

Rerum Novarum (Leo XIII), 26n7, 104n2, 121–22n5

"Resource Cost of Irredeemable Paper Money, The" (Friedman), 80n34

Return Heart of Europe, The (Connolly), 229n5

Ricardo, David, 21, 30n12, 78n30
  Principles of Political Economy and Taxation, 22n1
  "Proposals for an Economical and Secure Currency," *Works and Correspondence*, 41n8, 57–58n3
  Works and Correspondence, 9–10n15

Rist, Charles
  Histoire des doctrines économiques, 177n2

Rittmann, Herbert
  Deutsche Geldgeschichte seit 1914, 209n1

Robertson, James
  Creating New Money, 15n24

Roots of Inflation, The (Rushdoony), 16n26

Roover, Raymond de
  Business, Banking, and Economic Thought in Late Medieval and Early Modern Europe, 12n18, 52n10, 122n7

Rose, Tom
  God, Gold, and Civil Government, 16n26

Rothbard, Murray, 13, 50n7, 105n3
  America's Great Depression, 66n15
  Case Against the Fed, The, 10n16, 240n5
  Das Schein-Geld-System, 227n4
  Economic Thought Before Adam Smith: An Austrian Perspective

  on the History of Economic Thought, x, 11n18, 53n10
  Ethics of Liberty, The, 24n4
  "Gold-Exchange Standard in the Interwar Years, The," 214n8, 215n11
  History of Money and Banking in the United States, A, 144n21, 203n6, 213n7
  Man, Economy, and State, 10n16, 66n15, 70n19, 77n29, 115n1
  Mystery of Banking, The, 10n16, 161n3
  "New Light on the Prehistory of the Austrian School," *The Foundations of Modern Austrian Economics*, 11n18
  What Has Government Done to Our Money?, 10n16, 58n6

Rueff, Jacques
  The Monetary Sin of the West, 216n13

Rugina, Angel
  Geltypen und Geldordnungen, 24n3

Rushdoony, R.J.
  "Hard Money and Society in the Bible," *Gold is Money*, 3n5
  Institutes of Biblical Law, 16n26
  Roots of Inflation, The, 16n26

Ryan, John, 15n24

Saggio teoretico di diritto naturale appogiato sul fatto (d'Azeglio), 6n8

Salin, Pascal, 105n3
  La concurrence, 115n1
  La vérité sur la monnaie, 11n17, 144n19

Salins, A. de
  Le développement moderne des activités financiers au regard des exigencies éthiques du Christianisme, 181n4

Sandoz, Albert, 122n7

Sapori, Armando, 122n7

Sargent, T.J.
  The Big Problem of Small Change, 3n4

Say, Jean-Baptiste, 50n7
   Traité d' économie politique, 60n9
Schneider, J.H.J.
   "Oresme, Nicolas," 8n11
Scholastic Analysis of Usury, The
   (Noonan), 13n21, 52n10
"Schöne neue Zeichengeldwelt"
   (Hülsmann), 227n4
School of Salamanca, The (Grice-
   Hutchinson), 12n18
Schumpeter, Joseph A., 122n7
   *Capitalism, Socialism and Democ-
   racy*, 68n18
   History of Economics Analysis, x
   *Theorie der wirtschaftlichen
   Entwicklung*, 181n5
Schwartz, Anna
   *A Monetary History of the Untied
   States* (with Friedman), 62n11
Selgin, George
   "Fiscal Theory of Government's
   Role in Money, A," 103n1
   "How Would the Invisible
   Hand Handle Money?," 104n1
   Less Than Zero, 66n16
   "On Ensuring the Acceptability
   of a New Fiat Money," 30n11
Sennholz, Hans, 105n3
   Age of Inflation, 10n16, 240n5
   Lustre of God, The, 240n5
   Money and Freedom, 10n16,
   240n5
*Short History of Paper Money and
   Banking in the United States to
   which is prefixed an Inquiry into the
   Principles of the System, A,*
   (Gouge), 10n15, 24n3, 30n12,
   80n34, 186n8, 203n6
Skousen, Mark
   *Economics of a Pure Gold Stan-
   dard*, 11n17
Smith, Adam, 4–5
   Wealth of Nations, 24n2, 38n5,
   122n6
Smith, Vera
   The Rationale of Central Banking,
   199n1, 201

The Social Problem, vol. 2, Eco-
   nomics and Finance, 140n15
Socialism (Mises), 22n1, 26n7, 53n10
Sollicitudo Rei Socialis (John Paul II),
   221n17
Spinelli, F.
   A Monetary History of Italy,
   145n22
Spirit of Democratic Capitalism, The,
   (Novak), 64n12, 161n1
Spooner, F.
   "Prices in Europe from 1450 to
   1750," 74n21
Sprenger, Bernd
   Das Geld der Deutschen, 202n4,
   209n1
*Stabilized Money: A History of the
   Movement* (Fisher), 76n28
Steuart, James
   *An Inquiry Into the Principles of
   Political Economy*, 30n12
Stop the Legal Tender Crime (Zube),
   126n1
Strohm, Christoph
   "Götze oder Gabe Gottes?
   Bemerkungen zum Thema
   'Geld' in der
   Kirchengeschichte," 49n4
Suhle, Arthur
   *Deutsche Münz- und
   Geldgeschichte von den Anfän-
   gen bis zum 15*, 134n7
Summa Theologica, 101n16
Sumner, William Graham
   *History of Banking in the United
   States*, 31n13, 203n6

*Theorie der wirtschaftlichen Entwick-
   lung* (Schumpeter), 181n5
*Theorie des Geldes und der Umlaufs-
   mittel* (Mises), 10n16
Theory of Money and Credit (Mises),
   24n2, 60n9, 78n31, 100n14, 142n16,
   160–61n1, 240n5
*Theory of Money and Prinicples of
   Commerce, The* (Wheatley), 9n15,
   58n5, 91n2, 202n4, 203n5

Theory of Money Institutions, The (White), 144n20

Theory of Socialism and Capitalism, A (Hoppe), 24n4

Tocqueville, Alexis de
L' Ancien régime et la Révolution, 176n1

Tortajada, Ramon
"La renaissance de la scolastique, la Réforme et les théories du droit naturel," 12n18

"Toward a General Theory of Error Cycles" (Hülsmann), 169n10

Traité d' économie politique (Say), 60n9

"Traité de la monnaie" (Copernicus), 36n2

Traité de la première invention des monnoies, de Nicole Oresme . . . et Traité de la monnoie, de Copernic, 36n2

Traité des monnaies et autres écrits monétaires du XIVe siécle, 111n3

"Treatise on the Alteration of Money, A" (Mariana), 9n14, 104n2

"Treatise on the Origin, Nature, Law and Alterations of Money, A" (Oresme), 4n6, 38n4, 46n2, 50n6, 52n9, 56n2, 59n7, 61n10, 99n12, 100n14, 101n16, 104n2, 111n2, 121n4, 124n9, 127n2, 129n3, 136n9–10, 142n16, 149–50n23–25

"Une introduction à la pensée économique médiévale" (Lapidus), 75n25

Untersuchungen über die Methode der Socialwissenschaften und der politischen Oekonomie insbesondere (Menger), 10n16

"Usure" (Passage), 53n10

Vademecum zu einem Klassiker der mittelalterlichen Geldlehre, 8n11

Value of Money, The (Anderson), 32n16

Vaubel, Roland
"The Political Economy of the International Monetary Fund," 220n15

Velde, F.R.
The Big Problem of Small Change, 3n4

Veritatis splendor (John Paul II), 100n15

Vermeersh, A.
"Interest," 53n10

Vieira, Edwin
Pieces of Eight, 240n5

Viner, Jacob
"Religious Thought and Economic Society," 4n7

Vom Geld und vom Kapital (Nell-Breuning and Müller), 15n24, 75n26

Wagner, Adolph
Die russische Papierwährung, 31n13, 80n33

Walters, Alan
Do We need the IMF and the World Bank?, 220n15

Wealth of Nations (Smith), 24n2, 38n5, 122n6

Weber, Wilhelm
Geld und Zins in der spanischen Spätscholastik, 12n18

What Has Government Done to Our Money? (Rothbard), 10n16, 58n6

Wheatley, John
The Theory of Money and Principles of Commerce, 9n15, 58n5, 91n2, 202n4, 203n5

White, Lawrence H.
"Federal Reserve System's Influence on Research in Monetary Economics, The," 17n27
"Fiscal Theory of Government's Role in Money, A," 103n1
"How Would the Invisible Hand Handle Money?," 104n1
Theory of Money Institutions, The 144n20

Williams, Jonathan
Money: A History, 31n14

Wittreck, Fabian
Geld als Instument der Gerechtigkeit. Die Geldrechtslehre

des Hl. Thomas von Aquin in ihrem interkulturellen Kontext, 8n12

Woods, Thomas

Church and the Market, The, 14, 15n24, 85n1, 162n3

"Money and Morality: The Christian Moral Tradition and the Best Monetary Regime," 186n8

Works and Correspondence (Ricardo), 9–10n15, 41n8

Yeager, Leland B.

Ethics as Social Science: The Moral Philosophy of Social Cooperation, 4n7

"From Gold to the Ecu: The International Monetary System in Retrospect," 217n13

International Monetary Relations, 210n3, 213n7, 214n8

Zube, John

Stop the Legal Tender Crime, 126n1

"Zum Ewigen Frieden—ein philosophischer Entwurf" (Kant), 177n3

Zur sittlichen Beurteilung von Inflationen (Beutter), 14n22, 162n3

Index of Subjects

American colonies, 203–06
American Constitution, 204–06, 242
American Federal Reserve. *See* Federal Reserve (Fed)
American Revolution, 204, 242
American War of 1812, 205
Austrian School, ix, 10–14, 238–39

Banco d'Italia, 229
Bank for International Settlements (BIS), 231n6
Bank for Mutual Redemption, 145
Bank of Amsterdam, 38, 93
Bank of England, 147–48, 156, 162, 199–200, 215–16
Bank of Hamburg, 40
Bank of Japan, 164, 180
Bank of Scotland, 95
Bank of Stockholm, 94
banking
    deflation and, 67–68
    fractional-reserve. *See* fractional-reserve banking
    government's role in, 16
    international systems. *See* international banking systems
    as national producers of paper money, 203–06
    regulations, 145, 171–72, 231n6
bankruptcy, 128, 142–43, 153–57, 169–70
Banks of the United States, 205
Banque de France, 228–29
barter economy, 21–22, 224n1
Basel II Agreement, 231n6

Biblical references
    Biblical commandments. *See* Commandments, Biblical
    Deuteronomy 25:13–16, 99n11
    Isaiah 10:1, 124
    Isaiah 1:22–25, 150
    Isaiah 5:20, 121
    Isaiah 60:17, 241
    Leviticus 19:35–36, 98n11
    Luke 14:28–30, 71–72, 141
    Luke 19:23, 92n5
    Matthew 22:17–21, 123–24
    Matthew 25:26–30, 52
    Matthew 25:27, 92n5
    Proverbs 20:10, 72n20, 99n11
    Proverbs 20:23, 99n11
    Romans 3:8, 100n14
bimetallism, 129–31, 159, 210
bond dealers, 183–84
bonds, 225–26
Bretton Woods system
    dissolution of, 141, 207, 228
    as gold-exchange system, 216–19
    reform of, 17
    world money and, 235
British currency reform of 1717, 130
bullion, 35–36, 50, 116–18, 133
business cycles, 139–42

capitalism, 237–40
cartels
    as credit money producers, 197–98
    fractional-reserve banking, 144–45, 206–07

as paper-money producers,
228–30
Catholic Church, teachings of. *See
also* Christian doctrine
attitude toward capitalism,
237–40
comparison to Austrian economics, 14
concept of social justice, 6n8
ethical implications of social
science, 4
hoarding, 64n12
inflation, 87
international banking systems,
221
private property, 25–26
usury compared to interest,
52–53
central banks
gold-exchange standard, 214–16
government's role in, 16
international banking systems,
210–16
introduction of paper money
and, 159–64
legal tender laws, 142–48
private debt and, 183–84
as producers of paper money,
199–206, 230–32
public debts and, 166–68
central planning of economy, 172
centralized governments, 176–77
certificates of deposit, 39
certificates of money. *See* money
certificates
certification of money, 89–91
charities, 26, 220
checking accounts, 39
Christian doctrine. *See also* Catholic
Church, teachings of; Jesus Christ,
teachings of
Austrian School economics and,
14–16
desire for money, 2
money and banking and, 52
producing money, 49nn4–5
Civil War (United States), 205

Coinage Act of 1834, 209
coins. *See also* precious metals
addressed in American Constitution, 204–06
debasement of, 133–36
legal monopolies and, 116–24
as medium of exchange, 23
monetary reform and, 241–42
money certificates and, 35–38
production of in ancient times,
3–4
use of in free market, 46
weights of, 50–51
Cold War, 225n2
colonial America, 203–06
Commandments, Biblical
Eighth, 122
Ninth, 25, 50, 98, 112
Sixth, 25
commodity money. *See also* natural
money
comparison to paper money, 23, 55
costs of, 79–81
definition, 29–32
monetary stability and, 72
Constitution of the United States,
204–06, 242
cost calculations, 141–42
counterfeiting
benefits of in free society, 97–98
debasement of money. *See*
debasement of money
ethics of, 98–101
fractional-reserve banking and,
91–97
legalization of, 109–13
credit
for businesses, 179–82
effects of paper money on, 69
for governments, 177–78
for individuals, 182–85
credit cards, 39
credit money
cartels as producers, 197–98
comparison to natural money,
28–29, 128
comparison to paper money, 29
financing of wars and, 178
legal-tender laws and, 138–39

creditors
  debasement of money and, 135
  distribution effects of money
    and, 47
currency boards, 226, 227n3, 230–33
currency substitution, 127–28

debasement of money. *See also*
  counterfeiting
  ethics of, 98–99
  inflation and, 89–91
  legal-tender laws and, 133–36,
    146
  legalization of, 109–13
debtors
  debasement of money and, 135
  distribution effects of money
    and, 47
  governments as, 225–27
debts
  deflation and, 67
  private, 182–85
  public, 166–68, 177–78, 188, 205,
    242
deflation
  debasement of money and, 135
  gold standard and, 212
  governments as beneficiaries,
    107–08
  legal-tender laws and, 127, 130
  paper money and, 64–68
demand deposits, 137n12
division of labor
  in barter world, 21–22
  production of money and, 46
dollarization, 226–27, 232–33

ECB (European Central Bank), 164,
  229
economic growth, 60–62
electronic bank accounts, 39
electronic money, 33, 55–56. *See also*
  paper money
EMS (European Monetary System),
  228–30
ESCB (European System of Central
  Banks), 229

ethics
  of counterfeiting, 98–101
  of euros, 229–30
  of fractional-reserve banking,
    98–101, 238–39
  of legal monopolies, 119–24
  of legal tender laws, 148–51
  of legalized suspensions, 157
  of money production, 49–51
  of paper money, 172–73, 238–39
European Central Bank (ECB), 164,
  229
European Economic Community,
  228–30
European Monetary System (EMS),
  228–30
European System of Central Banks
  (ESCB), 229, 234
euros, 226–30
exchange rates
  under gold standard, 211–12
  Gresham's law, 126–27
  international paper-money sys-
    tems and, 226, 232–33
  legal-tender laws and, 135–36

Federal Reserve (Fed)
  banknotes of, 40n7
  fractional-reserve banking and,
    139n15
  international banking systems
    and, 215–16
  international paper-money sys-
    tems and, 226, 232–33
  legal-tender laws and, 141
  paper money and, 164–65,
    171n11
fiat inflation. *See also* inflation
  consequences for businesses,
    179–82
  consequences for governments,
    176–79
  consequences for individuals
    and families, 182–91
  governments as beneficiaries,
    103–08
  legal monopolies and, 115–24
  legal tender laws and. *See* legal
    tender laws

legalization of debasement and
  fractional reserves, 109–13
fiat monetary systems, 199–207
fiat money
  defined, 106–07
  inflation of. *See* fiat inflation
  paper money and, 160–61n1
fiorino d'oro, 197
Fisherian stabilization movement,
  76
Fort Knox, 218
fractional-reserve banking
  bankruptcy and, 153–57
  currency substitution and, 128
  defined, 41
  effects of deflation on, 68
  ethics of, 98–101, 238–39
  inflation and, 90–101, 180–82
  as institutional usury, 53
  international banking systems,
    211–13
  international paper-money
    standards and, 231n6
  legal monopolies and, 117–18,
    147–48
  legal-tender laws and, 130–31,
    136–45
  legalization of, 109–13
  national monetary systems and,
    206
  origins of, 93–97
francs, 228
fraud, 153–54
free economy, defined, 26
free market
  defined, 26, 86
  gold standard and, 213
  monetary orders and, 195–98
  paper money and, 29–33
French francs, 228

German Bundesbank, 229
German marks, 226, 229
gold as money. *See* commodity
  money; natural money
gold coins. *See* coins
gold standard
  deflation and, 212

fractional-reserve banking and,
  143n17
international banking systems
  and, 209–16
legal monopolies and, 117
national monetary systems and,
  205, 231
paper money and, 160
textbooks and, 2
governments
  benefits of monetary system to,
    238–39
  false money certificates and,
    99–101
  inflation and. *See* fiat inflation
  international banking systems
    and, 209–13
  international paper-money sys-
    tems and, 224–27, 230
  legalization of debasement and
    fractional reserves, 109–13
  paper money and, 30–31
  public debts, 166–68
Great Depression, 14
greenbacks, 31, 107, 205
Gresham's law, 126–30, 137n13

hoarding, 62–64, 133, 182–85
hyperinflation, 90n1, 165–72, 232–35

illiquidity, 154–55
IMF (International Monetary Fund),
  218–22
indirect exchange, 22–23
inflation
  addressed in American Consti-
    tution, 204–06
  debasement of money as, 89–91
  defined, 85–88
  families, effects on, 185–91
  fiat. *See* fiat inflation
  forms of, 5, 88
  fractional-reserve banking and,
    90–101, 180–82
  gold standard and, 211–13
  gold-exchange standard and,
    215–16
  governments as beneficiaries,
    86–88, 103–08

See also fiat inflation
historical case against, 7–17
hyperinflation, 90n1, 165–72,
   232–35
international paper-money systems and, 226
origin of, 85–88
paper money and, 159–62
stagflation, 69
insolvency, 154
interest
   compared to usury, 52–53
   distribution effects of money
      and, 47
   effects of paper money on,
      69–72
international banking systems
   Bretton Woods system, 141, 207,
      216–19, 228, 235
   gold standard, 209–13
   gold-exchange standard, 214–16
International Monetary Fund (IMF)
   and World Bank, 218–22
International Monetary Fund (IMF),
   218–22
international paper-money systems
   consequences of mergers,
      235–36
   emergence of standards, 223–27
   mergers, 228–30
   multiple standards of, 230–34
international trade agreements, 221
IOUs, 94–95
Italian lira, 228

Japanese yen, 226
Jesus Christ, teachings of
   coins and government, 123–24
   cost calculations, 141
   stewardship of money, 51–52
justice
   inflation and, 87
   money production and, 1–7

labor market, 14
labor unions, 68–69
Latin Currency Union, 210
laws
   of association, 21

of diminishing marginal value,
   43
Gresham's, 126–30, 137n13
legal tender. *See* legal-tender
   laws
of production, 21
legal monopolies
   coins and, 116–24
   economic versus legal, 115–16
   ethics of, 119–24
   legal-tender laws and, 116–19,
      145–47
   social justice and, 6
legal tender, defined, 125
legal tender laws
   bankruptcy and, 156
   bimetallism, 129–31
   business cycles and, 139–42
   central banks and, 142–44,
      147–48
   credit money and, 138–39
   ethics of, 148–51
   fractional-reserve banking and,
      130–31, 136–45
   government coercion and, 31,
      148–51
   inflation and, 112–13
   legal monopolies and, 116–19,
      145–47
   money certificates and, 131–37
   overview, 125–29
   paper money and, 107, 163–64
   social justice and, 6
lira, 228
London goldsmith bankers, 93–94

marginal value, 43
marks, 226, 229
materialism, 187
medium of exchange, defined, 22
mergers of international paper-
   money systems, 226–30, 235–36
monetary orders, 195–98
monetary reform, 240–42
monetary stability, 72–79
monetary systems
   fiat, 199–207

international. *See* international banking systems; international paper-money systems
national, 203–06
money
certification of, 89–91
credit. *See* credit money
debasement of. *See* debasement of money
desire for and Christian doctrine, 2
electronic, 33, 55–56. *See also* paper money
fiat, 106–07, 160–61n1. *See also* fiat inflation
natural. *See* natural money
origin of, 22–23
paper. *See* paper money
warehouses, 93–94
money certificates
coinage and, 35–38
debasement of money and, 89–91
fiat, 106–07. *See also* fiat inflation
legal monopolies and, 118–19
legal tender laws and, 131–37
as money substitutes, 38–41
money production
central banks and, 163
commodity money, 79–81
distribution effects of, 46–49
ethics of, 49–51
justice and, 1–7
natural money, 5, 7–17, 195–98
prices and, 43–45
scope and limits of, 45–46
money supply, effects on economic growth, 60–62
monopolies, legal. *See* legal monopolies
moral hazard
defined, 144
hyperinflation and regulation, 168–72
international paper-money standards and, 226

international paper-money systems and, 231, 234
paper-money systems, 236
public debts and, 166–68
mortgage corporations, 183–84

national monetary systems, 203–06
nationalistic ideologies, 176
natural laws, 11
natural money. *See also* commodity money
arguments for, 55–59
comparison to paper money, 56–59, 160–61, 165
monetary reform and, 240–42
money supply and, 61
overview, 24–28
production of, 5, 7–17, 195–98
North American colonies, 203–06

Oresme, Nicholas, teachings of
alteration of coins, 37, 50n6
distribution effects of money, 46–47
false money certificates, 99–101
first treatise on money, 4
Gresham's law, 127n2
inflation and governments, 104, 179
legal monopolies, 121, 124
legal tender laws, 129, 135–36, 142n16, 149–51
legalization of debasement and fractional-reserves, 111–13
money supply, 61
production of money, 56–59, 61
ways of gaining through money, 52n9
origin of money, 22–23

paper money. *See also* electronic money
addressed in American Constitution, 204–06
comparison to commodity money, 80
comparison to credit money, 29

comparison to natural money, 56–59, 160–61, 165
deflation and, 64–68
economic growth and, 60–62
ethics of, 172–73, 238–39
fractional-reserve certificates. *See* fractional-reserve banking
free market and, 29–33
hoarding and, 62–64
interest rates and, 69–72
international systems. *See* international paper-money systems
legal tender laws and, 107, 163–64
limits of, 164–66
monetary stability and, 72–79
origins of, 159–62
producers, 199–206, 230–32
public debts and, 166–68
purchasing power of the money unit (PPM) and, 168–72
reverse transubstantiations, 162–64
sticky prices and, 68–69
payments, suspension of, 6, 153–57
PPM (purchasing power of the money unit). *See* purchasing power of the money unit (PPM)
precious metals. *See also* coins
bimetallism, 129–31
counterfeiting and, 98–99
as medium of exchange, 23
as natural monies, 27, 35
paper money and, 29, 159
stability of money and, 72–73
prices, 43–45, 68–69
private inflation, 5
private property. *See also* property rights
as basis of capitalism, 238
inflation and, 86, 88
international banking systems and, 220–21
natural monies and, 25–27
paper money and, 160
product quality, effects of inflation on, 187–88
production of money. *See* money production

property rights
Austrian School as advocates of, ix
coinage and, 38
inflation and, 99–100, 179
as mission of government, 16
natural monies and, 25–27, 241
paper money and, 30–31, 172–73
public debts, 166–68, 177–78, 188, 205, 242
purchasing power of the money unit (PPM)
commodity money and, 79–80
effects of paper money on, 70–73
hoarding and, 185
inflation and, 183
paper money, 168–72
stability of money and, 73–79

real-estate boom, 170–71
reform, monetary, 240–42
regulations, banking, 145, 171–72, 231n6
reserves, defined, 39–40
rights, property. *See* property rights

savings, 182–86
Scriptural references. *See* Biblical references
silver as money. *See* commodity money; natural money
silver coins. *See* coins
silver standard, 209–11
social assistance. *See* welfare state
stagflation, 69
standards of international paper-money, 223–27, 230–34
states. *See* governments
stockbrokers, 183–84
stock-exchange, 170
Suffolk Bank, 145, 198n1
suspension of payments, 6, 153–57, 200

taxation, 178, 190
Third World, 220–21, 225n2, 237–38
token coins, 39–41

U.S. Coin Act of 1834, 130–31
U.S. Constitution, 204–06, 242
U.S. dollars. *See* dollars
U.S. Federal Reserve. *See* Federal
    Reserve (Fed)
usury
    Christian doctrine on, 2
    compared to interest, 52–53
    legal tender laws and, 149

wages, 68–69
War Between the States, 205

War of 1812, 205
warehouses, money, 93–94
wars, as consequence of inflation,
    177–78
weights of coins, 35, 50–51, 118,
    120–24
welfare state, 14, 188–91, 228
Western military bases, 221
World Bank, 218–22

yen, 227, 230

Made in the USA
Monee, IL
08 May 2023

33104215R00164